REFLECTION: JOURNEY THROUGH THE PSALMS

G. H. ROESENER

WESTBOW
PRESS®
A DIVISION OF THOMAS NELSON
& ZONDERVAN

WestBow Press books may be ordered through booksellers or by contacting:

WestBow Press
A Division of Thomas Nelson & Zondervan
1663 Liberty Drive
Bloomington, IN 47403
www.westbowpress.com
844-714-3454

Scripture quotations taken from The Holy Bible, New International Version® NIV® Copyright © 1973 1978 1984 2011 by Biblica, Inc. TM. Used by permission. All rights reserved worldwide.

Scripture taken from the King James Version of the Bible.

ISBN: 978-1-6642-3259-4 (sc)
ISBN: 978-1-6642-3258-7 (hc)
ISBN: 978-1-6642-3268-6 (e)

Library of Congress Control Number: 2021908472

Print information available on the last page.

WestBow Press rev. date: 5/28/2021

FOREWORD

This book would not be possible if it were not for the assistance of various individuals throughout the process. My journey through the Psalms began just as a simple Bible study for me to review the Old Testament song and prayer book. But it quickly became more than that. My eyes were opened to the beauty of God's Word through its various authors, not only to the people of old but to you and me today.

First to the cover. The cover design was completed by three of my grandchildren – Katie and Nicholson Miller and Molley Wilkins. I provided some basic concepts and left the design to their imagination. The title of the book, *Reflection: Journey through the Psalms*, was conceived by my good friend, Karen "Schultz" Alter, CEO, Borshoff, Indianapolis, Indiana. Borshoff is dedicated to creating powerful brand experiences through advertising and public relations since 1984.

My former pastor and mentor, The Reverend W. E. Lauterbach served as my trusted adviser. He also provided a copy of Dr. H. C. Leupold's *Exposition of the Psalms*, who also served as his Hebrew professor in seminary. My good, Christian friend, Stephen Koepper, served as my editor providing a wealth of work (and advice) to bring this project to fulfillment.

The cover itself is meant to reflect the royalty of David in his prime as God's chosen leader for His people, Israel. His kingship was an earthly reign of some 40 years, but his LORD is King forever. His earthly crown was not that of a bejeweled treasure, rather, it was a crown of thorns as our King of kings was born to die for you me. His clothing was stripped off and replaced with a scarlet robe. But He overcame death and rose victoriously, and LORD reigns forever seated at the right hand of God in all His majesty. Many of the psalms, including David's, point to the Messiah as the One to come as the Savior of the world.

I was born to Christian parents and was fed the Word of God from my youth. I was fortunate to attend a Lutheran Christian Elementary School. I continued my education in a secular high school and then attended professional training as a pharmacist at Butler University. Following my marriage to my grade school sweetheart, I became an active participant in my church's activities in all facets – including Bible study leader and elder. I have also served our corporate church, both state and national, in various capacities. I started studying God's Word in earnest in 1990 and began writing weekly reflections on my life and faith, called *Saturday's Notes*.

Connected in Him, I stand
G. H. Roesener
Saturday's Notes Publishing

REFLECTION: JOURNEY
THROUGH THE PSALMS

Author: G. H. Roesener
Saturday's Notes Publishing

The subsequent notes on each of the 150 chapters are meant to examine their language from thousands of years prior to today and how meaningful they can still be. This beautiful book in the Old Testament (referred to as "O. T.") was Israel's Song and Prayer Book. It can be that for you and me today.

Personally, I am not a pastor, nor do I have a Ph. D. in theology but I do have the blessing of the Holy Spirit, who has endowed me with the gift of His Word and understanding of Holy Scripture. I have studied His Word for decades and have been taught and mentored by various pastors who have assisted me in unlocking the mysteries of His Word. I trust that my journey on each psalm will be a blessing to you.

My suggestion is that you read the psalm in question first. Then read the notes and its various other biblical references, then return and re-read the psalm again. Like me, I trust that your eyes and mind will be opened to the beauty of these 150 chapters in God's Word.

Over the years, I have used multiple references in my study and have done so here also. I have various electronic dictionaries, study guides, and various printed materials that I use regularly. Notably, I have *Henry Halley's Bible Handbook* and *HC Leupold's Exposition of The Psalms*. I continue to like the NIV version of God's Word and will generally quote from this version, although I have memorized some verses from other translations.

Saturday's Notes Publishing is an informal unit of mine that was started in late 1990 when I first started writing. At first, I would write and share only with very trusted friends but then began to expand and eventually wrote weekly for almost eight years to a large subscriber list. Selected issues have been published (internally generated) in three volumes of *Saturday's Notes*. My signature, "Connected in Him, I stand" has been used for over 30 years now during my various writings. I am connected in Him by faith and I stand (lower case) blameless before His throne by grace due to the blood of the Lamb of God. I will not fully "Stand" until the coming of our LORD in the eternal victory celebration of all believers.

"And now unto Him who is able to keep you from falling and to present you blameless before His glorious throne with great joy; to the only God our Lord Jesus Christ be glory, majesty, power, and authority, through Jesus Christ our LORD both now and forevermore. Amen." (Jude 24-25 paraphrased)

Peace
Connected in Him, I stand
G. H. Roesener

CONTENTS

PSALMS, BOOK I
From Beginning to End

The Bible is a composite of 66 books containing hundreds of thousands of words. God's Word is absolute and His love for His creation is nothing less than tremendous. The Bible contains a total of 1,189 chapters and over 30,000 verses. But . . . only the first two and the last two chapters are perfect in terms of God's intention for His creation. The middle of His Word is found in Psalm 117 which also is the shortest chapter in Scripture. Listen to this beautiful Psalm:

> *Praise the LORD, all you nations;*
> *extol him, all you peoples.*
> *For great is his love toward us,*
> *and the faithfulness of the LORD endures forever.*
> *Praise the LORD.* (Psalm 117:1-2)

I am beginning a personal study of the Book of Psalms. The 150-chapter book is divided into five sections or Books as they are called. Each book concludes with a song of praise or doxology. Most theologians agree that each of the five books represents a theme from Moses' Pentateuch. Book I similar to Genesis and so on.

God's Word begins in Genesis with His marvelous creating work in six days. His final creating was man and woman. His creation was perfect but quickly changed its tune as sin entered the world. The evil one planted a seed of doubt in Adam and Eve's mind that they too could be like God! As such, their fall manifested in a recognition that sin's finality is separation from God and eventual death. As they hid themselves from God, their physical nakedness was also a sign of their absolute despair and their nothingness! But, God in His wisdom and mercy, provided a way out. The Great Protoevangel (Gen 3:15) shows God's immense love for His creation and a promise for a Savior.

Now let's look at Psalm 1. The author shows us two roads in life. The first describes a man who does not walk in the counsel of the wicked. He delights in the law of the LORD. He prospers like a tree planted by the streams of water. Here the author reminds you and me that we are to walk in line with God's purpose for us and promises fruit from our life in Christ. The second person is the opposite, i.e. a wicked man whose life is like the chaff that is groundless and has no future. It blows away and cannot withstand judgment. The final verse is God's promise as He watches over his righteous ones and ignores the wicked.

As we move to the end of His Word in Revelation, we see a beautiful vision provided to St. John. John saw the new heavens and the new earth (chapter 21). This new creation pictured as the new Jerusalem prepared as a bride beautifully dressed for her husband. This picture reminds us of God's perfect creating in Genesis 1 and 2 where creation was beautifully adorned in splendor. Their human nakedness was of no consequence in perfection! The picture of perfection is once again seen in the vision where there is no more death or mourning or crying and pain. John's vision is completed in chapter 22 and the Lamb himself is pictured here saying, "Come!" "Whoever is thirsty, let him come. Whoever wishes, let him take the water of life." This beautiful gospel language is a continuing invitation to anyone – for God wants all to be saved. This living water provides an everlasting fruit similar to the psalmist in chapter 1. John concludes with his short benediction, "The grace of the Lord Jesus Christ be with God's people. Amen!

Now let's take journey back to the concluding chapter in Psalms. The entire chapter is the doxology in Book V. All of God's creation is pictured here giving praise to the creation that God intended. Here the author opens with praising God in His sanctuary and his mighty heavens. His acts of power are only surpassed by His greatness. This final chapter reminds you and me of His final coming in the new

Jerusalem where all creation will be in constant praise of the Lamb! I am reminded of a sermon (8/25/1996) that reminds us that the 10-string instrument listed here parallels our human senses (also 10) giving praise to the Almighty (2 eyes, 2 ears, 2 hands, 2 feet, mouth and heart).

May we be in constant harmony with our Creator and Savior who has given us life eternally through the blood of the Lamb. May we use our senses to be the fruit of a thankful member of the household of faith. "Let everything that has breath praise the LORD." (Ps 150:6).

Peace
Connected in Him, I stand
GHR

PSALM 2
David's Prophesy

This psalm is often quoted in various New Testament books and is the first of Messianic Psalms. The Talmud suggests that this psalm is a continuation of the first. In part, the word "blessed" begins the first and is the ending of the second. The author of this psalm is attributed to David and is quoted by the Apostles in Acts as words of King David. We all think of David as the shepherd boy, a warrior and of course the great king of Israel. His reign was perhaps the greatest time in Israel's history of size, stature, and wealth. Now, we see David in his prophetic psalm looking to the King of Israel, that is God's Son the Anointed One promised long ago and to be a descendant of King David.

The opening verse begins with a rhetorical question, "Why do the nations conspire, and the peoples plot in vain?" From an earthly view, Israel appears as a target by many foreign rulers. These first two verses are also prophetic as we see in Luke's Acts where he tells of the Jewish rulers imprisoning Peter and John for healing a crippled man. Luke uses the word, "disturbed" describing the Jewish leaders' fears of the apostles' teaching Jesus and his glorious resurrection. Once released and back with their followers, Peter quotes David's psalm.

Why do people think they can gain freedom by ignoring God? God laughs at their stupidity and rebukes them in anger. He reminds us that His Son is the eternal king (verse 3). The first six verses speak to the threat against Christ's kingdom. But God promises that He will rule! Freedom is only available through the cross of Jesus Christ for his atoning sacrifice that frees us from sin's bondage.

Verse seven is quoted again in Acts 13 by St. Paul during his first missionary journey in Asia Minor's Antioch (Pisidia). That same verse is also quoted in Hebrews relating to God's superiority. This O. T. reminds you and me that the power and glory of the Son was vividly manifest when the Father raised him from the dead. As the resurrected Christ ascended to His Father, He assumed his role as King having conquered sin, death, and Satan himself. David continues with kingly language using the term "iron scepter." A scepter was a ceremonial staff that was a symbol of power and often adorned with jewels. This iron rod is pictured here as destroying any would-be ruler like a rod would shatter pottery.

And yes, here it comes. When the word "therefore" is used it means "here it comes!" The final verses are a counsel to you and me and to all who are ruling. First, David says, be wise. What is wisdom? Human wisdom is folly to God. True wisdom is defined in Solomon's proverbs. Listen, "The fear of the LORD is the beginning of wisdom, and the knowledge of him is understanding." Yes, to be wise is to know God and have faith in His Son Jesus Christ who is King Eternal.

Secondly, David reminds us to be a servant. We serve the Almighty by serving others. And we can rejoice in our true service. Finally, David uses the phrase, "Kiss the Son." Theologians generally agree that the phrase means to surrender fully to Christ as the King Eternal and king of our hearts and lives.

Yes, David was prophetic in his psalm. And his words were quoted on numerous occasions in different circumstances by multiple individuals. In fact, Handel's Messiah Part II quotes Psalm two.

The concluding verse is a promise of blessings to those who take refuge in Him. That same term is used in Psalm 46, "God is our refuge and strength, an ever-present help in time of trouble." Be wise, surrender to his leadership and serve Him.

Peace
Connected in Him, I stand
GHR

PSALM 3

David's Trust

What is trust? The dictionary defines the term in various ways, but in general it's a firm belief, confidence or reliance in something(one). It also can mean a reliance on something in the future (hope). The third psalm is again one of David's. The psalm is in the setting of an unsettled time in David's life with his son (Absalom) plotting to overthrow his father as king. Absalom's rebellion is recorded in 2 Samuel 15-18 that concludes with his son's death hanging in a tree.

Let's look back into David's life. While David was certainly in God's favor, he was not without guilt. 2 Samuel also tells of his grievous sin with the lust for Bathsheba and having her husband killed in battle. Nathan confronted David with his sin and while David was sorry for his sin, consequences were to follow for David. Nathan reminded David of all of God's blessings including His divine deliverance from his enemies and making him king over Israel and Judah. Nathan prophesied to David, "Now, therefore, the sword will never depart from your house, because you have despised me and took the wife of Uriah the Hittite to be your own."

The beginning of consequences was not long, as a baby of David and Bathsheba died. Turmoil continued in his family with the rape of his daughter Tamar by Amnon and then Absalom killing Amnon. What more can happen in David's life? Absalom plotted to take over from his father. His plans were succeeding causing David to flee, but then Absalom died by hanging in a tree.

Psalm three was written with this backdrop of David's confiding in

God. He inquires about the number of his foes and how they continue to rise up against him. His enemies are confident that God will not deliver him by ignoring him! Wrong! David immediately expresses his confidence in God and states that God is a shield around him! Quite a statement of faith despite his troubles and the threats against him. This "shield" is the famous promise of God to Abram in Gen 15:1. This shield is then used in St. Paul's total armor listing in Ephesians. The shield is none other than FAITH. His reliance on God is manifested in David's statement "lifts up my head." Yes, when you are in total despair, turning to God and having faith is sure, as he surrounds each of us so that we can hold up our head in confidence.

Verse four shows David's total reliance by "crying aloud," confident that God will answer. The subsequent verse is a statement of David's faith in how God protects him even in his sleep. His plea for God to deliver him from his enemies does not go unheard. His concluding verse is one of a confident deliverance and His blessing on His people.

The psalm begins with complaints and ends with rejoicing in the power and glory of God (Matthew Henry's Commentary). We too can be confident in God's abundant blessings even in times of human despair. God will neither leave nor forsake His own. So, as you read Psalm three, do so with all confidence that God is in control even when troubles occur in your life. Read Ephesians 6:10-17 as Paul defines the total armor of God and concludes with the great offensive weapon which is the WORD of God.

Peace
Connected in Him, I stand
GHR

PSALM 4

David's Prayer for Mercy

King David was sorrowful at times but sought God's intervention, knowing full well that his God was a merciful God, full of compassion for His sheep. Theologians believe this psalm was written about the same time as Psalm three. The theme of trust also seems to continue into this psalm as well.

David opens with a plea for God to answer him in his time of need and to "give me relief" from his distress. The first verse concludes with his plea for mercy. In the Jewish faith, this psalm is often referred to as a "Shema." Shema's are said morning and evening. This psalm is an evening Shema. The term refers to the phrase, "Hear O Israel, the LORD is your God."

When you consider David's troubles with his son Absalom, verse 2 takes on a special meaning. Absalom was gathering support for himself and attempting to separate men from David. David uses the term delusions (false beliefs) and seeking false gods. He expresses his confidence that God has set apart the godly and as such will hear and listen to their prayers.

This term "set apart" is very important. Why? God set Abram apart from his family and friends. He, like Christians today, is called and set apart for His purpose. This theme of being set apart is to remind God's followers that we are not of the world but in the world. St. Paul reminds us in Romans 12: 1 that we are to be "living sacrifices, holy and pleasing to God." We are not to continue to conform to the worldly standards.

St. Peter, in his first epistle, reminds his readers that we who are called are holy, and as such are to act in that same manner.

That term "trust" is used again in verse five – like the theme in the third psalm. *Halley's Bible Handbook* says it this way, trust in God is:

- a gladness of heart (joy) – verse 7
- a peace of mind – verse 8
- a communion with God in our bedtime meditation – verse 4
- a confidence that God is watching – verse 8.

O. T. sacrifices were a regular part of their worship. God looks in our hearts for our sacrifices. Remember the gifts of Cain and Abel? God saw the heart of Abel and his gift. Hebrews 13:15-16 says, ". . . let us continually offer to God a sacrifice of praise – the fruit of lips that confess his name. And do not forget to do good and share with others, for with such sacrifices God is pleased." David expresses his joy in God and is more thankful for His abundant joy - more so than all the grain and new wine.

David's plea can be our plea too. First, answer me when I call, and hear my prayers. Second, seek his mercy and grant relief in times of trouble. God has called us out of darkness into his marvelous light, says Scripture – and we are to be transformed and set apart for the kingdom's work.

In your bedtime prayers, remember this evening Shema and David's plea for peace in our sleep resting in God's promise that we are in His hands!

Peace
Connected in Him, I stand
GHR

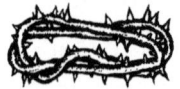

PSALM 5

A Morning Prayer of David

David continues to plead to his God for mercy and deliverance from his enemies. "Give ear to my words," says David. "Listen to my cry for help, my King and my God." David implies here in verse three that he goes to his God in prayer each morning, laying his requests on God's throne of grace and waiting expectantly for His answer.

David was very concerned over the deceitful hearts of those who take pleasure in evil. They cannot stand in God's presence, as God abhors sin. By God's grace and mercy, David is totally reverent when he reminds us today that we are to seek God's righteousness – making straight His way before us. Making "straight" is a term that is used over and over in Scripture. Solomon's great Proverb 3:5-6 reminds us to trust in the LORD versus our human understanding; and, if we acknowledge Him, He will make our paths straight. John the Baptist quotes the Prophet Isaiah (40:3). Making our paths straight means to remove all obstacles that may encumber our journey. John was certainly the forerunner of the Anointed One as prophesied in the O. T.

David was Israel's powerful king, yet he is asking God to lead him. He acknowledges that his own understanding is not God's wisdom. Have you ever thought about how wealthy he must have been? For example, his wealth included 100,000 talents of gold. That's approximately equivalent to 5,000 Tons. In today's price of gold ($1,729.78 per ounce – June 18, 2020) that would price David's wealth at $276.8 Billion U. S. Dollars. But, with all his wealth, he could not buy wisdom. Wisdom is only available from God himself. (NOTE: Fort Knox has 4,600 Tons of gold in its safekeeping).

David concludes with his request that all should take refuge in God and in Him alone. Let us all sing for joy as our expression of gratitude for His protecting care. And finally, David is confident that God will bless the righteous and surround them with His shield.

As we awaken each day, let us too take David's example of seeking God's divine guidance and protection. Martin Luther said it this way in his Morning Prayer:

I thank You, my heavenly Father, through Jesus Christ, Your dear son,
that You have kept me this night from all harm and danger;
and I pray that You would keep me this
day also from sin and every evil,
that all my doings and life may please You.
For into your hands I commend myself, my body and soul,
and all things.
Let Your holy angel be with me, that the evil
foe may have no power over me.
Amen.

Peace
Connected in Him, I stand
GHR

PSALM 6

An Individual Lament of David

This is the first of penitential psalms. Again, David is the author. We see a continuing theme of his anguish over sin and pain - even illness. Halley's Handbook entitles this psalm as a "Cry of a Broken Heart." David opens his psalm with requests: "Don't rebuke me in your anger; do not discipline me in your wrath; heal me; turn and deliver me; and Save me!" Each of these requests is out of his faint heart (verse 2). David cries for mercy to his LORD.

David questions God just as we do from time to time. "How long, O LORD, how long?" He states he is worn out from groaning. The dictionary defines groaning as, "a prolonged stressed dull cry expressive of agony, pain or disapproval." His cries for mercy reached heaven but not before he wets his bed clothing with tears.

This psalm has been set for stringed instruments. A *sheminith* is an eight-stringed instrument or can be a musical style or octave. Verse three is quoted by Jesus in John 12:27-28. Jesus is in one of his dialogues explaining to his followers why he must die! Listen to the words of our Lord, "Now my heart is troubled, and what shall I say? Father, save me from this hour? No, it was for this very reason I came to this hour. Father, glorify your name!" Immediately, a voice from heaven said, "I have glorified it and will glorify it again." The crowd heard but were confused as to its origin.

Notice the similarity of David and his heir, none other than the Messiah. Each portrays a heavy heart and each request, to be saved from anguish and pain.

The first seven verses are an outright cry for mercy. Then the mood changes beginning with verse eight. David now shifts to a confident tone. Why? Because of his knowledge of God's unfailing love for His own, promising to answer our prayers. We too can be confident through the blood of the Lamb, who pleads to the Father for us making us righteous in His sight. Amen!

Just as David says, "Away from me, all you who do evil," our LORD also says this in Matthew's gospel (7:23). Jesus is teaching about those who build houses on rock or sand. Jesus shows His righteous judgment indicating that those whose heart was evil will be separated, "Away from me, you evildoers." This same phrase is used in the acrostic Psalm 119:115.

We can also pray in all confidence, going from a groaning spirit to a joyful heart, knowing full well that our prayers have been heard. Like David, we, too, can say, "The LORD has heard my cry for mercy; the LORD accepts my prayer."

This psalm of lament (audible grieving) is one that can be heard around the world. God's people everywhere are plagued by evildoers who have subjected them to harm and danger, yes, even death. May the God of all grace and mercy hear our prayers for the sake of His Son, our Savior. Amen and Amen.

Peace
Connected in Him, I stand
GHR

PSALM 7

The Righteous Judge

David continues his authorship in this psalm, It is again another individual type of lament. The title affixed to this psalm indicates this is a cry, or lament, concerning Cush, a Benjamite. Historically, Cush was a son of Ham and grandson of Noah. It might be that he was one of Saul's officers who was pursuing David.

As in other previous psalms of David, he begins by petitioning the LORD. But he first states his trust in God, admitting he takes refuge in the LORD. "Save and deliver me," asks David. He fears being torn apart as a lion tearing apart his prey. The central theme here is "God is a Righteous Judge." (see verses 8b-9). This psalm is used in the Jewish faith during Purim which is also called Festival of Lots. This holiday commemorates a saving of God's people from Haman as recounted in the Book of Esther.

Like many other psalms, David's Psalm 7 is quoted in other parts of Scripture - St. John's Revelation (2:23). In this chapter, John is instructed to write to the various churches. Verse 23 is directed to Thyatira where he states, ". . . I AM He who searches hearts and minds." (emphasis added) This righteous judge concept from Psalm 7:9.

As I read through this lament, I prepared a list of key words and phrases.

- ✓ Take refuge in the LORD
- ✓ Evil pursues me
- ✓ Rise up against the rage of my enemies

- ✓ Decree justice
- ✓ Judge Me!
- ✓ My shield is God
- ✓ Evil destroys itself (14-15)
- ✓ Thanks, and praise be to the LORD

Perhaps the most relevant verse to me is the concluding verse where David re-affirms his belief in God's righteousness and sings His praise to the LORD Most High. The prophet Isaiah (chapter 42) presents a vision of the coming Messiah and His work. Israel was the servant of the LORD and was manifested in none other than Jesus, the Lamb and Righteous One. Isaiah reminds Israel that He has called them in righteousness. He will take hold of their hand as they are to be a covenant to His people and to the Gentiles.

David's concluding verse is very thankful that God is a righteous judge. This statement comes just after David reminds you and me that evil only "digs a hole" for itself as trouble recoils on itself. Yes, the LORD is the one and only righteous judge. We, like David, sing His praises as we trust in Him and His promises.

As I read back through my key phrases, I am reminded that evil cannot and will not overtake me, even if I die in its wake! God is my refuge and strength an ever-present help in time of trouble (Psalm 46). Continue to seek His face as the Righteous Judge will endure forever. Amen!

Peace
Connected in Him, I stand
GHR

PSALM 8

How Majestic is Your Name!

As I read through this psalm, I immediately thought about the hymn, "How Great Thou Art." King David has a wonderful grasp of God's greatness and glory. This psalm is a distinct departure from the previous psalms of lament. The term majestic implies royalty. The dictionary defines it this way, "impressive or beautiful in a dignified or inspiring way." King David was royalty himself but stood in awe of the wonders of God and uses creation as his backdrop in describing His wonders, making humans exceedingly small in comparison.

The faith and trust of children are stated here in verse two. Here children sing His praise. Jesus uses this quote in Matthew 21:16 during one of His many conversations with the Chief Priests and Scribes. David compares God's creation – including the moon and stars – to lowly man! David is in awe of how little he is compared to God's great creation of the heavens and earth. If you sit back and look at what we know today about the heavens, it's no wonder David was in awe. The moon is about 2,160 miles across and 238,857 miles away from earth. The sun is 93 million miles away from earth . . . and so large that 1,300,000 earths would fit in it!

The son of man noted in verse four is mankind in general but is also used both in the O.T. and the New Testament (referred to as "N. T.") as a reference to Jesus in his true man state.

Jesus, as Son of Man, is the only person who truly reflects God's image. St. Paul talks to his church in Colossae (1:15-16). "He (Jesus) is the image of the invisible God, the firstborn over all creation. For by him, all things were created: things in heaven and on earth, visible and invisible, whether thrones or powers or rulers or authorities; all things were created by Him and for Him." The N. T. uses this psalm in other places where the Son of Man is a "little lower than the angels," and then also where He has His glory restored and has "placed all things under His feet."

The word "glory" has always intrigued me. My weekly *Saturday's Notes* dating back to 1991 begins with my address to a charity auction for the Indianapolis Lutheran High School. The theme was based on Isaiah 60:1. I was struggling with the word glory and asked my mentor and uncle (Late Reverend Robert Trautmann) this question: "What does glory mean to a Jew?" His response was a stack of books earmarked with references to God's glory. Well, here's what I wrote in my address: "The word 'glory' was special to the Israelites. While it had several meanings, the word implied the PRESENCE OF GOD. God's presence was the cloud in the wilderness, later the Glory of the tabernacle and His temple. God's glory continues to be with us in His temple, our bodies, as believers in Jesus Christ, the only Glory of God the Father."

This psalm is used frequently in the N. T. referring to Christ. He entered this world in less than a kingly majestic manor and yes, made a little lower than the angels. But His work of salvation was in God's plan. Unlike Abraham when his sacrifice of his only son was interrupted, God went all the way with His one and only Son sacrificed for your sins and mine!

O LORD, our Lord, how majestic is your name in all the earth?

Peace
Connected in Him, I stand
GHR

PSALM 9

God's Eternal Faithfulness

The O. T. is full of instances where God's chosen people (Israel) have waxed and waned in their faithfulness. It was seemingly easy for them to quickly forget how God delivered them from their enemies time and time again! Why? The question is rhetorical of course, as we know it is sin! But, God, in His agape love for those who trust Him, is eternally faithful.

The first portion of Psalm 9 offers praise to God for his greatness, wonders and ever-presence. The second portion shifts to one of pleas for action and deliverance from his enemies. This psalm was evidently set to music and has been entitled, "The Death of the Son." Theologians are uncertain of its meaning, but some manuscripts (Septuagint) have this psalm combined with Psalm 10, as together they make an alphabetic acrostic, that is, using each letter of the Hebrew alphabet.

Praise is a part of most psalms and used numerous times in the N. T. St. Paul opens his encyclical letter to the church at Ephesus with words of praise. Following his opening greeting, verse three begins with "praise." His words of praise tell of God's greatness, having called us to be His own, out of grace, through the death of His Son on Calvary's cross. He has endowed each with gifts to serve Him by serving others. Verse 12 of that letter reminds you and me that we are to give God all the praise and honor for having heard the word of truth and received the gospel of salvation and sealed by His Holy Spirit. Amen.

David's words of praise are from his heart, that is, a true form of worship. He promises to tell of God's wonders and continue to sing praises to the Most High. The psalm may have been written following Israel's victory over the Philistines. Israel had many encounters with the Philistines. The first is recorded in 1 Samuel 4-7. The Israelites were defeated with thousands of casualties. Then, they remembered that the LORD's covenant (Ark) was not present. When the Ark was brought into their camp, their shouts of joy made the earth tremble as of an earthquake. When the Philistines heard the news, ". . . were afraid." But they were successful with even more casualties and the loss of the Ark. The Ark of God (His presence) brought death and destruction to various cities where it was placed. Finally, they said, "Give it back to the Israelites." Eventually, Samuel told the people, "If you are returning to the LORD with all your hearts, then rid yourselves of the foreign gods . . .and commit yourselves to the LORD and serve Him only." Their return to faithfulness yielded victory over the Philistines.

The last encounter is with the young shepherd boy, David, and the great Goliath. We know that David was outsized, but he said, "I come against you in the name of the LORD Almighty."

These stories of victory show that God's presence is all-powerful even though outnumbered. He reminds us (verse 10) that those who know Him and trust in Him will never be alone nor forsaken by God! Just as the LORD never forgot the Israelites in their plight, with the Philistines, David reminds us that he will not ignore the cry of the afflicted (verse 12). God's people are referred to as Zion (also refers to Jerusalem). The Daughters of Zion is a phrase showing the loving and caring relationship as a father to his child(ren). Israel was never forgotten nor forsaken by the LORD. Rather He continued to show His great kindness to them when they returned with a contrite heart.

As those who are called by His Spirit, we need to continue to seek Him and pray for God's mercy and grace to those who have not seen nor heard of Him. I am reminded of the Great Faith Chapter (Hebrews 11) and the author's description of those O. T. people who had faith in God's promises. Then in verse 6, the author states, "And without faith it is impossible to please God, because anyone who comes to Him must believe that He exists and that He rewards those who earnestly SEEK him (emphasis added).

Like David, we too can with all confidence offer praise to the Almighty for His wonders and deliverance. Seek and ye shall find, knock and door will be unlocked.

Listen to the hymnist re: faithfulness:

> Great is thy faithfulness, O God my Father;
> There is no shadow of turning with Thee.
> Thou changest not: Thy compassions they fail not;
> As Thou has been, Thou forever wilt be,
> Great is Thy faithfulness! Great is thy faithfulness!
> Morning by morning new mercies I see;
> All I have needed Thy hand hath provided;
> Great is Thy faithfulness, Lord, unto me!
> (LSB: 809 v. 1)

Peace
Connected in Him, I stand
GHR

PSALM 10
The Afflicted

Psalm 10 has no title per se as most do in Book I, but the theme is surely obvious. The author is anonymous. However, most agree it's David since ancient texts combine Psalm 9 and 10 together as an alphabetic acrostic psalm. David was a very compassionate man and King of Israel. His compassion shows here for those who have been attacked by the wicked. He begins his psalm questioning why God is standing so far off.

Does God really ignore those in need? Well, let's look at times past, going back in time to when the Israelites were slaves in Egypt. The 3ʳᵈ chapter of Exodus begins to tell the story of the LORD appearing to Moses in the burning bush. (Theophany). Listen to verse 7ff, "I have indeed seen the misery of my people. . . I am concerned about their suffering. . . I will rescue them . . . to a land of milk and honey . . . the cry of Israelites has reached me." Was not God concerned?

Psalm 10: 1-11 recount the mind of the wicked in their attack of those most vulnerable. David asks, "Why do you hide?" (Psalm 10:1b) The wicked lie in wait as a lion, in cover to catch the helpless. The wicked brag of their conquests, boasting that their God has forgotten and has covered His face! I am reminded of Job and his plight. God allowed Satan to destroy everything in Job's life. Job refuses to give up on God, yet he does not understand why all this is happening to him. Is God listening?

We, too, have the same issues as Job did and then later, in David's time. The wicked seem to be all-powerful. They seem to succeed and nobody's listening. Let's look at Jesus himself, the Son of God, the

Messiah! The gospel of Mark is written showing Jesus' compassion. Mark tells about Jesus' baptism, his appearance on the mountain with Moses and Elijah (The Transfiguration) and of course, his death. In the first two instances, we see God's voice saying, "This is my beloved Son in whom I am well pleased." In the last situation God was silent. Jesus cries out, "My God, My God, why have you forsaken me?" But God remains silent. The act of atonement was necessary so that your sins and mine are wiped away, presenting us blameless before His glorious throne. Was God really ignoring His Son? The quietness of God was for you and me! He has heard our plea for help and deliverance from the wicked one. He uplifts the afflicted even as David cries out in Psalm 10.

In verse 12 and beyond, David's tone changes to one of confidence in God's presence. "Arise, LORD! Lift up your hand O God. Do not forget the helpless." (Note: This verse mirrors the same theme in Ps 9:12). David's confidence builds as he states that God does see and calls God the helper of the fatherless. Then, in the concluding verses David builds the crescendo. Listen, "The LORD is King for ever and ever; You hear O LORD the desire of the afflicted."

Our God is a compassionate, loving and all-seeing God. He knows the plight of the afflicted. He hears the cries of those who come to Him. We know that God promises to hear us and answer our prayer.

Pray with me. O God, our loving LORD, who has never ignored those who seek His face. Make us ever mindful of your eternal presence - especially in times of trouble. Protect the homeless, the helpless and those in need. Make us servants according to the needs of others. Let us always rejoice knowing full well that You are in control. Your will be done. Amen.

Peace
Connected in Him, I stand
GHR

PSALM 11

Can Wickedness Prevail?
Even in Hiding?

Who will rule? The wicked or the righteous? That seems to be the $64,000 question. David elaborates in this psalm, as he continues to seek refuge in the One who is his LORD and protector. We are not sure when this psalm was written, but it could have been when King Saul was in pursuit of David, who was in hiding. Perhaps some of David's advisers were suggesting that he flee from his adversaries (verse 1b).

David goes into some detail about those who seek his fate, even using bow and arrows shot into the shadows (hiding). The righteous here are described as upright in heart. If the wicked survive in destroying the foundations of the righteous, where can they hide?

David may be anticipating his adviser's recommendation to flee; and then he reminds himself that the LORD is on His throne, implying that He is in control. The key word here is "look." If we look AT the world and its temptations and delusions, then we can, like David, become afraid. But if we look UP to the LORD above, we can in all confidence as to who He is and that He continues to be in control.

What are the results of the LORD's observations? Well, the wicked are doomed to destruction and described as suffering from "burning coals" and "burning sulfur." The burning or fiery coals may be a metaphor that describes God's judgment and/or spiritual purification. The burning sulfur is extremely dangerous, as its melting point is 239 degrees F. with the brimstone and the smoke extremely dangerous.

David's advisers were less than optimistic. Their view was to flee from the "arrows" of his enemies. We see in verse 7b that David says, "The upright will see His face." The upright are the righteous, and our LORD (Jesus) speaks of them in the Sermon on the Mount in Matthew's gospel. In Matt 5:8, He says, "Blessed are the pure in heart for they shall see God."

So, let us see what David's options are. The wicked will see, or experience coals of fire and sulfur heaped on their heads. The righteous will see His face. Let's see? What does he do? The answer is the same for you and me today. We can live a life of the world (wicked) or can rely on the righteous. Which is it?

St. John, in his first epistle, reminds us that hope keeps us pure; and St. Paul says, "Hope does not disappoint us (Romans 5:5)." John reminds his readers that the children of God will be like Him! Thus, trust in God versus wickedness or the worldly pressures.

As David was in fear of his enemies, we too can take comfort in the truth that God is in His temple and has promised to protect us, as our hope in Him is true! Amen.

Peace
Connected in Him, I stand
GHR

PSALM 12

Deceiving Lips

David has a trilogy of psalms beginning with Psalm 11 that relate to wickedness. My title for Psalm 11 was "Can Wickedness Prevail?" This psalm focuses on the lips where David says, "Everyone one lies . . . flattering lips speak with deception."

The first four verses are petitions to the LORD for help and a request to destroy accusers. The final four change gears where we see a promise to action and the confidence of David.

"Help . . . for the godly are no more," is almost a cry of despair by David. The prophet Isaiah devotes several chapters (56-59) on the sins of his day. Chapter 57:1 is similar to David's cry for help. Listen! "The righteous perish, and no one ponders it in his heart." Each author is dismayed over evil and the apparent loss of anyone righteous. David continues his cry for assistance by requesting that the accusers be destroyed. He says, "Cut off the flattering lips and . . . boastful tongues." Scripture is rich with references to the mouth and lips. The table below lists several references and a brief summary of the content.

Lip References

Source	Summary
Psalm 140:3	Viper's poison on lips
Psalm 141:3	Keep watch. . . my lips
Proverbs 10:32*	Lips righteous: know what is fitting Lips wicked are perverse

Proverbs 12:22*	Lord detests lying lips
	Lord delights in truth
Proverbs 13:3*	Guarding your lipsàguards your life
	Rash lips àruin
Romans 3: various	NO one is righteous:
	throats are open graves
	tongues are deceitful
	lips are poisonous/vipers
	mouths are cursing/bitter

*Antithetic

David's prayers are answered. Beginning with verse five, the LORD has heard the cries of the weak and needy. He says, "I will now arise . . . I will protect them from those who malign them." Comforting the needy is a common trait of our LORD. The N. T. is ripe with examples of how the LORD seeks out the needy. Healing the sick, the blind, the deaf and the paralytics are among the many examples of our compassionate LORD.

The final verses express David's confidence in the LORD's promise to act. Why? Because David knows that the words of the LORD are flawless and compares them to a purified silver that has all impurities removed through its seven-step process. We can also remain confident that those who speak lies with their lips will end in ruin says the Proverb (see table above).

Peace

Connected in Him, I stand

GHR

PSALM 13

How Long?

This psalm concludes the trilogy with Psalms 11 and 12. Deliverance sometimes takes longer than we, as human beings, expect. David was no different. His opening words are, "How long?" In other words, "What are your waiting for?"

The first few lines of this psalm continue to expound on his question of "How long?" Listen! "How long: will you forget me? will you hide your face (refuse to listen)? wrestle with my thoughts? will my enemies' triumph?" All these questions are still true today. As Christians we ask, "How long?" just as David did centuries ago. David is perhaps expressing his fear of death from his enemies. David is concerned that his enemies will continue to seek him out if the LORD waits too long. He says, "My enemies will rejoice when I fall."

God does promise to answer prayers - but in His time. David says, "I trust in your unfailing love . . .and my heart rejoices in salvation." The word trust is defined as a firm belief in something or someone, or having confidence placed in one. David continues to trust in the LORD . . .and couples it with His unfailing love (agape). The word trust is commonly used in Scripture, especially in the O. T. including the Psalms. David's son, Solomon, says, "Trust in the LORD with all your heart and lean not to your own understanding." (Prov 3:5). The prophet Isaiah also says, "I will trust in the LORD forever." (Is 26:4). and again, the author to the Hebrews quotes Isaiah from another section.

David may have feared death, but it is here referred to as "sleep." This concept is very dear to the Christian. As I have learned from my mentors, unbelievers die but believers fall asleep in Jesus. Amen! Our Lord Jesus uses this concept of sleep in relation to two of his resurrections (Daughter of Jairus and Lazarus). St. Paul picks up on this concept in his resurrection chapter 1 Corinthians 15. Listen. "But Christ has indeed been raised from the dead, the first fruits of those who have fallen asleep." (1 Corinthians 15:20) St. Paul here reassures all Christians that we who have expressed our faith in the Messiah will literally be sleeping (temporary) vs eternal death (permanent).

David concludes with his vote of confidence, "I will sing to the LORD for He has been good to me." Amen and Amen.

Peace
Connected in Him, I stand
GHR

PSALM 14

Fools Rush In!

David opens with a very strong word→fool. A fool in Hebrew is one who is morally deficient. In Scripture, it also refers to unbelievers. The balance of verse one continues the nature of the fool. He is corrupt and his deeds are vile. The conclusion is that no one does good.

Does the LORD care? Of course, He does. David reminds his readers that the LORD looks down from above to see if there are any who seek Him. St. Paul picks up on this section in his letter to the Romans (3:10). Romans 3 begins talking about God's faithfulness and never-changing nature. Then, Paul reminds his readers that neither Jew nor Gentile is righteous by nature, as they are all under sin. Verse 10 then quotes Psalm 14, indicating there is no one who is in the likeness of God and are all-together worthless.

Many areas of the ancient world were polytheistic, that is, worshiping many gods. This was especially true of ancient Greeks and Romans. Furthermore, they believed that no god would hold them to account. David even asks a rhetorical question, "Will the evildoers never learn?"

The Psalmist is confident that God is present in the company of the righteous. While the fool frustrates the poor, the LORD is their refuge. Matthew details the Sermon on the Mount and in chapter 5 quotes Jesus: "Blessed are the poor in spirit (sinners) for theirs is the kingdom of God." The "poor in spirit" recognize their sinfulness and seek refuge in the Almighty. As Christians, we too recognize that without the Holy Spirit, we cannot call Jesus LORD. The Spirit of God calls us to faith and leads us to a righteous state through the blood of the Lamb of God.

David expresses great joy in the thought that the called people of God will bring salvation to its people through the Son of God, the promised Messiah. Let's go back and review God's call to Abram and His promise. "I will make you into a great nation and I will bless you; I will make your name great, and you will be a blessing. I will bless those who bless you . . .and all peoples of the earth will be blessed through you." (Gen 12:2-3).

Indeed, God was faithful in His promise to Abraham, Isaac and Jacob. David now recalls God's promise and awaits the LORD's restoration of His people. As the world is drifting away from the true God, I pray that the fools who rush in to corrupt, might come to the knowledge of the truth for God wants all to be saved! Amen.

Peace
Connected in Him, I stand
GHR

PSALM 15

Ten Commandments of the Righteous

Psalm 15 takes a big departure from the various psalms of lament of David. This psalm uses a question & answer type format, examining the blameless. Historically, President Thomas Jefferson said that this psalm is "The picture of a true gentleman."

The psalm begins with a question, "Who may dwell in your sanctuary?" David begins listing what I call the "Ten Commandments of Psalm 15." Five of the 10 are listed as positive traits and the balance as what not to do. The table below summarizes the list.

Positive	Negative
Blameless	Does not slander
Does what is righteous	Does no wrong to neighbor
Speaks truth	Does not slur fellow man
Despises vile/honors those who fear Lord	Does not overcharge (usury)
Keeps his oath	Does not take bribes

The use of the term "blameless" is common. It does not suggest that we are perfect (sinless); rather one who is blameless is a virtuous person and above suspicion. Various other psalms use this term often as an adjective with the noun walk. (Psalm 26:1; 26:11; 84:11; 101:2, 6; and 119:1).

What then shall we say? A person of faith is blameless before the throne of grace by way of the atoning sacrifice for sin by the Lamb of God. Alone, it is impossible to please God. A person of faith must always seek the Lord's guidance to "walk the narrow path." In that way, we can speak truths, maintain our promises, and do whatever else is righteous. The antithesis is that the person of faith avoids those traits that are negative or that we are not to do.

The Ten Commandments of the Righteous will not be shaken! That's the conclusion.

O God, I am a sinful human being and deserve eternal destruction for my sin. You have promised to make me holy and blameless by the blood of Your one and only Son, who bore my sins and those of the world so that we can become righteous in your sight. Help me to live as a righteous man. Amen.

Peace
Connected in Him, I stand
GHR

PSALM 16
Prophetic and Fulfilled

No other psalm can be as enlightening as this psalm of David. This *miktam* of David is golden! The term miktam carries various possible meanings. Dr. H. C. Leupold refers to it as "a mystery poem," while other call it "golden" and "engraving." Regardless of its true meaning, the psalmist uses this platform to tell you and me that regardless of what life may bring, God (el) will keep us safe and is our eternal refuge. The term *el* means "The Strong One." The plural form often used in scripture is *Elohim*. Personally, I like the combination of YHWH ELOHIM which might be translated "the Lord God Almighty.

This Psalm 16 is quoted by various N. T. writers including St. Peter and St. Paul. We can also point a relationship to the "Suffering Servant" chapter in Isaiah 53:10-11. Listen to the prophet: "Yet it was the LORD's will to crush him (Jesus) and cause him to suffer, and though the LORD makes his life a guilt offering, he will see his offspring and prolong his days, and the will of the LORD will prosper in his hand. After the suffering of his soul, he will see the light of life and be satisfied by his knowledge my righteous servant will justify many, and he will bear their iniquities." David here could be pictured as the O. T. Christ.

David begins with confirming statements of his absolute trust in God himself. And, "Apart from you, I have no good thing." (verse 2b) Christ himself totally relied on His Father in doing His holy and complete will for His Son. Jesus had complete faith just as his ancestor, David, had hundreds of years earlier. David speaks of those faithful (saints) as ones in whom God takes pleasure or delight. Then there is everyone else.

Verse 5 reminds you and me that, like David, we too have been assigned our portion in life; and that, by faith, our "lot is secure." We can take solace that this faith is by far our greatest possession. David continues to praise his LORD, who is always before him and at his right hand (place of honor). This place of honor (right hand) is in Hebrews 10:13 referring to Jesus' act of salvation for mankind and being rewarded His place of honor as a job well done and assuming his place of honor at the right hand of God. Just as David's faith is not shaken (v8), our LORD himself did not walk away from the road of horror in front of him.

And so, here it comes. THEREFORE is the key word that the Bible uses frequently to let its readers know that something very important is coming. David says, "My heart is glad . . .my tongue rejoices. . .my body will also rest secure." David is certainly firm in his faith and his entire being rejoices. The balance of verse 10 is quoted by St. Peter in his Acts 2 sermon on Pentecost. Listen to Dr. H. C. Leupold in his book: *Exposition of the Psalms*, "David did lie down and die, and so in a sense this statement was never fulfilled in regard to him. But in Christ it was fulfilled; and the best statement of the resurrection of the Christ." "Thus, Christ's resurrection has vindicated David's bold assertions in faith," continues Dr. Leupold.

What then can we say? Listen to St. Paul in his first letter to the church at Thessalonica: "May God himself, the God of peace, sanctify you through and through. May your whole spirit, soul and body be kept blameless at the coming of our Lord Jesus Christ. The one who calls you is faithful, and He will do it." (1 Thessalonians 5:23) These words of Paul echo David in his belief that his whole being is confident and will be filled with joy in God's presence in the place of honor.

After reading and re-reading this 16th psalm, I am more confident in my faith, as Christ's ancestor, David, proclaims unfailing love and trust in *Elohim* – The strong one. Let me close with one of my favorite doxologies. "May the God of peace, who through the blood of the eternal covenant brought back from the dead our Lord Jesus, that great shepherd of the sheep, equip you with everything good for doing his will, and may he work in us what is pleasing to Him, through Jesus Christ, to whom be glory for ever and ever. Amen." (Hebrews 13:20-21)

Peace
Connected in Him, I stand
GHR

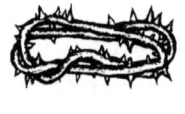

PSALM 17

The Face of Vindication

This psalm of David is similar to the previous psalm but could be interpreted as being more intense. David continues to pray for his safety from Saul's opposition (1 Samuel 23). David opens this personal lament with a plea to God to hear him and listen to his cry for help amongst his enemies in hot pursuit. David is confident that his walk has been in God's path (verse 5), versus those of his enemies.

In subsequent verses, David is asking God for extraordinary deliverance. Listen to David's plea: "Show the wonder of your great love, You who save by Your right hand those who take refuge in You from their foes." (verse 7) Oftentimes, the right hand of God is in reference to His omnipotence and almighty power. David is assured of his LORD's love and that His right hand (power) will be his rescuer. This confidence in the Lord's deliverance continues: and in verse 13, he says, "Rise up, O Lord . . . and bring them down!"

This psalm is concluded in high fashion. "And I – in righteousness I will see your face." What a powerful statement from an O. T. God-fearing man. This statement foretells David's ultimate time with his LORD in eternity. Because of God's righteousness blanketing you and me by the blood the Lamb, we too shall see Him "face to face." (Revelation 22: 4) David lived in faith of the promises of God a thousand years prior to his Lord's walk on this earth as the ultimate deliverer from sin, death, and the evil one.

A few hundred years later, Isaiah was commissioned as a prophet. Listen to his commissioning statement: "I saw the LORD seated on a throne, high and exalted, and the train of His robe filled the temple . . . the seraphs covered their faces . . . and said, "Holy, holy, holy is the LORD Almighty; the whole earth is full of his glory." (Is 6:1-4) The face of God is perhaps a symbol of spiritual protection and blessing. Remember Aaronic blessing? Listen, "May the LORD bless you and keep you; the LORD make his face shine upon you and be gracious to you; the LORD turn His face toward you and give you peace." (Numbers 6:25-26).

The O. T. is rich with other references concerning God's face. "Seek his face always." (1 Chronicles 16:11) The psalmists also refer to God's face, including God hiding his face from our sin. The gospel writers tell us that Jesus' face shone like the sun in His transfiguration on the mountain (Matthew 17:2). St. Paul reminds us that God's light shines in our hearts (the light of faith). And he says, "Give us the light of the knowledge of God in the face of Christ."

Yes, David's final vindication is the knowledge of the eternal blessings promised to all who love Him and profess their faith in the Holy One. In the final chapter of St. John's Revelation, he sees the river of the water of life, as clear as crystal, flowing from the throne of God and the Lamb. Then, we like St. John, will see His face, which will replace the need for the light of the sun. Revelation 22:16 concludes with our LORD's sign-off and points to his relationship to David, "I AM the Root and Offspring of David, and the bright Morning Star." Amen and Amen.

May the God of all grace and mercy continue to shine eternal love on you and may you (like me) see Him face to face in the resurrection.

Peace
Connected in Him, I stand
GHR

PSALM 18

The Strong One! – A Hymn of Thanksgiving

The tone of this psalm moves from one of lament to one of thanksgiving for God's powerful deliverance from David's enemies. The first two verses set the overall tone of David's love for and praise to God for His safety, deliverance, and divine protection.

The opening words are fruits of his faith! "I love you, O LORD, my strength." There is no way that a faithless person can say, "I love you" as David did! I am reminded of the great reformer's explanation of the Apostle's Creed when he said, "I believe that I cannot by my own reason or strength believe in my Lord Jesus Christ or come to Him. The Holy Spirit has called me by the gospel, enlightened me with His gifts, and sanctified me . . ." (Martin Luther, 3rd Article, paraphrased). The words chosen here to show confidence in the LORD's deliverance are many. Strength, Rock, Fortress, Deliverer, Shield, and Horn (symbolizing strength). It's a biblical Thesaurus!

The rock is often used in both the Old and New Testaments as a symbol for God. Here the Hebrew word could be defined as "crag." A crag is a rugged massive rock that surely defines strength. Jesus used the term to describe his great Apostle Peter (Matthew 16:18): "On this Rock I will build my church . . . and the gates of hell will not overcome it." The rock is none other than the Lord himself, as the foundation to all who are in faith. In the same sentence David adds fortress to define how God has protected him.

The conclusion of verse two adds "shield" and "horn" to his terms of strength. The use of shield in the O. T. goes back to Moses' opening book in Genesis 15:1. Here the LORD promises Abram that He is his shield and exceeding great reward. In the N. T. St. Paul uses the term to describe faith (Ephesians 6 – Armor of God) - the shield of faith to extinguish the arrows of the evil one. The term "horn" is a symbol of strength and power. David uses the term in the phrase "horn of my salvation, my stronghold."

The Latin word *paean* has been used by theologians to describe Psalm 18. Paean is a fervent expression of joy and thanksgiving. This psalm of thanksgiving also mirrors 2 Samuel 22, which is referred to as David's Song of Praise.

The next section elaborates on various negative terms of destruction and despair, but then are quickly followed by the LORD's recompense. Terms like "cord of death/grave, "torrents of destruction," "snares of death," and "earth quaking and trembling" are eloquently stated but are no match for the Strong One! David describes how the LORD thundered from heaven; the voice of the Most High resounded; his arrows scattered the enemy; giant bolts of lightning routed them, and finally, the blast of breath from His nostrils laid bare the foundations of the earth. What more can we say concerning God's strength versus the world?

"As for God, His way is perfect; the word of the LORD is flawless!" "And who is the Rock except God?" This is a powerful statement, followed by a rhetorical question. David is firm in his belief that his power and strength are from none other than the LORD himself. Faith in the Almighty is able to withstand all and yes, even in death, we overcome its finality based on the promises of God to take us to be with Him in eternity.

"The LORD lives! Praise be to my Rock! Exalted be God my Savior!" Unlike the gods of this world, our God is ever living and has been exalted to the right hand of the Father. David's crescendo is powerful and gives us confidence in the modern-day to praise God to all (nations) because of His unfailing love and kindness, shown to all who believe in Him. Amen.

Peace
Connected in Him, I stand
GHR

PSALM 19

The Word Creates and the Law Guides

"And God said" are the opening words in Genesis 1, describing His wonderful creation. God's Word created. This wonderful psalm begins with the author's wonder at God's glory. "The heavens declare the glory of God; the skies proclaim the work of His hands." And verse two speaks to his ever-creating nature as we see how "day after day" and "night after night" creation speaks!

The sun! David tells us that God pitched a tent for the sun and like a champion, runs its course (created by God!), making its daily circuit. Let's examine some statistics about the sun. First, one million earths could fit inside the sun. Secondly, it contains 99.86% of the mass in the solar system. It's almost a perfect sphere with temperatures reaching 15 million degrees Celsius. But here's the biggest number you may ever see. The mass of the sun is 1.9885×10^{30}kg. I converted that number to Tons and the number is 451,900,000,000,000,000,000,000,000. Yes, that's 451.9 octillion. (numbering naming source: www.almightyguru. com). And yes, nothing is hidden from its heat.

If the Word indeed creates, then the Word indeed can set forth laws. God delivered the decalogue to Moses at Mt. Sinai. Here David indicates, "The Law of the Lord is perfect. . . and his statutes are trustworthy." What else can be said? God's laws set guidelines as lights to our path and daily walk. Listen to David's list of the Law's function:

revives the soul; makes us wise; gives us joy; gives light to the eyes; provides warnings, and rewards those who keep them.

This psalm discusses God's Law and is similar to Psalm 119 in a sense. Listen to the often-quoted verse (105): "Your word is a lamp to my feet and light to my path." David understands the purity of His laws. Yet, David also understands that he is a sinful human being. His prayer is that God would "forgive his hidden faults."

St. Paul uses language similar to David in his letter to the Romans (1:18-20) as nature proclaims God's existence and power. Man indeed has no excuse according to Paul's stern statement. I believe that the Apostle John took some guidance from David related to the Word of God in His creating and His perfect laws. Read this beautiful dialogue in John 1:1-14. The Word (Greek=Logos) here is capitalized indicating a reference to our LORD. And then this great Word became flesh and tabernacled among us.

May this great Word proclaimed remind you and me that His word is creating, lawgiving and yes, saving! It's the Word made flesh that came to fulfill God's great promise to redeem the world in His Son.

Peace
Connected in Him, I stand
GHR

PSALM 20
Eternal Victory

Psalm 20 and 21 are companion psalms of victory that God had directed for His servant, David, over his enemies. Requesting victory from God over life's many challenges and adversaries was seen by David as more reliable than any human power. This psalm may refer back to the times listed in 2 Samuel 8 or 10 which describe David's armies and their victories over multiple nations including, Philistines, Moabites, Edomites and the Ammonites.

It would appear from the language here that Israel was praying for its king. The first five verses are requests of God. Listen to the nine different requests offered up in this payer:

- Answer when in distress
- Protect you
- Send you help
- Support you
- Remember your sacrifices
- Accept your offerings
- Give you desires of your heart
- Successful plans . . ., and
- Grant all your requests.

Prayer is a divine communication between God and His people or believers. It is a privilege to be able to talk to your LORD. This was the case then, as it is now in modern times. These requests were made first, then in later verses we see their statement of faith, "We trust in the name of the LORD our God."

If this psalm and its companion (21) relate the times listed in 2 Samuel 8 and/or 10, then listen to 2 Samuel 8:14: "The LORD gave David victory wherever he went." The psalms also state that many would place their trust in chariots and horses; but as we saw in II Samuel, they did not win out over God's people. It was not due to the superior Israelites, but rather it was God's power (verse 6) that provided victory.

It is this power that overcame sin, death, and the evil one in the victory posted by none other than God's Son, Jesus, who suffered agonizing death on the cross of Calvary. This perfect sacrificial death provided the sin sacrifice that would not need to be repeated. God then showed His power over death by raising His Son to life to reign forever and ever. This sacrifice brought eternal victory to all who trust in the LORD.

So we, like David and his constituents, can pray as they did to answer our prayers of deliverance in times of trouble. God's right hand of strength delivers all who trust in Him. While David's enemies were brought to their knees, we rise up and stand firm! Amen and Amen.

Peace
Connected in Him, I stand
GHR

PSALM 21

Victory's Wisdom

This psalm is a likely continuation of the previous psalm however; this psalm is one of thanksgiving for God's deliverance. David opens his psalm with a statement of thanksgiving for God's strength in granting victory and the joy expressed by its author. David's prayer to his LORD shows his great thanks for God's gifts to him as king. His thanks for his physical gifts are noteworthy; however, his thanks for his "eternal" blessings made him glad with joy, due to His presence. How often do we recognize God's gifts to each of us especially our eternal salvation?

David reminds each of us (v. 7) that he trusts in the LORD; and because of His unfailing love, we cannot be shaken! The *Life Application Bible* notes this: "His wisdom is the best strength you can have." David's son, Solomon, reminds us in his book of wisdom that, "Wisdom preserves the life of its possessor." (Eccl. 7:12b)

While earthly oppressors appear to succeed at times, we like David can be assured that victory and judgment are the LORD's. The verses (8-10) describe his confidence in the LORD's power and acts of judgment. I am reminded of St. Paul's Resurrection Chapter (I Cor 15) where Paul is bold in stating Christ's victory over his enemies. For just as Christ was raised from the dead, we too will be raised to newness in life. Then in the latter verses comes the most powerful statement: "Where O Death is thy sting; where O Death is thy victory? For the sting of death is sin and the power of sin is in the law. But thanks be to God! He gives us the victory through our LORD Jesus Christ."

(1 Corinthians 15:55-57)

The leaders of the Jews indeed plotted evil against our Lord, but they did not succeed (verse 11). David too was giving thanks that his enemies plotted against him and the land of Israel, but they did not win!

David's final verse is one of confidence and one that showed his people that the LORD is the God of Israel, promised long ago. The LORD is exalted on high and the land of Israel will sing His praise.

Our accolades today cannot be too lengthy as we get reminded that our blessings are not our doing but God's! Our victories are not ours, but His alone! Our stewardship is a definite recognition of the source of our very being and all that He has given us. May we all continue to give thanks for victory over our enemies and especially over the evil one.

Peace
Connected in Him, I stand
GHR

PSALM 22

Suffering Servant. . . And Delivered!

The term "suffering servant" is generally a label assigned to Isaiah 53 in which the O. T. prophet describes the Messiah as a lowly servant, versus a kingly type, to deliver His people. Yet in Psalm 22, we can also see this same type of suffering language in two-thirds of the psalm. But the gospel-like language is also present in the concluding verses where deliverance is found.

Earlier, my notes suggested Psalm two was the first of the Messianic psalms. The LORD frequently referenced the psalms in His earthly ministry. The *Life Application Bible* lists 18 different psalm references that are Messianic and four of them are in this very psalm. The first verse in this psalm is certainly the most memorable as we go forward 1,000 years to the crucifixion of our LORD: "My God, my God, why have your forsaken me?" (Matthew 27:46) While hanging in agony on Calvary's tree, Jesus looked up and, in indescribable pain, asked His Father why He had left him alone?

David is certainly prophesying of his Savior's misery and suffering. But was he personally suffering? And from what? Or whom? Evidently, David had some great trial that we don't understand, but clearly is describing his LORD's ultimate sacrifice for humankind.

In my Bible study called, *The Gospel of Mark, The Compassionate Christ*," Lesson #2, entitled "Mark: The Voice: Present and Absent," I remind my readers to think about the Father who sent His only Son into this world to save them from this inevitable damnation! The voice prophesied by Isaiah would prepare the Way as one like Elijah. Indeed,

John the Baptist did. And the voice from heaven above was prominent in two events. First at His baptism, the Spirit descended as a dove and spoke of His pleasure. Secondly, on the mountain of Transfiguration, the voice spoke again saying, "This is my Son, whom I love. Listen to Him!" (Mark 9:7) But in the final situation on Calvary the voice was noticeably absent, thus Jesus' cry as depicted in Psalm 22:1.

Theologians have divided this psalm in two sections. The first includes verses 1-21 and describes a sense of being forsaken. Then the second section in verses 22ff describes a deliverance. In some way, it's the Law and the Gospel of Psalm 22. The Law shows us our sin, i.e. being forsaken or separated from God by way of sin. The Gospel shows us our Savior, i.e. being delivered from sin by the Messiah's rescue event on Calvary and His glorious victory resurrection on the third day.

David makes reference to being lower than a man, vis-à-vis, a worm in verse six. Being the lowest of the low (worm) echoes his feeling of being rejected, scorned, and despised. Yes, just as our LORD was in His earthly walk to Calvary's cross. The worm reference is also shown in Isaiah 41:14 and Job 25:6 again showing a feeling of helplessness and frailty.

This feeling of utter helplessness is also shown in David's description of being poured out like water in verse 14, followed by bones out of joint and his heart turned to wax. His strength is dried up and is compared to a piece of shattered pottery (potsherd), that fails in its duty to hold water.

According to various lists, the Messianic references are as follows:

Psalm Verse Reference	Description	N. T. Quote/Use
1-21	Agony on the cross	Matthew 26 and 27
18	Casting lots for clothing	Matthew 27:35 John 19:23
15	He thirsts on the cross	John 19:28
22	He will declare God's name	Heb 2:12

Source: Life Application Bible Table, p.923

The Servant King was definitely despised and rejected by men but also left alone to suffer for your sins and mine. . . and those who are afar off. This is the same Suffering Servant that Isaiah prophesied – and, by the way, used past tense verbs – as if it had already happened! That's a guarantee that God's earlier Messianic promise is a sure thing!

The future appears bright to the author in later verses, as he professes his confidence that future generations will be told about the LORD. And they too will proclaim His righteousness just as David did. "For he has done it!" Amen and Amen.

Yes, the Suffering Servant was sacrificed and totally ignored by His Father. Yet, we too know that He was delivered from the totality of the grave on the third day as death could not hold Him down. He arose victoriously and was witnessed by many who continued to proclaim that Jesus is the Messiah, the Savior of the world. May all who know His name praise the LORD, and may those who have not heard receive the Good News of Him crucified.

Peace
Connected in Him, I stand
GHR

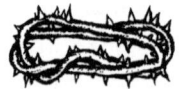

PSALM 23

The Shepherd, A Beginning Trilogy

Is there anyone who has never heard of the 23ʳᵈ Psalm? Likely not at least in some form. But in order to get the whole meaning of this short psalm of David, one needs to read the six verses not only individually but in a collective manner. I have chosen to entitle this note "A Beginning Trilogy," for reasons that you will read later. For now, let's just enjoy of the beauty of this song of David.

1 Samuel 16 reminds us that David was a shepherd himself, tending his father's flock. He was chosen by God to replace King Saul and was anointed (spirit-filled) as the heir apparent to rule over God's people. Some might suggest that this psalm was written as the boy David while others indicate that it was written sometime after his anointing. Regardless, the meaning doesn't change in my view.

Sheep are relatively unintelligent animals, more so than pigs or cattle, and as such are pastoral (need shepherding). They tend to flock together and are often reluctant to move due to predators. They are afraid to move out of light to darker areas. They have a diurnal (24-hour day and night difference/cycle) type of activity; as they tend to graze from dawn to dusk, while stopping periodically to rest and chew their cud.

This short psalm provides a look at the various functions of a shepherd. First, David explains that he too needs a shepherd for guidance, just as he provided guidance for his flock. Beginning in verse two, we see that a shepherd provides rest and guidance to his flock. The terms green pasture and still waters show how the shepherd provides an area for rest (to lie down). Verse three reminds us that the shepherd also guides his flock into the "right" places, just as our Good Shepherd (John 10) leads us into paths of righteousness. The true shepherd not only provides for physical guidance but also providing a spiritual component. His "name sake" here refers to character or reputation according to theologians.

Verse four shows us the protecting feature of a shepherd. Again, a shepherd is careful to guide his flock through areas of darkness where danger lurks. A shepherd provides a strong sense of reassurance to sheep as they pass through darkened areas which could mean death or extreme danger.

A shepherd had to provide food or sustenance for his flock as well as oil as a remedy for anointing and gentle healing. Sheep tend to overgraze a pasture (heft) and thus may have to be moved to a new grazing area. David uses the phrase, "My cup overflows," which reminds me of how a shepherd provides for every need, and in abundant supply.

So we have a shepherd who provides rest and guidance, food and sustenance, and protection. Now we see in the concluding verse a summary showing "goodness and mercy" for the flock and most importantly, a fellowship with God himself as the eternal Shepherd.

Now to the "trilogy." King David said, "The LORD is my shepherd." When our LORD became flesh and dwelt among us, He said, "I AM the good shepherd," (John 10:11 KJV, emphasis added). Here Jesus reminds us that the man who enters by the gate versus other means is the shepherd and the others are thieves and robbers. Then, the doxology of Hebrews says it this way: "May the God of peace who through the blood of the eternal covenant brought back from the dead our LORD Jesus, that **great** shepherd (emphasis added) of the sheep, equip you with everything good for doing his will, and may he work in us what is pleasing to Him, through Jesus Christ, to whom be glory for ever and ever. Amen." (Hebrews 13:20-21)

Thus, we have an increased emphasis on the status of the shepherd – from no adjective through "good" to "great"!! Also, St. Peter gives some advice to under shepherds (pastors) in his first epistle when he said, ". . .

And when the Chief Shepherd appears, you will receive a crown of glory that will never fade away." (1 Peter 5:4)

Peace
Connected in Him, I stand
GHR

PSALM 24

The Presence of God

Psalm 24 is one of the greatest psalms of David. It most likely is a psalm of praise to God for having delivered the Ark to its proper place in the City of David, Jerusalem. Tradition suggests this psalm was sung on the first day of each week in the temple services.

In modern times, this psalm is the subject of a centuries-old hymn written by a German Lutheran pastor. Georg Weissel (1590-1635) wrote this hymn that is traditionally sung during Advent season of the church year. Bach used this hymn in Part V of *Christmas Oratorio*.

This movement of the Ark of the Covenant is described in 2 Samuel 6, where we are told the Ark was moved from the home of Obed-edom to Jerusalem, or the holy hill of the LORD. The Ark was symbol of God's presence. When the Ark was stationary, it was placed in a sacred tent called the Tabernacle. The Ark contained the 10 Commandment's, Aaron's rod, and a portion of manna.

The beginning of David's song of praise is a statement of God's ownership and control over His creation. David states, "He founded it." If God owns everything, then we are his stewards (managers), using His gifts wisely. David asks somewhat rhetorical questions in verse three: "Who may ascend to the hill of the LORD?" And, "Who may stand in His holy place?" 2 Samuel 6 tells us that Uzzah brought out God's anger when he touched the Ark. And God struck him down! This action may have been the source of David's questions raised in verse three.

David is quick to answer his question about worthiness. He says, "He who has clean hands and a pure heart." The combination leads me to believe it's not only cleanliness outwardly but also an inward purity and recognition of God's holy presence. I am reminded of my mentor's closing blessing following church services when he reminded us that our body is a temple of the Holy Spirit. As such, David continues, we are not to worship idols nor swear falsely.

Blessings surely follow, says David, for those who are prepared to enter His presence. He will surely bless them and indeed will redeem or vindicate us by His beloved Son, Jesus. The term "seek his face" is a term that shows me an earnest effort to seek God. No one has ever seen God, but David is attempting to invade or penetrate the very presence of God.

"Lift up your heads," says the psalmist. The gates of Jerusalem welcome back the Ark to the City of David. The gates are opened wide to accept God's glory in the form of the Ark of the Covenant. Yes, LORD, please come in and abide with us. That can be our prayer today as Christians we have the very presence of God in us as in faith the Holy Spirit abides in us.

Listen to the hymnist as he writes this beautiful Advent hymn.

Lift up your heads ye mighty gates!
Behold, the King of glory waits.
The King of kings is drawing near;
The Savior of the world is here.
Life and salvation He doth bring;
Therefore rejoice and gladly sing.
To God the Father raise
Your joyful songs of praise.
(LSB 341, verse 1)

Fling wide the portals of you heart;
Make it a temple set apart
From earthly use for heavn's employ,
Adorned with prayer and love and joy.
So shall your Sov'reign enter in

And new and nobler life begin.
To God alone be praise
For word and deed and grace!
(LSB 341, verse 4)

Peace
Connected in Him, I stand
GHR

PSALM 25

Deliverance

This psalm takes on the character of one seeking help or deliverance from his enemies. One of my Bible footnotes indicates that 72 of the 150 psalms speak of enemies. This psalm of King David is called acrostic which means each of the 22 verses begins with each letter of the Hebrew alphabet.

Dr. H. C. Leupold, in his *Exposition of the Psalms* suggests that, ignoring verse 22, the remaining 21 verses are divided into three sections of seven verses each. The first section seeks God's help and guidance and then concludes in the final verse of this section imploring God not to remember his sins because of God's agape love. I am especially focused on three specific verbs of action from David's mouth: **show me, teach me** and **guide me.**

> **Show me→your ways**
> **Teach me→your paths**
> **Guide me→in truth**

Just as God's mercy and love date back to His people of old, David is indeed confident that God is his Savior and will indeed continue to show him (give direction); teach him (to walk in God's path); and guide him (in all truth), as he continues to govern and lead God's people.

The second section begins with David's acknowledgment of God's goodness, as He continues to instruct sinners in the way of righteousness. Again, David requests that God would forgive his shortcomings just as in the first section. Like David, we too indeed sin much and fall short of the Glory of God. And like David, we must seek His continuing forgiveness for our sins. The final verse in this section is very powerful. "The LORD confides in those who fear him; He makes His covenant known to them." That word "confides" gives comfort to His own, showing a very close relationship with every person in faith!!

King Solomon also uses the thought of "confides." (Proverbs 3:32) "For the LORD detests a perverse man but takes the upright into his confidence." Indeed, the Lord has taken all who believe in Him into His confidence. The mysteries of the Almighty are made known to us. The I AM of old is the same I AM who died on Calvary's tree for the sins of King David and yes, for you and me.

The final verses again state a petition. Listen again to David's verbs: **Turn to me and be gracious; Look upon my affliction; Take away my sins; Guard my life and rescue me.** David is very confident in his hope in the LORD.

The final verse is like an epilogue as David summarizes his petitions and confession as he pleas to God to redeem Israel from all their troubles. This psalm of David is one that the people of Israel needed to hear, as their leader was confident in his faith in the LORD. He pleaded for God's continued deliverance from its enemies, just as the God of old delivered His people from slavery under Egypt's iron hand.

"I believe, help my unbelief." (Mark 9:24). This is my prayer, as I believe that human nature casts doubt on faith and unbelief comes ever so close.

Peace
Connected in Him, I stand
GHR

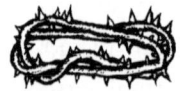

PSALM 26

Bold Petition vs. Boasting

This psalm starts out with a bold petition for vindication, as he has led a blameless life. Is this a bold petition or is it boasting? David was certainly not sinless (as no one is!) but claims to be blameless by confessing his sin before God and pleading for his mercy and forgiveness.

This David was certainly one of Israel's greatest and perhaps even the greatest in the entire O. T. But he too also had his misgivings, just and you and I have. What does the word vindicate mean? The simple definition is to "clear of accusation or blame." Does David's opening in verse one sound like boasting? Let's take a minute to look at the prophet Jeremiah. Listen to the prophet's instruction on boasting: "Let not the wise man boast of his wisdom or the strong man boast of his strength or the rich man boast of his riches, but let him who boasts boast about this: that he understands and knows me (Lord), that I am the LORD, who exercises kindness, justice, and righteousness on earth, for in these I delight." (Jeremiah 9:23-24)

David continues in this petitioning psalm to state his trust in the Lord without wavering. Then comes verse three with his three BOLD verbs: test me, try me, and examine my heart and mind. David is confident about God's examination as he has continually walked in truth. The KJV uses the term fidelity vs. truth. I specifically think the term fidelity has a stronger meaning, that is, "unfailing fulfillment or strict adherence." His atonement is noted in verse six where he states he has washed his hands and gone to the LORD as an absolved man of faith.

David's faithful walk with his LORD is one which we too should emulate. His faith is even noted in the Great Faith Chapter (Hebrews 11:32). In his concluding verses in Psalm 26, David repeats his bold statement (blameless life) all because of God's merciful redemption.

We too can be confident, as David, that we will receive the reward of faith by the blood of the Lamb who died once, for all! David certainly struggled over his life before and after his kingship. He states in his final verse that he is standing on level ground as God has heard his plea and leveled out the rough places in his walk.

May we, like David, be bold in our faith especially as we continue to seek to be blameless before God by confessing our sin and asking for God's agape love and forgiveness based on His Son's atoning sacrifice. Then, we like the great assembly of believers, praise the Lord. Amen.

Peace
Connected in Him, I stand
GHR

PSALM 27
The Light of Life!

"The LORD is my light and my salvation - of whom shall I fear?" (verse 1) This is a profound statement of confidence from the great David. The question here is rhetorical, as David knew the answer. The two key personalities assigned to the LORD are light and salvation. If those attributes are true, then what can anyone fear?

This psalm of David is one of mixed emotion. First, he states his confidence and then he shifts to a lamenting type tone. But one might suggest a single-minded type of approach. As we have seen in the previous Davidic psalms, his confidence in the LORD is unmatched. In verse one, his statement and rhetorical question is unmatched in today's world. ". . . My light and my salvation - of whom shall I fear?"

First, light is the beginning of the creating work of the LORD. Darkness is in reference to the world's temptations, and the light is the liberation from eternal damnation by the blood of the Lamb. Light yields faith and salvation yields reward. Agree? Or disagree?

We too have a single-minded focus in life. The LORD is my stronghold. . . How can I be afraid in the house of the LORD which is His stronghold? David continues with what lies before him – evil men; enemies; armies. Only ONE thing he asks, "That I will dwell in the house of the LORD all the days of my life." (verse 4b)

God's dwelling place is his temple, i.e. our bodies, which are the dwellings of His Holy Spirit who dwells among us! David says, "For in the days of trouble He will keep me safe in His dwelling." (verse 5) What else can we say?

His tone changes to one of a lamenting type. "Hear my voice when I call. . ." He continues with his plea to be merciful and answer his request. David continues to seek His face but is in fear for his enemies who might destroy him. He even suggests that his mother and father may forsake him. . . the LORD will "NEVER" forsake him! Amen. David concludes in his crescendo: "I am still confident of this: I will see the goodness of the LORD in the land of the living. Wait for the LORD; be strong and take heart and wait for the LORD." (verses 13-14)

St. Paul also talks about God's light in terms of Christ's return (Romans 13:12). "The night is nearly over; the day is almost here so let us put aside the deeds of darkness (sins) and put on the armor of light."

Whether it's David's earthly enemies or his spiritual trials (or ours?), let us put on the armor of His light, awaiting the final return of the Lamb of God, the eternal Son of the Father, and Salvation to the world. Amen.

Peace
Connected in Him, I stand.
GHR

PSALM 28

The Rock. . . A Fortress of Salvation

I have concluded that David's prayer life is unequaled! Most of the psalms in Book I are written by King David. This psalm begins with powerful words like many others before Psalm 28. "To you I call, O Lord my Rock." David is comfortable with his Lord as The Rock and it's in this sense that he begins this psalm with a prayer for help.

The word "rock" is used in Scripture over 100 times according to my word search and its use. In the O. T. Hebrew, the term is (eben). The first character, Aleph represents God or Heavenly Father. The remaining characters means Son (or Jesus Christ). Thus, a stone means the Father and the Son. The Greek use of rock takes on both the masculine and feminine forms of the noun. The *petros* is the masculine form and is a piece of rock, shifting or rolling and insecure. The *petra* is the feminine form and is a solid, immovable rock. Thus, all the names for the LORD where Rock is capitalized is the feminine form meaning a solid, immovable rock.

The Rock here is capitalized and thus a name for our God. David requests his LORD not to turn a deaf ear to him and his needs. He realizes that if God does, then his fate is sealed for the pit (Sheol). Here David is looking heavenward, with his hands lifted up to God's Most Holy Place. While not necessary, David reminds the Rock that the evil one shows no respect for the LORD, nor His works. (verse 5)

I have listed just a few references to the Rock used in the O. T. in the table below. Here we see various songs from Moses, David, and Isaiah as well as an oracle against Damascus.

Source	Author	Content
Deut 32:4	Song of Moses	He is the Rock; his works are perfect
II Samuel 22:3	Song of David	The LORD is my Rock, my fortress, and my deliverer, my shield, and my horn of salvation.
Isaiah 17:10	Oracle against Damascus	You have not remembered the Rock, your fortress.
Isaiah 26:4	Song of Isaiah	Trust in the LORD forever, for the LORD, the LORD, is the Rock eternal.

These O. T. references are interesting from noted writers. Moses reminds us that the Rock's words are perfect and without error. David's use in 2 Samuel lists Rock first, indicating its importance in the list followed by qualities that he ascribes to the Rock. And then Isaiah reminds us to trust in the Rock forever and even repeats the LORD for emphasis, showing that this Rock is eternal.

The balance of David's psalm (verses 6-9) gives praise to his LORD for having heard his cry for mercy. Like in 2 Samuel, David calls his Rock strong and his shield. Yes, it's He that he trusts and Him alone! David reminds Israel the LORD is their strength their fortress for salvation through the Anointed One to come.

May the LORD, the Rock eternal, continue to be your fortress and shepherd to carry you to be with Him in His second coming.

Peace
Connected in Him, I stand
GHR

PSALM 29

The Voice!

If there was any idea or suggestion that God is not in control, then please read Psalm 29 before you reach any rash decision to the contrary. The first two verses of David's psalm ascribe or assign glory and strength from all creation including the "mighty ones" (KJV heavenly beings). "Worship the LORD in the splendor of His holiness." All God's creation bows to the glory of the Mighty One.

David then begins verse three by describing the "voice" of the LORD. His voice is like that of thunder. The KJV translates it this way, "The God of glory thundered." The voice of the LORD is then described in a powerful sense over various aspects of nature. Examine the seven uses in the table below

Voice	Description
1. Voice over the waters	stormy mighty waters and thunder
2. Voice is powerful	strength over nature
3. Voice is majestic	even heavenly beings worship
4. Voice breaks cedars/ Sirion (Mt Hermon)	breaks Cedars of Lebanon into pieces; Mt. Hermon to skip like a deer
5. Voice strikes like lightening	striking more quickly than a lightening flash
6. Voice shakes Desert Kadesh	mighty deserts obey His voice
7. Voice twists oaks/strips forests bare; alternate: makes deer give birth	more powerful than forests and can control nature (birth)

After you read through the list, think about these facts. First, the Cedars of Lebanon are mighty trees, and can reach 120 feet tall, and are up to 30 feet in circumference. Sirion or Mt. Hermon is a cluster of three summits, each approximately 9,232 feet in height, where the voice can dance like a wild ox.

The O. T. has multiple references to the "Voice of the LORD." In David's Song of Praise, recorded in 2 Samuel 22, he states, "The LORD thundered from heaven; the voice of the Most High resounded." (verse14). In Job he states, "God's voice thunders in marvelous ways; He does great things beyond our understanding." (Job 37:5)

David shifts his thought back to the Great Flood in the days of Noah. The flood waters rose with 40 days of rain and even covered the highest mountains by 20 feet (see Genesis account). The waters flooded the earth for 150 days and it took almost eight months before Noah stepped on dry ground.

As David recounts the strength of the LORD and His absolute control over creation, then cannot God also control our so-called troubled times that we often refer to as storms in life? The only time the voice of God was absent was while His Son was hanging on Calvary for your sins and mine. Unlike at Jesus' baptism or his transfiguration when the voice echoed its pleasure, Calvary was desolate, leaving our Lord alone.

This parallel of how God's control over nature and our lives, points to David's final verse. "The LORD gives strength to his people; the LORD blesses his people with peace."

Peace
Connected in Him, I stand
GHR

PSALM 30

The Living Stone

The O. T. is rich with references to God's presence, which is sometimes referred to as "glory." This psalm of David was likely written at the dedication of the site for the future temple. His plan to build a house was to be tabled for the time being. David was concerned that his LORD had to live in a tent! By today's standards, David had amassed "billions of dollars" in materiel for the Temple of God. (See 1 Chronicles 22).

The LORD's vision to Nathan (2 Samuel 7) is worth reading when considering this psalm. Listen to the LORD's words: "I have not dwelt in a house from the day I brought the Israelites up out of Egypt to this day. I have been moving from place to place with a tent as my dwelling." (v. 6). The LORD's house is not dependent on a building! The Church of God is not a building, but its people with God as the Living Stone, or foundation, of the church. Each believer represents a stone in the spiritual house of God. Israel was God's living stone in the O. T. St. Peter, in his first epistle, reminds us that Jesus is the "living Stone" that was rejected by men. (1 Peter 2:4) Peter quotes the O. T. prophet Isaiah (28:16).

David opens his psalm of praise with a notation of exaltation! Why? Because the LORD has lifted him out of the depths (preserved from his enemies). David uses the phrase "O LORD" seven times and twice more with the "O LORD my God." The nine uses are primarily cries for help and mercy. We know that David was the warrior king of Israel, and with the LORD's mighty arm, conquered the enemy's advances. Verse six reminds us all that human security and its reliance can lead to destruction. It's only when we realize that when the LORD makes the mountains stand firm, we can feel secure in God's ever-living presence. He not only delivered David from his various trials, but also delivers you and me from the eternal "Pit."

Yes, the Living Stone became flesh and dwelt among us (John 1:14), and He was born to die for us. He is the capstone that the builders rejected (Psalm 118:22). Yes, the O. T. living stones failed to see the foundation of their deliverance.

David closes with a statement of praise and joy. He says, "You have turned my wailing into dancing; you removed my sackcloth and clothed me with joy." Sackcloth was worn as a token of sorrow, but David gives thanks to the LORD his God for having clothed him in joy and will give thanks forever!

Maintain your house on a firm foundation, relying on God's presence for deliverance. We should always remember that a Christian's joy is eternal while the earthly happiness is only transient.

Peace
Connected in Him, I stand
GHR

PSALM 31

Preservation of the Faithful

This psalm of David was written in a time of stress, perhaps during a period when Saul was in pursuit of David. 1 Samuel 23 recounts David's conquering of the Philistines at Keilah. God was with David and told him to attack and that he would be victorious. In the end, the people of Keilah were not grateful, as they were willing to hand David over to the pursuing Saul. Again, the LORD intervened and saw to it that David and his men left Keilah to avoid Saul's capture. Saul's son Jonathan also helped his friend to avoid his father's pursuit.

With that background, listen to the verbs used in the first few verses of this psalm: **deliver me; lead me; guide me; free me; and redeem me.** David's trust in God Almighty is perhaps unequaled. His first sentence reminds you and me that he has taken refuge in the LORD. He continues his plea for rescue, acknowledging that God is his Rock and fortress (citadel). Verse five should be very familiar since our Lord repeated it on Calvary's cross, "Into your hands I commit my spirit." (Luke 23: 46) In fact, the N. T. reminds us that Stephen, one of the seven chosen to assist the apostles, was stoned and prior to his death, he said, "Lord Jesus, receive my spirit." (Acts 7:59). Each use in the N. T. reflects a confirmation of faith in the One True God, like David's in this psalm.

David reminds us that God did not allow him to be handed over to his enemies but allowed him to remain free in a spacious place. We too, are free from sin (enemies) as our Lord has provided a space for us in the Book of Life. Yes, our Lord Jesus Christ hung on Calvary's cross to prepare a place for us.

David continues to admit he is stressed and overcome with grief and sorrow. (verse.9) His life is consumed with anguish and his strength is dissipated. He elaborates how his enemies continue to conspire against him and plot to take his life. (verse 13) In today's world, the evil one attempts to snare sheep from the pen and take their life from eternal bliss to that of fire. But, David says, "I trust in you, O LORD; I say, You are my God." (verse 14) He commits his time to God's hands as his savior from his enemies. The phrase "Let Your face shine," is one of total recognition of the LORD to an issue. The opposite would be to turn your back to something.

Verse 19 begins a new section with a rhetorical question: "How great is your goodness?" David knows that God's goodness for His flock is "abundant" (stored up). David is abundantly joyful to be in the shelter of God's presence.

What then can we say? "Praise be to the LORD, for he showed his wonderful love to me when I was in a besieged city (Keilah)." (v. 21). "Love the LORD, all you saints," says David. (verse 23) That statement like many others in Scripture applies to you and me today. Why? Because the LORD **preserves the faithful.** Verse 23 is antithetical, i.e. polar opposites. He preserves the faithful . . . and repays the proud in full. Be strong and take heart is the suggestion David makes to those of us who hope in the LORD.

Peace
Connected in Him, I stand
GHR

PSALM 32

Joy of Forgiveness

As a healthcare professional, I know and have observed how someone benefits (gets relief) from a medication or treatment for a particular condition. In David's case, he experiences the pure joy in knowing that his sins are forgiven! This marvelous psalm of David's is one of a deep penitential attitude toward his egregious sin. According to *Life Application Bible,* this psalm is one of 10 such penitential psalms. I am particularly taken by the word "covered." The word is used 109 times in Scripture, and most are in the context of shame. Jeremiah also points out in Lamentations 3:44 that the LORD can cover His presence with a (cloud) so that no prayer can get through - but not in David's case.

As David begins his verse, he is obviously confident that God has made him blameless before the throne of grace. Listen to his words: "Blessed is he whose transgressions are forgiven; whose sins are covered. Blessed is the man whose sin the LORD does not count against him and in whose spirit is no deceit." (verses 1-2) These opening verses were quoted by St. Paul in Romans. The lawyer-like Paul uses Father Abraham as an example of justification (works or faith?). He says, "If" Abraham were saved by his works then he could indeed boast. But, instead, he was justified by faith and it was "credited" to him as being right with God. The Abraham example then leads into David's Psalm 32 and these verses. (Romans 4:7-8)

Our LORD also used similar words in John's gospel as he noted that Nathanael was a true Israelite in whom there is nothing false (or deceitful). (John 1:47)

As David moves into verses 3ff, he relates the effects of his sin and its effects, without forgiveness. Listen to his words: **my bones wasted away; my strength was sapped**. Verse 5 shows his contrition and acknowledges his sin. Thus, the joy of forgiveness. No longer did he suffer his bodily loss of strength but experienced God's great love for a contrite sinner.

Here comes the "therefore" which suggests some revelation. David says to us, "If it worked for me, it can for you too!" (paraphrased). The final verses are reminders from God himself, who suggests we should not be like a horse or mule that must be led by bridle, rather let the LORD lead you in your walk in faith.

A pastor (under shepherd) of Jesus Christ, uses this psalm (v. 5b) in the confession and absolution portion of a liturgical service. (LSB, Divine Service #3, p. 184). With this confession, we too can be joyful in knowing that our sins are covered. Let's listen to David's final verse in this eloquent psalm of forgiveness: "Rejoice in the LORD and be glad, you righteous; sing, all you who are upright in heart." (verse 11)

In closing, I am reminded of another of David's psalms that is appropriate here. "Create in me a pure heart, O God, and renew a steadfast spirit within me. . . Restore to me the joy of your salvation and grant me a willing spirit, to sustain me." (Psalm 51:10,12)

Peace
Connected in Him, I stand
GHR

PSALM 33

Praiseworthy!

Did you know that a lyre is a type of harp? The lyre is a U-shaped type of harp that has a varying number of strings (4, 7 or 10). The harp also has multiple types and has more strings than its lyre counterpart (14 to 17). The use of stringed instruments dates back into antiquity, in some cases to 3,000 B. C. The Bible mentions the first harpist (father of all harpists) as Jubal, Lamech's son in Genesis 4:21. The O. T. term *nevel* is translated as harp (lyre with a skin membrane). A *kinnor* is a nevel with thinner strings.

Psalm 33 opens with the words "Sing joyfully… it is fitting to praise Him." The harp and ten-stringed lyre are mentioned in the following verse as instruments used in this new song of praise. The author of this psalm is listed as anonymous, but some experts attribute it to David as he was indeed an accomplished musician. David was chosen by King Saul to be in his service as a musician (1 Samuel 16:15).

Regardless of the author, it is noteworthy that our God is praiseworthy as verse four says, "The word of the LORD is right and true; He is faithful in all He does." The word "true" has multiple meanings including exact conforming to a standard or a pattern. The author then begins to elaborate on how the LORD, by His word created the world and all that there is therein. He also is a deliverer as He "foils" the plans of the nations and thwarts their purposes. But the LORD's plans stand firm forever! (verse 11)

So, the LORD is the creator and the deliverer but is also LORD over all - and most importantly, He is the Savior! All these attributes are praiseworthy, and the author encourages nations to seek God as their LORD. All the nations who choose Him will be blessed and receive an eternal inheritance.

The author also reminds his readers that we are never alone, for the eyes of the LORD are always on those who fear (revere) Him. That's comforting! Now, as with those before the Christ, we can all await in the sure and certain hope for our deliverance, as He is our help and shield.

"In Him our hearts rejoice, for we trust in His holy name." (verse 21) The final blessing in verse 22 is comforting and reassuring. We continue to place our hope in Him for His unfailing love that rests upon all who call Him LORD and Savior. Amen.

Peace
Connected in Him, I stand
GHR

PSALM 34

Taste and See: A Lifetime of Goodness

The story of David and his travels to avoid Saul's attempts to kill him are many.

1 Samuel 21:10 – 22:4, records a time when Saul was in pursuit. David escaped to Abimelech (King Achish) in Gath. The Gath people wondered why they should befriend such a man who has blood on his hands – more so than Saul! So, David left and found shelter in a cave. Eventually, he found favor from the king of Moab for his family. The account in 1 Samuel tells us that David feigned madness for fear of what King Achish might do to him. The whole story sounds bizarre especially as a backdrop to this beautiful psalm.

Psalm 34, like others, is acrostic, with the 22 lines representing each letter of the Hebrew alphabet. After reviewing the verses, I have entitled my notes as *Taste* and *See: A Lifetime of Goodness*. Why? First, David says he will "extol (exalt) the LORD at all times," and his praise will always be on his lips. That sounds quite the opposite from a man running for his life and having to appear mad to escape harm.

"I sought the LORD, and he answered me!" Verse 4 reminds you and me today that we too can seek rescue in His presence, regardless of the enemies or foes that surround us – or our status in life, rich or poor. God is indeed our strength but is also our nourishment. Listen to David, "Taste and see that the LORD is good; blessed is the man who takes refuge in Him." (verse 8) The *Life Application Bible* makes a great analogy here re: taste and see. "It's a warm invitation, 'Try this; I know you'll like it'" (34:8 footnote).

The senses of the righteous are indeed keen. St. Peter uses this same language in his first epistle regarding being holy. He opens chapter two with a reminder to rid ourselves of all kinds of evil and to crave the spiritual milk like newborns, and growing to adult food. Then, he says, "Now you have tasted that the LORD is good."

The author of Hebrews (6:5) also warns about tasting the goodness of God in His Word and then falling away. "It is impossible for those who have once been enlightened, who have tasted the heavenly gift, who have shared in the Holy Spirit, who have tasted the goodness of the Word of God...to be brought back to repentance."

We know that God does provide protection and delivers us from evil, but that does not mean that troubles won't beset us from time to time. David reminds his readers in his beautiful psalm of the following:

Function (He, the LORD)	Result
Delivers – v. 4	from fears and troubles
Saves – v. 6	from troubles
Guards - v. 7	encamps his angels around us
Supplies – v. 9	all our needs/lack nothing
Listens – v. 17	when we talk to Him
Redeems – v. 22	the righteous/servants

David's psalm offers-up a lifetime of praise with the Word of God always on his lips. He invites you and me to "taste and see" that the LORD is good. In his final line of verse, we too can take solace that "no one who takes refuge in Him will be condemned."

Peace
Connected in Him, I stand
GHR

PSALM 35

Without Reason

While David had many external enemies, it appears in this psalm that he also had internal ones. While David was an ancestor of the LORD, he was not without trials and tribulations – even internally just as Jesus had both internal and external enemies. David was a righteous and good king. He attempted to be ruling with justice but experienced those who were against him – even hated him! In today's politic (USA and beyond), we have the same tenor, that is, hatred without reason.

This psalm has been listed by some as being "imprecatory." That means cursing or to invoke evil upon someone. If you examine the first few verses, you will see David's requests:

Verb (Request)	Result
Oppose (contend)	those who oppose me
Fight	those who fight me
Come to	take up shield/buckler
Brandish (Block)	weapons against those that pursue me

I remember a time in my personal life when I felt that people were dumping all their troubles on my back. And I asked myself, "Why me?" I happened to meet a colleague shortly thereafter, and when asked, "How are you?" I replied, "I feel like I have been dumped on." She looked at me and said, "You know why?" I said, "No." She said, "It's because you have JESUS written on your back." Was this an angel of the LORD? I'm sure David had thoughts, too, as he felt the pressure of internal friction and troubles.

Initially, David felt abandoned as he cried out for deliverance from those who hated him. The table above shows the requests he made for the LORD to fight in his defense. The term "angel of the LORD" is used here in two situations and like the psalm before it, are the only two in the book of Psalms that reference our LORD as the "angel of the LORD."

David requested that the angel of the LORD drive away and pursue his enemies. This term is one that often refers to our LORD Jesus Christ (preincarnate) with multiple references in both the Old and New Testaments. The angel appeared to Abraham and interrupted his sacrifice of Isaac, appeared in the burning bush to Moses, and many more.

David was quick (verse 3) to request that God would remind him that "I AM your salvation." (Psalm 35:3 – emphasis added) This is the same I AM that appeared to Moses in the burning bush (a theophany) and one and the same that died on Calvary for your sins and mine!

Verse 17 would suggest David was a little impatient as he wanted the LORD to act quickly. "O LORD, how long?" This question was offered up to the LORD by David in two previous psalms (6:3 and 13:1). In the first reference, David asks, "How long, O LORD, how long," as his soul was in deep anguish. The latter reference David asks, "Will you forget me forever?" David was eager to have his pursuers (referenced as lions) be put to shame. The LORD Jesus Christ himself asked His Father, "If you are willing, take this cup from Me; yet not My will but Yours be done." (Luke 22:42)

As the psalm continues, the pitch and plea appear to increase. "Be not silent. . . Do not be far from me, O LORD." (verse 22) Then, he says, "Awake," "rise," and contend." All these words were urgent pleas by David. We too appear anxious at times when we wonder how long the LORD will wait until He acts? David remains confident in the LORD as he begins the final section (verse 26) He reminds God that when vindicated, all those who are on his side will praise the LORD for having saved His servant, David. And then the concluding statement promises that he will not ever stop praising God for His righteous deeds.

You and I can be sure that God is not far away (verse 22) for the LORD himself promised us, "And, lo, I am with you alway until the close of the age." (Matthew 28:20 KJV).

Peace
Connected in Him, I stand
GHR

PSALM 36

Love is Priceless!

This psalm has a contrasting theme, first addressing the sinfulness of the wicked, followed by the faithfulness of God toward those who love Him. The author is again seemingly David, although some may suggest otherwise. The author opens with the word "oracle" which has various meanings but, in this case, might well be a wise statement(s). The issue is the wicked who have no fear of God (v. 1), and the faithfulness of God and His priceless love toward those who fear Him.

The opening four verses describe the personality of the wicked. Listen to David's description: **no fear of God; self-flattering; deceitful mouth; evil plotting and a sinful path.** Verse 1b is quoted by St. Paul to the Roman Christians (3:18). Chapter three goes into detail re: God's faithfulness to His creation. As Paul goes deeper into the chapter, he asks a question: "What shall we conclude then?" (Romans 3:9) "Jews and Gentiles alike are all under sin (law)." (verse 9) He then describes in detail how we as humans are unable to seek or love God, as there is no one who is righteous or who seeks God. He concludes his various quotes from the O. T. with this Psalm 36:1b.

But David knows that his God's love is priceless! He uses terms that defy human understanding like: His **love reaches to the heavens; righteousness is like a mighty mountain; justice is like the great deep and then concludes with his unfailing love that is priceless**! If God's love were not absolute, then the law's condemnation would rule and there would-be no-good news of His grace! But, "God so loved the world that He gave His only begotten Son, that whosoever believeth in Him could not perish (from the law) but have eternal life." (John 3:16)

Verses 8 and 9 have beautiful language regarding that wonderful living water that springs from the river of life. That is the living water that the Messiah himself spoke about to the Samaritan woman at the well (4:10ff), then later, when Jesus reminded the crowd at the feast that "If a man is thirsty, let him come to me and drink. Whoever believes in me as the Scripture has said, streams **of living water** will flow from within him." (John 7:37) (Emphasis added). David describes God's love and faithfulness as a fountain of life that is never ending. This fountain provides fresh, cleansing water that leads to spiritual life.

David completes his psalm with a plea that God would continue to love those who know you (i.e. righteous and upright in heart) and that the evil or wicked will fail in their attempts to drive them away.

To God be the glory.

Peace
Connected in Him, I stand
GHR

PSALM 37

Temporary or Permanent?

This rather long psalm of David is perhaps one of my favorites. It reminds me of my college days in a lecture hall, where the professor was instructing his students. This psalm, while it may appear as the wicked have some success, is very mindful of the eventual outcome, which lasts forever. Our life is but a blink of the eye in the LORD's time, and thus it seems that our adversaries are successful. David reminds us otherwise.

This psalm is also acrostic although it is every other verse. This psalm is one of comfort to those who wait "patiently" for the LORD. David opens with the phrase: "Do not fret." Immediately, we have some comfort language as to who may be impatient waiting for the LORD to act. (see also verse 7). This phrase is repeated three times in the first few verses. He quickly reminds us that we are to "trust in the LORD" and to "do good." This concept of trust appears in multiple verses throughout the psalm (verses 3, 4, 5, 7, 34 and 39). Trusting is coupled with patience which when combined, are often an enigma to modern-day Christians, as we expect immediate action.

Patience is an attribute that is often ignored, and even in my case, is difficult to maintain. When things appear that God is not acting, we are reminded that God will act in due season and that punishment will overtake the wicked. Verse five is one that I remember from catechism class and still recall it from KJV: "Commit Thy way unto the LORD. trust also in Him, and He will bring it to pass." Keep your eyes on the road and don't veer from the narrow way. Then verse seven opens with a familiar phrase: "Be still." This phrase is repeated in Psalm 46:10 where the author reminds all of us that we are to be still and listen! Why? Because God is God!

If you look more closely at what it means to follow God, you will see that multiple things happen. It maybe not at first be evident, but in repetition it comes home. Examine the table below for some examples.

Following God:
1. Inherit the land (six times)
2. Enjoy great peace
3. Upholding the righteous (twice)
4. Will not wither in times of trouble/disaster
5. Steps are firm (not to stumble or fall)
6. Utters wisdom (tongues speak wisely)
7. Stronghold/deliverance

If repetition is important, then certainly the author reminds us that following God will allow His heirs to inherit the earth. Remember the LORD's Sermon on the Mount? Matthew 5:5 repeats David's phrase of the "meek" that will inherit the earth. And why does he repeat it so many times? Because it's so important to remind us that while the wicked may appear to be successful, they are like the grass that will wither away!

The latter portion of this lengthy psalm (v. 34) has three key words/ phrases: "**Wait. . . Keep His way. . . He will exalt you.**" Wait again points back to the word "patience." The author continues to remind us to keep His way and do not stray from the path before us. The result? He will exalt you! Amen.

The final exaltation comes from the Savior himself as Christ was the final sacrificial lamb that atoned for the sins of the world. His death and resurrection would erase the sin punishment from the law and grant an inheritance that will endure forever.

If we ponder these words of David, we too can remember that we are to be patient and endure the sufferings of this world so that we may inherit the land (eternity) that has been prepared for us by the Lamb of God.

Peace
Connected in Him, I stand
GHR

PSALM 38

Sin's Consequences –
Grace's Reward

David's sin had consequences! They were apparently both physical and mental pain and anguish. Dr. H. C. Leupold in his *Exposition of the Psalms* says that David's health issues are not mentioned in the historical books of the O. T. But it's clear in this psalm that he has extreme anguish over his sin(s). Some have suggested that this psalm was following his sexual sin with Bathsheba. Regardless of the time, his pain is extreme. Figuratively, he says, "Arrows have pierced me." (verse 2)

His opening verse has two similar requests. First, he begs, "Do not rebuke me in your anger." And then, "(Do not) discipline me in your wrath." The word rebuke is a harsh term that reflects a sharp disapproval or reprimand. David attributes his health issues as consequences of his sin, that is, "no health in my body." Ezra, an O. T. priest, scribe and leader, was one of the key leaders in the Israelite's return from captivity in 538 BC. The Persians, having overtaken the Babylonians, allowed the Israelites to return to their homeland. Ezra led a group back to Jerusalem from Persia. In Ezra 9:6, he writes, "O my God, I am too ashamed and disgraced to lift up my face to You. . . because our sins are higher than our heads." Ezra's comments were made over intermarriages of God's people with foreigners.

The sacrifices and offerings in the O. T. were many; but two were "Sin and Guilt" Offerings. The latter was one that often was for a sexual sin. The fat of the animal was burnt on the altar.

David's description is very vivid. My bones have no soundness; burden too heavy to bear; wounds fester; searing back pain; feeble; pounding heart; failing strength. A term used in modern medicine called "malaise" may well describe David's various complaints. Malaise is general bodily discomfort that is experienced at the beginning of an illness, or it can be a general sense of unease - even depression. His so-called friends are avoiding him and his condition. David was vocal, but our Lord was silent before his accusers.

Verse 15 begins to show some confidence that God will not ignore him. "I wait for you ...You will answer, O LORD my God." He again confesses his iniquity (v. 18) as he continues to be very troubled. He concludes (verses 21-22) with an ultimate cry for help. "O LORD do not forsake me; be not far from me, O my God. Come quickly."

God is the only hope from sin. David, like you and me, suffered consequences from sin, yet God has promised to answer our prayers as a contrite and forgiven sinner. Remember GRACE is an acronym; "God's Righteous at Christ's Expense." The Messiah has made the ultimate sacrifice for sin so that all who believe in Him will share eternity with their Savior. Listen to St. Paul in his great Resurrection Chapter (1 Corinthians 15): "O death where is thy sting? O grave, where is thy victory? The sting of death is sin, and the power of sin is the law. But thanks be to God. He gives us the victory through our LORD Jesus Christ."

Peace
Connected in Him, I stand
GHR

PSALM 39

The Breath of Life

This psalm could be classed as a resolution that was not kept, according to Dr. H. C. Leupold in his *Exposition of the Psalms*. But, as you read this beautiful psalm of David, it is clear that he also notes how short this life may be but that those who trust in our LORD have a "Breath of Life."

David is very humble as he opens his psalm. "I will watch my ways. . . and keep my tongue from sin." The Bible is long with references to the mouth/tongue and its wickedness. King Solomon in his book of Proverbs says, "The tongue of the righteous is choice silver." (Proverbs 10:20). And again, "A perverse tongue will be cut out." (Proverbs 10:31) The prophet Jeremiah also remarked, "The tongue is a deadly arrow." (Jeremiah 9:8)

What then can we say? David was aware that whatever he might have said would be taken out of context. He chose to keep a muzzle on his mouth. . . but then reversed his decision later in the psalm. He notes in verse four, "Show me, O LORD, my life's end." He knew his life was as fleeting as the "breath of life." He remarks that a man's life is like a breath. But, he knows that his hope is in the LORD. (verse 7b)

What is life? It's a short span of human years on this earth that, for the Christian, is one of serving our LORD by serving others. King Solomon remarks in his opening words of Ecclesiastes, "Vanity, vanity. . .utteringly meaningless." (Paraphrased). If we look back to David and his words of wisdom to his son Solomon we see these words; "Walk in His ways and keep his decrees, and commands, His laws and requirements." (1 Kings 2:3)

Verse eight begins with a plea to "Save me." He knew that regardless of life's span, he needed to be saved from sin's transgressions and punishment. He noted that man's sin is rebuked and disciplined. What then is the next step?

"Hear my prayer. . .listen to my cry. . . be not deaf." (verse12) David states he is but an alien on God's earth and his service is but a breath in God's timeframe. We too are but an alien on this earth and here to serve God by serving others. But we also have the promise to convert from alien to resident. Yes, heaven is my home!

Listen to the hymnist as he brilliantly broadcasts the gospel message:

> Therefore I murmur not, Heav'n is my home.
> Whate'er my earthly lot, Heav'n is my home.
> And I shall surely stand
> There at the Lord's right hand; Heaven is my
> fatherland. Heav'n is my home.
> (LSB: 748 v. 3 – Thomas Taylor 1807-35)

My God grant you the breath of life to know Jesus as your Savior from sin and who can change you from an alien to an heir of Salvation.

Peace
Connected in Him, I stand
GHR

PSALM 40

Waiting. . .Not Easy!

This psalm of David is one of deliverance. But there are two distinct portions. The first part is past tense, "I waited patiently for the LORD." Then beginning in verse 11 the tone changes to present tense where he prays "to save me," and "to help me." Some may have suggested this was not intended to be the same psalm but regardless it is agreed to be that of David.

As I read the opening verse, I was reminded of the old saying, "Give me patience and give it to me right now!" Yes, waiting is not easy for you and me and certainly not for David. If we examine the benefits of his patient waiting, we can see that God indeed stepped in and delivered David. The table below lists God's deliverance.

The LORD's action	Benefit to David
Lifted me	Out of the pit
Set my feet	On a rock/firm stance
Put a new song in my mouth	Praise to the Almighty

Blessed is a key word beginning in verse four. David once again points to the man who continues to walk in the path of righteousness, versus the proud, who worship false gods. Like David, those who follow and believe in the LORD are lifted up with their feet firmly entrenched on solid ground. The NIV uses the word "trust" which implies a firm belief.

No one can count His wonders! The blessings of Almighty God are more numerous than the grains of sand or stars in His universe. David indeed cannot even fathom how and where to begin to recount God's divine blessings.

Verse six begins a section (6-8) that refers to 1 Samuel 15:22ff and the Prophet Samuel's rejection of Saul as King over Israel. Samuel says, "To obey is better than sacrifice." David knew of God's various sacrifices, but he also knew that the heart must be in the right place. He states, "Here I am, I have come" which many believe he had come to God's sanctuary.

The author of the Book of Hebrews reminds us of Christ's ultimate sacrifice, once for all times! Hebrews 10:5-10 are like Psalm 40: 6-8. The key verse in Hebrews 10 is: "We have been made holy through the sacrifice of the body of Jesus Christ once for all." (Hebrews 10:10)

David is indeed faithful in his witness as verse 9 reminds us. He does not seal his lips but rather tells of the glory and majesty of his LORD. He is ever conscious of his enemies and pleads to his LORD to save him. "Come quickly," (verse 12) says David. He recalls how many want him dead and out of their lives. Yes, "Do not delay," says David. (verse 17)

How quickly we can forget God's great mercy when things appear good. Then when troubles come, we find it difficult to be patient for the LORD's plan for us. Jesus' Sermon on the Mount (Matthew 5-7) reminds us that our petitions to God do not fall on deaf ears. Listen to the Messiah, "Ask and it will be given to you; seek and you will find; knock and the door will be opened to you." (Matthew 7:7) Going to the throne of grace in prayer is comforting, knowing full well that He listens and will respond. Waiting. . .Not easy!

Peace
Connected in Him, I stand
GHR

PSALM 41

Abandoned

Psalm 41 concludes Book I of the Psalms. Most are authored by David at various times of his life. David's plea is stated as one from a position of weakness. He reminds us all that the ones who attend to the weak are blessed in God's sight. He also states that God delivers in times of trouble.

David is confident that God protects and preserves his life even when his enemies surround him. He also sustains the sick and restores him from illness. David continues to be drowning in sorrow for his past sin(s). While God forgave his sin with Bathsheba, the consequences of his sin remained. Some suggest this psalm was written during the time of Absalom's rebellion. 2 Samuel 15 records the rebellion against David by his son. He wanted to overthrow his father and assume the throne.

The difference between David and his son Absalom was that David was contrite and forgiven. Absalom, on the other hand, was not contrite and continued in his sinful ways. Eventually, Absalom lost his life. David asks for God's mercy (v. 4) and confesses he has sinned. His enemies want him dead! In verse 9, David says, "Even my close friend, whom I trusted," has lifted up his heel against me. Who this might be is not known but it points to the N. T. Messiah and his betrayal by one of the 12. We know that Judas Iscariot spent three years with Jesus. He was the group's treasurer but eventually betrayed our LORD for money. In John's gospel, Jesus is teaching his disciples (chapter 13). This is the time he washed his disciples' feet. The lesson was for them to be servants to others. In his concluding verses, he quotes David's 41st psalm: "He who shares my bread has lifted up his heel against me." (John 13:18)

David is sure in his ultimate victory. He knows God is pleased with him since he continues to deliver him from his enemies. But we also see that David talks about his eternal salvation, that is, being in God's presence forever.

Abandoned? No! David was a contrite sinner. God saved him from his enemies and will ultimately save him into eternity. While we may fall asleep in Jesus, we are not abandoned to the grave but wait expectantly for the return of our LORD, when all those who have fallen asleep in Him will rise to life everlasting.

As with all the five book sections in psalms, Book I conclude with a doxology. "Praise be to the LORD, the God of Israel, from everlasting to everlasting. Amen and Amen."

Peace
Connected in Him, I stand
GHR

PSALMS: BOOK II PROLOGUE

Psalm 42 begins the second book in Psalms continuing through Psalm 72. David continues to be the major author in this Book II; however, we see the sons of Korah, Asaph, Solomon and several unknown authors. In my opening notes on Psalms, *From Beginning to End*, I noted that each of the five books within Psalms somewhat mirror the five books of Moses.

In Book II, the themes of "ruin and rescue," are similar to Exodus, the 2nd book in the Bible. Book II opens with several psalms from the sons of Korah. These three men have an interesting background from Scripture. First, who was Korah? Korah was a Levite in the time of Moses who among others, led a rebellion against Moses. Levites were temple (tabernacle) servants. Numbers 16:1ff tell us of the rebellion with the outcome of 250 being killed by the hand of the LORD for their rebellion. However, we are not told why the sons of Korah survived. But nonetheless, they continued to be God's servants in the temple and authored 12 (sometimes recorded as 11 since #42 and #43 are combined in some texts) psalms.

The three sons of Korah were Assir, Elkanah and Abiasaph. (Exodus 6:24) Some of the most memorable verses from Psalms are contained in the Korah-authored psalms. I have included some of them in the table below.

Table: Korah's Sons: Memorable Verses (Not all included in Book II)

Psalm Location	Text
Ps 46:1	God is our refuge and strength, an ever-present help in trouble.
Ps 46:10	Be still and know that I am God
Ps 48:1	Great is the LORD, and most worthy of praise
Ps 84:10	Better is one day in your courts than a thousand elsewhere
Ps 84:11-12	For the LORD God is a sun and shield; the LORD bestows favor and honor; no good thing does he withhold from those whose walk is blameless. O LORD Almighty, blessed is the man who trusts in You.

PSALM 42

A Spiritual Thirst

Psalm 42 appears to be connected to the next psalm as *Halley's Bible Handbook* considers these "one poem." Regardless, this psalm opens with a deep desire for God. This desire is compared to a deer (masculine form "hart") that seeks streams of waters, so the soul pants for God. The Sons of Korah were a musical guild formed by King David. In this psalm, they use various verbs (pants, thirst, pour out) that relate to flowing water.

How much water does one human need per day? The National Academy of Sciences determined that an adequate intake is 15.5 cups for men and 11.5 cups for women. (A cup is 8 ounces). Daily physical needs are one thing, but what about our spiritual needs? The authors here use the verb "pant" suggesting a significant form of dehydration and/or need for drink (that is, a spiritual thirst). Here the authors note their intense thirst for the living God (verse 2). Jesus refers to the living water in the Gospels. First, he meets a woman at a well in Samaria (John 4) and talks about living water. Jesus responded to the woman who asks where she can find this living water, "Everyone who drinks of this water will never be thirsty again." Again, Jesus reminds the Pharisees that He is the living water that is eternal life (John 7:38).

Yes, the human needs both physical and spiritual water for this life and the life to come. Amen! The authors were discouraged as their enemies said, "Where is your God?" (verse 3) This question implied that their God had ignored them. The righteous have poured out their soul thirsting for peace that knows no understanding. If they can shout for joy and thanksgiving, then why are their souls downcast? Then, they quickly say, "Put your hope in God." (verse 5b)

The authors are quick to remember God and His promises for the Land of Milk and Honey. They say, "from the land of the Jordan. . . to the heights of Hermon to Mizar." Mount Hermon is physically important, as the snows from its peaks provide water to the Jordan River. Mizar is not totally known vis-a-vis its location. It could be the Hermon Hills and it is referred to as a small mountain in the Septuagint. Its meaning is "distress."

The "deep calls to deep" is a term that likely refers to a cataract, that is, water rolling over a steep surface). Literally, a cataract is a large or high waterfall (rapids) that provides a deluge or downpouring. The author compares this deluge to the griefs that have befallen him. But all is not lost! Why? Because God is at all times present – by day and by night. (verse 8) If that is true, then why are the authors mourning? Has their God (Rock) forgotten them? Again, the authors repeat the phrase, "Where is your God" that is a taunt from their enemies.

The final verse is one of confidence as the authors say, "Put your hope in God, for I will yet praise him, my Savior and my God." We too can confidently say that our God is our hope and salvation. This Jesus, the living and spiritual water, has provided our parched bodies with all that is needed to sustain us to eternal life. Unlike our daily physical needs for water, our soul's thirst is satisfied by the Living Water of Life.

Peace
Connected in Him, I stand
GHR

PSALM 43
Hope Prevails

The issue continues. Psalm 42 and 43 are often combined into one poem and generally considered one by most commentators. H. C. Leupold, in his *Exposition of the Psalms*, suggests that the two psalms have three stages: 1) Psalm 42:1-5, tension and pain are most severe; 2) The balance of Psalm 42 suggests healing; and 3) In Psalm 43 the waves of pain and tension have subsided, and peace is all but restored to the steps of the sanctuary. (H. C. Leupold's *Exposition of the Psalms*, p 342, Psalm 43).

The Sons of Korah open with an imperative: "Vindicate me!" To vindicate means to clear of accusation, blame, or suspicion. This clear plea is for God himself to go to their enemies. The authors here are quick to state that their God is their stronghold, but they are apparently unsure why He has rejected them. As God's children, we know that God does not reject those whom He loves. Otherwise, why would He have sent His Son to the cross for total atonement? As humans, we can feel all alone and rejected in times of stress and tension. Thus, the authors seek God and ask Him to send forth the light to guide them.

H. C. Leupold suggests that the use of the word "light" in verse three reflects God's mercy and/or His steadfast love. If true, then the second part of this section makes sense as God's light will bring him to the holy mountain (Mt. Zion, Jerusalem), as God's dwelling place, and to the altar of God. A feeling of restoration overcomes the authors as they are confident that God is their joy and delight. As such, they will ever sing His praises.

The concluding verses appear to repeat frustration referring to a downcast soul. "Why then am I so disturbed?" says the authors. But just as in Psalm 42, the concluding verse is repeated. "Put your hope in God." In times of trouble when all seems to be going wrong, do not fall into a trap believing that God, too, has forsaken you. Like the authors, we too can sing His praises as our Savior and our God. Amen!

Peace
Connected in Him, I stand
GHR

PSALM 44
Echoing Confidence

This psalm begins with a recounting of God's deliverance of His people from Egyptian captivity to the Promised Land. The oral history had been passed down from generation to generation as God's actions drove out nations; planted our fathers; crushed the peoples; made fathers flourish. Yet, it was not by the sword, but by the Word of God (His right-hand, suggesting strength).

When this psalm was written remains in question. Some suggest it was in the time of King Jehoshaphat while others think it may have been in the time of David or even during the revolt of the Maccabees. Regardless, God delivers His people from their enemies. The Kingdom of Judah/Israel always seemed to be in the sights of its neighboring enemies seeking to devour the smaller and weaker nation. Yet, God in His ever-promising and never-relenting nature, continues to deliver His people. Why then do we doubt? It's sin!

The authors rely on God's previous actions of His word (right arm) that has delivered His people from their enemies. It's this history that the authors are now drawing or echoing their confidence. Listen, "In God we make our boast all day long, and we will praise your name forever" (verse 8)

The authors are very distraught! They claim that God has rejected and humbled them. (v. 9). Subsequent verses expound on this devastation and rejection – scattered, sold, made us reproach. Why then has this happened, regardless of the nation's confidence in the LORD? "Our hearts have not turned back," say the authors. Pure anguish ensues.

Then comes a plea to "Awake, O LORD" (verse 23). Assuming that the LORD was asleep or hiding His face, the authors plead for God to rise up and assist in their misery and to redeem them, due to God's unfailing love.

We too can remember that He is not only our temporary (human) solution to troubles but also our eternal salvation from the evil one who can devour us in the lasting battle of unbelief. We must remember that He is our eternal refuge from the armies that may besiege us. With His right hand of strength and power and His love He can deliver His sheep from all adversaries.

Peace
Connected in Him, I stand
GHR

PSALM 45

A Wedding Song: Oil of Joy

Many theologians agree that this psalm is Messianic, i.e. Messiah's future in relationship to the church. Christ the bridegroom and His bride the church (body of believers). The Sons of Korah may have written this psalm for a special wedding of King David or Solomon and his bride. Verse 2 describes how God has blessed His Son i.e. He is blessed forever and has been anointed. Later in this psalm we see the term "oil of joy," which refers to an anointing oil. If you look back to Exodus 30:24 we see the formula for this anointing oil. (Rx written as I would have seen it on a prescription to compound)

Rx	Liquid Myrrh	500 shekels
	Cinnamon	250 shekels
	Fragrant cane	250 shekels
	Cassia	500 shekels
	QS hin w/ olive oil	

According to unitconverters.com, a biblical sanctuary shekel was equal to 0.402 ounces. And a hin is approximately equal to 4L or a little over a gallon in US measurement. (Note: As a pharmacist, I have used "QS" meaning a quantity sufficient of oil to make a total mixture of a hin).

The authors describe the king as being clothed in splendor and majesty and riding forth in victory as "truth, humility, and righteousness" prevail over the king's enemies. As such, this victory is eternal (verse 6) with his scepter of justice ruling over his kingdom. This verse points to the divine character of the bridegroom. The author of Hebrews quotes this psalm (Hebrews 1;8-9), describing the Christ as reigning forever, having been anointed with the oil of joy.

Beginning with verse 10, the authors address comments to the queen, or bride. These verses point to the rich blessings of this union of the bridegroom and the bride. Christ as the bridegroom and His bride, the church, are one!

Yes, our LORD has called us to be with Him eternally as a bride and bridegroom are united as one. Our union with our LORD is made perfect by the agape love of the Christ, who has gone to Calvary for His bride, so that we can live with Him in eternity.

Peace
Connected in Him, I stand
GHR

PSALM 46

A Battle Song. . . In All Confidence!

While this psalm's number may not be noticeable, the lines of this beautiful passage inspired the creation of one of the most memorable hymns in Christianity: *A Mighty Fortress is Our God* (Ein Feste Burg) written by the reformer, Reverend Dr. Martin Luther in 1529. The psalm contains 11 verses in its entirety, but H. C. Leupold suggests that verse one was the inspiring verse for Dr. Luther in penning his hymn.

While verse one was inspirational to Luther, we cannot ignore the other 10 verses of this psalm by the Sons of Korah. Various theologians have asserted that this psalm may be eschatological (predicting of end times), while others believe that it refers to a historical event.

The psalmists open with the word "God" and then follows with His defining functions of "refuge and strength." Yes, His help is indeed in times of trouble and is "ever-present." The opening verse is indeed an expression of human confidence in God himself in any time of trouble. Listen to Dr. Luther's opening lines in his hymn:

> A mighty fortress is our God,
> A trusty shield and weapon;
> He helps us free from every need
> That hath us now o'ertaken.

Luther points not only to God's shield (defense of enemy's weapons) but also to His offense against any enemy, large or small.

If this psalm was written in response to a historical event, some theologians believe it relates to the Assyrians and their attempt to overtake Jerusalem in the time of Hezekiah, king of Judah. The prophet Isaiah writes in his 37th chapter how the king's prayer reached His throne and Isaiah delivers God's response by delivering His people from the atrocities of Sennacherib and the Assyrians. God indeed was faithful to His promise by delivering Jerusalem from the hands of its enemies; "I will defend this city and save it, for my sake and for the sake of David my servant." (Isaiah 37:35) The angel of the LORD went out and put to death 185,000 men in the Assyrian camp. Verse two now takes on significance as we see confidence exuding: "Therefore we will not fear. . ."

In a slight departure, I am reminded of a story that was published in the *Washington Post* in 2011, following the 9/11 events. The Reverend Derrick Harkins presented his parish with a sermon using the opening verse in Psalm 46 in his "On the Far Side of Trouble." His message was inspired by the family members of Army Major Patterson who perished at the Pentagon in one of the 9/11 attacks. He reminded his parishioners that the Bible doesn't talk about the absence of calamity, but God promises His presence in trying times. He said, "September 11th was not the first, and sadly it will not be the last." Just as Hezekiah and his people were delivered in their time of trouble, so we too, in today's environment can be confident of God's presence and deliverance according to His good and faithful will.

Psalm 46 can be categorized into three major themes: 1) confidence in God; 2) sounds of praise of Zion because God dwells there; and 3) an invitation to all to recognize God's power and rule. (Source: H. C. Leupold's *Exposition of the Psalms*). Interestingly, the word "God" appears seven times in this psalm and the word "LORD" appears three times. Seven of course is a number associated with completeness or perfection, and three perhaps refers to the trinitarian nature of Yahweh (LORD).

God's acts of deliverance are infinite, and we may not even recognize them when they occur. But the author here reminds us that the "LORD Almighty is with us; the God of Jacob is our fortress." (verse 7) Dr. Luther's last phrase in the first verse amplifies God's superiority: "On earth is not His equal." And in the second verse, Luther states, "But for us fights the valiant One."

The psalmists conclude their verses with an invitation "Come." Verse 8 begins "Come and see the works of the LORD." He causes wars to cease and destroys all offensive weapons and their defenses with fire. The concluding verses require our utmost attention and to do so requires a quietness to ponder the greatness of His power and rule. Listen! "Be still, and know that I am God; I will be exalted among the nations, I will be exalted in the earth." (verse 10). Here the first two words are offset by a comma, causing us to pause. Just as God heard Hezekiah's plea for deliverance, He too hears you and me in our quiet times, as we go to Him in prayer. We can be assured that He is God. The world would have us believe that it's "us (we)" or even "I" but no one can ignore the I AM who is exalted among all nations and over the entire realm of His creation. Period!

Verse 11 is a repeat of verse seven amplifying our stated belief that Christians have an ever-present God who is always with us, especially in times of trouble when we need to seek his protecting care just as He promised in Days of Old to Jacob.

Footnote:

Dr. Luther is certainly well known for his leadership in reforming the Church. But this great man was also a musician and songwriter. He felt that music was of God, not man, and he was determined to restore congregational singing in the German language. While *A Mighty Fortress is Our God* is certainly his most notable, he wrote many other hymns. His first hymnal was published in 1524 and included eight hymns, four of which were his own. Our denomination's current hymnal has 23 hymns authored by Luther.

Peace
Connected in Him, I stand
GHR

PSALM 47

Awesome! The King of All

The Sons of Korah write this beautiful psalm to praise the Almighty, the King of All. Here we see the term "Most High" used. This term most high was referenced years prior by Melchizedek, the King of Salem (Jerusalem) in Genesis. He is referred to as the "priest of God Most High (Genesis 14:18). The Hebrew word is *El Elyon*. The term expresses the exaltedness and overwhelming majesty of God according to one dictionary source. *Elyon* signifies the supremacy of GOD over everything in heaven and earth. As Melchizedek blesses Abram, he says, "Blessed be Abram by God Most High, Creator of heaven and earth" (Genesis 14:19).

This psalm was likely written about the same time as its predecessor, concerning the victory of the Most High over the Assyrians. Just listen to the opening verses: "Clap your hands, all you nations; shout to God with cries of joy. How awesome is the LORD Most High, the great King over all the earth?" This sounds like the words of the early King of Salem as he blessed Father Abram.

Verse four reminds the readers that the Most High chose His people's inheritance for them by delivering them from the Assyrian raiders under Sennacherib. St. Peter also reminds his readers in 1 Peter 1 that "He has given us new birth into a living hope through the resurrection of Jesus Christ from the dead, and into an inheritance that can never perish." (verse 3-4) A comparison could be made here of the Most High coming down to deliver Israel from the Assyrians. Then ascending (verse 5) to His throne with the Son of God coming down in the form of man to deliver us from certain death from sin by His atoning death on Calvary. And finally, victory over the grave and ascending to the right hand of God.

According to Dr. H. C. Leupold's *Exposition of the Psalms*, he notes that the later Jewish tradition used this psalm for their New Year festival in early October. The traditional Christian use of the psalm is for the festival of Ascension.

Multiple references can be found of the *El Elyon* in the Bible. Moses writes in Deuteronomy that the Israelites were not to be afraid as the LORD your God who is among you is a great and awesome God. . . And will drive out those nations before you." (Deuteronomy 7:21-22) I was particularly drawn to Daniel and his time as interpreter for King Nebuchadnezzar. In Daniel 4:17, Daniel declares that the God Most High is sovereign, yes, even over the powerful Nebuchadnezzar. He has the power to control kingdoms of men and gives to whom He pleases. Daniel indeed interpreted the King's dream regarding his downfall if he didn't recognize *El Elyon*. Well, he indeed met his maker and was driven away from his people and ate grass like cattle. Then, he raised his eyes toward heaven, and his sanity was restored as he "praised the Most High." (Daniel 4:34)

God is indeed sovereign and King of All. Just as Moses referred to the Most High as a great and awesome God, so too the Sons of Korah remind you and me of just how awesome our God is. He has delivered you and me from the grave of the hopeless to eternal joy in heaven with the Most High. So just as the Sons of Korah repeatedly "sing praises to God," we too show our thankful hearts for His work of salvation on Calvary and ascending to the right hand of God in victory. Amen and Amen!

Peace
Connected in Him, I stand
GHR

PSALM 48

How Great?

This psalm pointed me to this title of "How Great?" I read and re-read this psalm over and over and kept thinking about our great God and His protection of those who trust in Him. I was immediately drawn to the famous hymn, "How Great Thou Art." Just listen to the first verse:

> O Lord my God, When I in awesome wonder
> Consider all the worlds Thy Hands have made;
> I see the stars, I hear the rolling thunder,
> Thy power throughout the universe displayed.

How Great Thou Art
This well-known hymn was the work of a British Methodist missionary, Stuart Hine. This hymn was based on a Swedish traditional melody and poem written by Carl Boberg (1859-1940). In 1931, Hine and his family were in Ukraine. It was there he heard the Russian translation of a German song (O Store Gud or O Great God). He translated it into English and then added verses, in part due to his experiences. The final version was published in 1949.

The psalmists begin with acknowledgment that our God is great and most worthy of our praise - especially in His city and His holy mountain. The prophet Micah prophesies about the last days. He says, "The mountain of the LORDS's temple will be established as chief among the mountains; it will be raised above the hills and peoples will stream to it" (Micah 4:1). The great city of Jerusalem was seen as the center of God's presence. It was not only beautiful but also very protective of its inhabitants. God is here referenced as our protector just as the city's citadels and ramparts protected its inhabitants.

Even as worldly kings approached her, they were astounded at her citadels and ramparts and fled in terror. At the end of this section (verse 8), the authors state, "God makes her secure forever." As such, those who put their trust and faith in our Great God meditate on his unfailing love. Jerusalem was in the land of Judah, the city of David and the lineage of our Savior. God has made Mount Zion secure forever and the psalmists say that we are to tell the next generation of His great love and protection.

"For this God is our God for ever and ever; He will be our guide even to the end." What a beautiful ending to this Psalm 48:14. St. Paul reminds you and me that we are not strangers but fellow citizens with God's people and members of God's household. Our faith is "built on the sure foundation of the apostles and prophets, with Christ as the chief cornerstone. In Him the whole building is joined together and rises to become a holy temple in the LORD." (Ephesians 2:19-21)

Just as Mount Zion (Jerusalem) was a fortress for its people, our fortress is our faith and trust in the Savior who has delivered us from sin's damnation. Our faith is the result of the indwelling of God's Spirit who lives and directs our lives until His promised return.

In conclusion, listen to the final verse of How Great Thou Art:

> When Christ shall come, with shout of acclamation,
> And take me home, what joy shall fill my heart.
> Then I shall bow, in humble adoration,
> And then proclaim: "My God, how great Thou art!"

Peace
Connected in Him, I stand
GHR

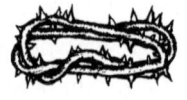

PSALM 49

Hear Ye, Hear Ye!

Psalm 49 indeed requires one to sit up and take note! Yes, because the authors give us an insight into life's futility and a reminder of Solomon's Book of Ecclesiastes. The chapter opens with a proclamation, "Hear ye, all you peoples." In other words, stop what you're doing, open your ears and LISTEN to what I'm going to say!

The term "all" means everyone - rich or poor, low and high alike. The introduction then shifts to remind their listeners that wisdom and understanding will be uttered from the lips and we're to give ear to the parable (or proverb). Verse five begins with a question: "Why should I fear? Fear is one of the two most dreaded words in Scripture. The other is doubt. In this psalm, the authors (Sons of Korah) take issue with those whose wealth appears to protect them from everything and everyone. Their trust is only in their wealth! Then, the authors utter their words of wisdom in verse seven: "No man can redeem the life of another or give to God a ransom for him." "The ransom for a life is costly – no payment is ever enough," says the psalmist. Slavery in the O. T. was commonplace and many a slave could be sold or freed as the owner wished.

Payment of the rich to free themselves from death's door is impossible. No amount of money can free men from sin's claim on their earthly life. The N. T. comments frequently about our servant (slave) condition. In Mark's gospel, he tells us that our LORD became man not to be served but to serve and (freely) give his life as a ransom for many. St. Paul also reminds the church at Ephesus that our freedom (redemption) came by Jesus' blood, in accordance with His pleasure and will. Finally, the author to the Hebrews states, "He entered the Most Holy Place (Holy of Holies) once for all by His own blood" (Hebrews 9:12).

The temple was in three parts: Outer Court, Holy Place, and the Most Holy Place. In the outer courts, priests offered sacrifices for sin and guilt. In the center of the Outer Court was the Holy Place which contained three objects – Lampstand, table for showbread, and the altar of incense. Then at the rear of the Holy Place was the Most Holy Place where only the High Priest entered annually. This Holy of Holies contained the Ark of the Covenant the top of which was the Mercy Seat which was the throne of God.

Verse 10 reminds all that sin caused death regardless of your earthly status. Despite a man's riches, he is like a beast that perishes. Leupold in his commentary makes a comparison to Solomon's Ecclesiastes where in spite of his wisdom, riches, and power, realized that all was meaningless! He then concludes his book with wisdom. Listen! "Fear God and keep his commandments, for this is the whole duty of man."

Verse 15 brings promise and Good News to those who follow God and His promises. "But God will redeem my soul from the grave; he will surely take me to himself." This verse parallels Solomon's wisdom in Ecclesiastes 12:13-14. Wisdom and understanding are key. Also, Solomon's Book of Proverbs says this: "The fear of the LORD is the beginning of wisdom and the knowledge of Him is understanding" (Proverbs 9:10).

In conclusion, I want to leave you with this statement made in the *Essential Bible Companion to the Psalms*. "The solution is not to be poor in wealth but to be rich in understanding, not trusting in riches one has nor envying riches one does not have."

Yes, we can enter the Most Holy Place that our LORD has prepared for us on Calvary's cross since He ransomed our soul from death's tyranny.

Peace
Connected in Him, I stand
GHR

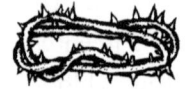

PSALM 50

Genuine Worship

This psalm could be entitled a faith barometer. The question: "Where do you fit on the true worship scale?" This psalm is ascribed to Asaph, one of King David's musicians. The authorship may have been David and Asaph was merely the transcriber. There are 12 different psalms ascribed to Asaph (50 and 73-83). Asaph was the son of Berechiah an ancestor of the Asaphites. They were also a descendant of Gershon, the son of Levi. They were a guild of musicians in the first temple. History suggests that Asaph was one of three Levites commissioned by King David to oversee singing in the house of Yahweh. It is also possible, this same Asaph served under David's son, King Solomon (2 Chronicles 5:12).

The psalmist opens this chapter with a beautiful collection of names of our LORD. He says, "The Mighty One, God, the LORD." This psalm is one of judgment and here the royal titles of the Judge are listed. The Mighty One (el); God (Elohim) and LORD (Yahweh). Singly, each is important; but combined they provide a powerful image of the Judge, Jury, and possible executioner. This God of Israel speaks and summons the earth! Like me, it might grab your attention! Unlike today's legal system with separate functions of legal defense/prosecution, jury, and judge, our LORD owns the universe and is perfect in His judgments.

I am reminded of a bargaining that occurred in Genesis when Abraham bargained with the LORD over Sodom and Gomorrah regarding the righteous who might be found in the cities to be destroyed by God. In Genesis 18:25, God said, "Will not the Judge of all the earth do right?" Rhetorical of course! The bargaining continues with the LORD being patient with His servant Abraham. St. Peter reminds us that our LORD is patient. He does not want any to perish but to come to repentance and "true" worship of the only God and Jesus Christ whom He has sent. (2 Peter 3:9 - paraphrased)

The psalmist continues to describe those who have true worship and those who are merely going through the motions. Leupold describes this chain of events this way: "True devotion (calling on Him) produces an act of deliverance, and that, in turn, leads to glorification of the Deliverer."

The Judge reminds His people (called consecrated ones) that He does receive their sacrifices and burnt offerings, but in fact, our LORD owns everything and is not in need of our sacrifice or gift. Rather, he is searching our HEARTS for our true devotion to the Deliverer. In verse 15, He reminds us that if we call upon Him in the day of trouble that He will deliver us. . .and you will honor me!

Not so with the faithless followers! A warning ensues to those Asaph refers to as the wicked. He is speaking to the people Israel who continue to follow their sacrifices with hollow hearts. Their "formalistic" worship yields evil and, if not reversed, it results in wickedness and separation from the Deliverer.

So, what is true worship? In 1 Chronicles 16, King David summoned Asaph and committed a long psalm of thanks. In verse 28-29, David says, "Ascribe to the LORD, O families of nations, ascribe to the LORD glory and strength; ascribe to the LORD the glory due His name. . .Worship the LORD in the splendor of his holiness." And in the final verse, David says, "Praise be to the LORD, the God of Israel from everlasting to everlasting." And all the people said, "Amen!"

St. Matthew reminds us that when Satan tempted our weakened (human nature) LORD, that we are to "Worship the LORD your GOD, and serve Him only!" (Matt 4:10 a quote from Deuteronomy 6:13) Yes, our true worship is to worship our LORD with all our heart, soul, and strength (Deuteronomy 6:5). And, if we ignore God, He will tear us to pieces (verse 22). In closing, Dr. H. C. Leupold, in his *Exposition of the Psalms,* reminds us: "Thanksgiving is so wholesome a matter that it is the mother of all other phases of true worship." Let us all remember that we are to worship our God in spirit and in truth and not with false pretenses or empty hearts.

To God be the Glory! Amen

Peace
Connected in Him, I stand
GHR

PSALM 51

Egregious Sin and Guilt

This psalm of David is perhaps one of his most telling. Why? Because he bears all the weight of his terrible sin of adultery and murder. And as King! David was weighted down by his sin but upfront about his confession, requesting the great mercy of God to forgive his egregious sin. As you read and re-read this psalm, do you feel his pain and the weight of his sin? More importantly, do David's words of confession remind you that we too need to confess our sin before God and beg forgiveness?

David opens this beautiful, penitential psalm with deep guilt and asks for mercy from his God. Why? Because he knew that his God has "unfailing" love and compassion. Here David uses the word "blot out" (wipe out) to ask God to remove his transgression as its weight is overbearing. The dictionary defines the word blot in this way: an association of disgrace with one's character or reputation. A synonym might be stain. David's disgraceful and public sin of adultery and murder was ever before him (verse 3). While his sin was human and damaged people, David acknowledges that his true wrongdoing was against God.

Sin is always with us as David admits but he asks for cleansing. David says, "Cleanse me with hyssop." Hyssop is an herb in the mint family with cleansing properties. The Bible mentions hyssop several times. In Leviticus, God commanded His people to use hyssop in ceremonial cleansing, including treating leprosy. Hyssop was also used in Exodus where the Israelites marked their doorposts with lamb's blood. God instructed them to use hyssop as a "paintbrush" due to its sturdiness. David's reference to hyssop here is more of a spiritual cleansing. And the result is "whiter than snow."

Yes, David's spiritual cleansing was done by blotting out his transgression, making him clean (whiter than snow). The lamb's blood on the doorpost was a sign for the Angel of Death to pass over their house. Jesus' blood was shed on Calvary's cross and saves you and me from certain death because of our sin.

Verse 10 begins a new life. A clean slate is granted due to God's mercy and unfailing love. David's request here is to create a pure heart and a right (steadfast) spirit within him. As such, he now enjoys the restoration and joy as someone made right with God and an heir of salvation.

Once forgiven, David feels a sense of relief and joy. Verse 13 reminds us that, like David, we too can tell others of God's forgiveness in Christ. David also asks God's blessing on His City and to make Zion prosperous and guarantee their protection. Finally, he asks God to receive their sacrifices from thankful hearts and "forgiven" members of His kingdom.

Psalm 51 is used in liturgy. In particular, verses 10-12 are used following the Sermon or Homily, asking God to create a clean heart within us having heard the Word of God. God indeed promises his grace and mercy to all who confess Him as Lord and Savior. As we daily sin much, let us ever be mindful to go to the throne of grace, asking for mercy and forgiveness and a new heart to do better the next day.

Peace
Connected in Him, I stand
GHR

PSALM 52

Unfailing Love Over Evil

This psalm references Doeg the Edomite who had gone to Saul to inform him of David's moves, especially to the house of Abimelech. 1 Samuel 21-22 records the story of Saul in pursuit of David. David penned this psalm in response to Saul's evil that was propagated through his servant, Doeg. Doeg the Edomite was the chief shepherd of Saul. Abimelech was a priest. David had gone to him in search for bread. None was available except for the consecrated bread. The priest complied with David's wishes and provided the sacred bread. After a short stay at Gath, he fled to a cave. His family heard of his whereabouts and followed. Being afraid of Saul, they stayed with the King of Moab as David returned to Judah.

Once Saul heard of Abimelech's actions, he needed confirmation and went to Doeg. His confirmation engendered an order by Saul to slaughter all the priests, killing 85 in all. One of Abimelech's sons escaped and told David of Saul's actions through Doeg. These evil actions were the genesis of David's psalm.

As you read through this psalm, it's obvious that David is incensed with evil and reminds himself that God will surely bring Saul down into everlasting ruin. (verse 5) His opening question is appropriate for Saul but could be said of today's rulers who seek evil rather than good. David says, "You are a disgrace in the eyes of God. Your tongue plots destruction like a sharpened razor – loving evil versus good." (verses 2-3)

Then David reminds us that "Surely God will bring down (evil) to everlasting ruin." Verbs such as snatch up; tear; and uproot are strong words from Jesse's son. Verse eight shifts to exclaim how the righteous act who are of the house of God. David begins with claiming he is like an olive tree. Why would he use such an analogy? First, the Olive Tree is a most beloved, sacred symbol of peace and friendship. It is a long living tree dating back thousands of years. David refers to the tree's flourishing in the house of God. Remember, following the flood, Noah sent out a dove who returned with a "freshly plucked olive leaf." (Genesis 8:11)

David restates his unfailing love for his God and trusts in Him for all things - even protection from his pursuer Saul. Today, we too can boast in the Lord as David did as we face trials that encircle us. God's love surpasses our human understanding. We cannot love as God loves us (agape). He knows our every danger and will deliver us from Satan's arrows as we continue to walk the narrow path in line with God's divine will for each of us.

May we, like David, continue to put our trust in the One who created us (humanly and spiritually) as the one and only wise God and Jesus Christ whom He has sent.

Peace
Connected in Him, I stand
GHR

PSALM 53

Ditto!

Am I dreaming or is this psalm the same as Psalm 14? The answer is yes and no. In many instances, the words are the same including the verse number designation, but after verse 4, more differences occur.

My notes on Psalm 14 were entitled, "Fools Rush In." My discussion related to the fool being an unbeliever and how the world was more polytheistic. This similar rendition of the earlier psalm has theologians questioning why this almost exact carbon copy was written. And by whom was it written? And when was it written versus the previous psalm?

I have prepared a table that examines the similarities and differences of the two psalms in question.

Comparison/Verse	Psalm 14	Psalm 53
v. 1	Same	Same
v. 2	LORD	God
v. 3	all	everyone
	turned away	turned aside
v. 4	LORD	God
v. 5b	For God is present . . .	God scattered the bones of those who attacked you
v. 5c	n/a	You put them to shame, for God despised them
v. 6	You evildoers frustrate the plans of the poor . . . similar to 5c in Ps 53	n/a
v. 7	LORD	God (verse 6 in this psalm)

So, what do the experts say? Some would say that David's initial copy was imperfect or defective and the later version issued corrections. while others say that alterations were made later to fit the situation prevailing at the time. If the latter is true, then some would suggest that it was around the time of the Assyrians (circa 722 BC) when they overtook the northern tribes (Israel) and led them into captivity, never to return. Sennacherib was threatening Jerusalem and the King of Judah attempting to continue his conquering of the land of Israel, both north and south. In my view, what if the message was so important that it was worth repeating?

Let's examine the table above to see the differences. What stands out is the change of the word LORD in Psalm 14 to God in Psalm 53. It occurs three times in the varying verses. The LORD related to YHWH and is a proper noun. It is the personal name for the God of Israel. The term, God (Elohim), is a common noun and refers to the true god. According to sources, it's an honorific plural form to honor the single referent (el).

If this psalm indeed refers to the time of the Assyrian attack on Judah, then verses 5 and 6 make sense. God did indeed destroy hundreds of thousands of Assyrians to protect His people (that is, scattered their bones) and put them to shame (as they had overpowering odds).

Regardless of its origin and authorship, this psalm ends with an exclamation of God's deliverance: "Oh, that salvation for Israel would come out of Zion! When God restores the fortunes of His people, let Jacob rejoice and Israel be glad!" As members of the household of faith (just as God's chosen Israel), we too have been restored through the blood of the Lamb of God, Jesus, who has redeemed you and me to a righteous state. Let us too be glad and rejoice.

Peace
Connected in Him, I stand
GHR

PSALM 54

The LORD . . . My Helper and Sustainer

This beautiful psalm of David has a two-pronged approach. First, David seems to be pleading to God to provide deliverance and then he shifts in the second portion of this psalm to one of confidence of God's help and sustenance. The entire psalm is noticeably short and very succinct – trouble comes, God's help is invoked, and God delivers. Period! End of story.

Some theologians disagree as to the origin of this psalm, but many would agree it was during one of the times when King Saul was in pursuit of David, God's anointed to succeed Saul. If true, then 1 Samuel tells us the story of the pursuit. Before we review the Samuel account, let's look at David's opening phrase, "Save me, O God." What more can we say even today but save me from the pitchfork of sin that pierces our very beings. "Save me" is followed by a continuing plea to vindicate him by God's unmatched might. Oftentimes, God's might is reflected just by His "right hand."

King Saul was in hot pursuit of David in the area of the town of Ziph, a town in Judah in the Negeb. Ziph is associated with a clan (family) associated with Caleb. The account in 1 Samuel tells us that while Saul was in hot pursuit, David had a chance to subdue and annihilate his pursuer. But he didn't! David refused to take the life of the LORD's anointed. Rather, he took the spear and water ewer of King Saul as evidence that he indeed had opportunity. But we see the

LORD's intervention here as, "He caused them (Saul + army) to fall into deep sleep." Later we see in the dialogue that Saul was gratified that David spared his life. (1 Sam 26:12b).

David now shows his confidence, beginning in verse four. Listen: "Surely, God is my help; the LORD . . . sustains me." Yes, the LORD was well aware that his anointed one David would spare the life of his pursuer as evidence that God is merciful. Furthermore, the continuing story tells us that Saul's pursuit was short-lived, as foreign invaders were approaching his turf.

God is indeed a gracious and all-knowing God. He is attentive to our every need and is our helper and sustainer. The dictionary defines sustainer as "essential support." Yes, God is essential to our every-step and movement. He responds to our plea for deliverance. He is always in a protective mode just as He caused Saul and all his followers to fall into a deep sleep allowing David to remove evidence of his presence.

1 Samuel also tells us of the conclusion of this incident in 26:24: "As surely as I have valued your life (Saul) today, so may the LORD value my life and deliver me from all trouble." Yes, David completes his psalm of praise and deliverance with a pledge to sacrifice a free will offering and to continue to "praise Your name, O LORD." (verse 6)

Remembering David and his pursuers, we too can be confident that God delivers you and me from ALL troubles as we go to Him in prayer for deliverance. Our creating God did not ignore the sin that entered the world in Genesis, rather He promised (Genesis 3:15) to send a Deliverer to save us from our situation of total separation from God. Jesus fulfilled that promise on Calvary's cross and now we look to His second coming, as He has promised to come and deliver us to be with Him forever and ever. Amen.

Peace
Connected in Him, I stand
GHR

PSALM 55

Cast the Care of Brokenness on the LORD

While David is listed as the author, some have disputed his authorship of this psalm of lament. The lament is quite revealing and very applicable to today. The author lays himself before the throne of God in complete anxiety and anguish. The author's enemies continue in pursuit. Some theologians belief that enemies here are Absalom, King David's third son, and a self-declared king. Absalom was attempted to eliminate his father. 2 Samuel tells the story of Absalom and his relationship with his father and the kingdom of Israel.

Enter Ahithophel. His name means "brother of foolishness," and at one time he was a trusted advisor to King David. But he defected to Absalom and became one of David's bitterest enemies. (Source: ATS Bible Dictionary). Dr. H. C. Leupold entitled his exposition of this psalm as, "Prayer in the Face of a Wicked Conspiracy Involving a Formerly Trusted Friend." Yes, a friend turned traitor. Sound familiar? Well, it could also be a Messianic type picture of how one of Jesus' inside 12 defected to the enemy of sin and greed, thus offering up his former friend to the enemy.

The author opens with his plea for God to listen and not to ignore him! He is very distraught and seemingly at death's door at the hands of his enemies. Just as David lived in a broken world, thousands of years haven't changed the world's situation. We live in a world of broken relationships - from marriages and family issues to internal country angst and continuous waring nation against nation. David compares his flight to that of a dove who escapes danger via its speed. Experts estimate their speed between 30 and 55 miles per hour.

But without a dove's speed, David counts on the LORD's deliverance and requests that the LORD would confuse his enemies. We're told in 2 Samuel 17:14 that "the LORD had determined to frustrate the good advice of Ahithophel." Beginning in Psalm 55:12, David is confused and distraught that his former friend would raise his hand against him. And again, theologians suggest this to be Messianic of Jesus and Judas as told in the gospels.

David's plea is followed by a prayer for judgment, ending in verse 15 with a plea for a judgment of death. Perhaps David's issues were a direct result of his previous sin and consequences with Bathsheba. Indeed, he endured multiple family issues, including a son's betrayal of his father, seeking power and glory for himself. God indeed confused the advisors as recorded in 2 Samuel. Their words were "smoother than butter," but war was in their hearts. (verse 21)

David concludes this psalm with an often-quoted verse. Listen! "Cast your cares on the LORD and He will sustain you; He will never let the righteous fall." What a crescendo ending this lament and now a powerful statement of faith that God will never forsake His servants. Yes, and with David we too can say, "I trust you (LORD)."

The N. T. continues to amplify the casting of cares on the LORD. St. Matthew's gospel says, "Come to me, all you who are weary and burdened, and I will give you rest," (Matthew 11:28) and then again in Peter's first epistle, "Cast all your anxiety on Him because He cares for you." (1 Peter 5:7)

Peace
Connected in Him, I stand
GHR

PSALM 56

In God I (We) Trust

I am reminded of old television show called, "Who Do You Trust?" In the show, a question was posed, and the man would have to decide whether to answer the question or "trust" the woman to do so. In this psalm, David opens his plea to God with the phrase, "Be merciful to me, O God." Why? Because men were in hot pursuit of him and his life. This psalm seems to be similar to previous psalms from the same author with his plea for mercy and deliverance from his enemies.

But his tune of fear in verses one and two quickly changes to one of trust! "When I am afraid, I will trust in you," says David. Then in verse four we hear this beautiful statement of praise: "In God I trust, I will not be afraid!" As a sinner, we face the consequences of total separation from God. That's true fear! But as a faithful follower of the One who has called us out of darkness into His marvelous light, our fears are erased! David then presents this question following his faith statement: "What can mortal men do to me?" Yes, men can cause an end to mortal life, but they cannot rob us of our relationship with the True God and the eternal future that we have with Him.

David reminds God to record his lament and list his tears on His scroll, not to be ignored! St. Matthew reminds you and me about God's omniscience in chapter 10 when he warns his disciples of the persecution that faces them. He says, "And even the very hairs of your head are numbered." Yes, He knows our every need without writing them down in His scroll. David's confidence grows as we read verses 10-11. David repeats the phrase, "In God I trust," as he does in the opening verses.

David concludes his psalm in thanksgiving, as He is assured of his deliverance from his enemies. Jesus reminded his disciples to be wary of one who can kill both body and soul (Evil One). (Matthew 10:28 KJV). David is ever thankful that his God has delivered him from stumbling and from Sheol. His future is a new life (newness) as he walks before God in true light. Listen to St. Paul's encouragement in Romans 6:4: "We were therefore buried with him through baptism into death in order that, just as Christ was raised from the dead through the glory of the Father, we too may live a new life."

During this Advent season, let us be very mindful that our LORD has promised to return and take us to be with Him into eternity. Like David, let us say, "In God I (we) trust."

Peace
Connected in Him, I stand
GHR

PSALM 57

Hidden in Your Presence

This psalm of David shows how adversity in the world continues to surround and even attempt to destroy the LORD's servant. Nevertheless, David seeks his LORD's protection and says, "My soul takes refuge." (verse 1). Historians are unsure of the exact location of David's flight, but he was hidden in a cave (1 Samuel 21-24). Verse 1b adds a new dimension to David's seeking the LORD's protection. This time it's in the "Shadow of His wing . . . until disaster passes." This could be referring to the wings of the heavenly host. Yes, David is seeking not only a physical hiding in the cave but also a spiritual one with the LORD, with His countenance providing divine protection to the chosen one to be leader of Israel.

The second part of the opening section tells us that David continues to cry out to His God for safety as he trusts that God has a purpose for his life. A purpose? Yes, each of us has a purpose that God has indeed ordained. Like David, we need to be in prayer and study to know His will for each of us. The Scriptures are full of examples of how God has a divine purpose for men and women who may have even initially had a confrontational or adversarial relationship with God himself.

Let's look at some examples of how God purposes a life for service. Saul, also known as Paul, was a Pharisee, a Roman citizen, a theologian trained by Gamaliel, and an adversary of the Christ. But God changed that in His personal visit to Saul on the road to Damascus. Peter and John were successful fishermen, but God chose them for His purpose to be disciples and apostles ("fishers of men"). Timothy, an assistant to

Silas and Paul, became a patriarch of the church at Ephesus. Lydia, a seller of purple and native of Asia Minor, moved to Philippi and became a founder of the new church in her city. And so on!

The verses that follow show a contrast from David to his pursuers. David, a faithful servant of the Almighty, relies on God for his deliverance, as opposed to his enemies who are described here as lions and ravenous beasts, having teeth like weapons and tongues like sharp swords.

Even as they have dug a ditch to trap David, the ultimate defeat is not for David but those who pursue him and have, themselves, fallen into the pit. As such, David sings out for joy (verse 7) as his heart is steadfast and his heart's music awakens the earth. The earth is a megaphone for God's glory, as its sounds awaken the dawn. Verse 10 reminds you and me that God's love is so great that it fills the earth to heaven's doors and his faithfulness reaches the skies. Listen to the hymnist as he writes about God's faithfulness:

> Great is Thy faithfulness, O God my Father;
> There is no shadow of turning with Thee.
> Thou changest not: Thy compassions, they fail not;
> As Thou hast been, Thou forever wilt be.
> Great is Thy faithfulness! (Repeat)
> Morning by morning new mercies I see;
> As I have needed Thy hand hath provided;
> Great is Thy faithfulness, Lord unto me!
> (LSB 809, v. 1)

(Note: the last five verses of Psalm 57 are so important that they are repeated as the first five verses in Psalm 108)

Peace
Connected in Him, I stand
GHR

PSALM 58

Perfect Justice . . . Surely!

Psalm 58 continues with David's issues with his enemies. This time, he opens with a question regarding the lack of justice (injustice) by Saul's advisers. Whether they were silent, offering no judgment and letting injustice rule, is not totally clear. But David asks a corollary question in verse 1b: "Do you judge uprightly among men?" The question is evidently rhetorical as he continues into verse two by answering, "No!" This is one of 19 imprecatory psalms. Other O. T. books have some imprecatory themes as in Hosea, Micah, and Jeremiah. An imprecatory psalm is calling for judgment or to invoke evil or a curse.

"Your hearts devise injustice and your hands mete out violence," says the author. David states that they have been evil from their birth. As sinful human beings, we are born into sin (original sin), but in this case their evil condition has continued and maybe even worsened. This total depravity of man is stated throughout Scripture. In Psalm 51, David admits being sinful from birth. The prophet Jeremiah says, "The heart is deceitful above all things." (17:9) St. Paul also remarks about our sinful condition. In Romans 3:10 Paul says, "None is righteous, no not one!" and then again in 1 Corinthians he says, "The man without the Spirit does not accept the things of the Spirit of God." (2:14)

Yes, we all have fallen short of the glory of God from birth; but thanks be to God for our spiritual washing in Holy Baptism, where we are washed clean and receive the Spirit of God, in faith! Amen!

Beginning in verse six, David seeks God's assistance in rendering his enemies powerless. He uses the example of the lion (from Psalm

57) and asks God to remove their fangs. Now without teeth, they are compared to water flowing away. And again, before the fire heats the pot, the wind has neutralized its effect.

David states that under God's divine (perfect) judgment, the righteous will be victorious as their enemies are avenged. "Surely the righteous still are rewarded; surely there is a God who judges the earth." (verse 11)

As we continue to live in a world where sin may appear to rule, let us be ever mindful that Christ is Supreme! He is indeed the righteous judge and will return in judgment between good and evil. In the opening section of Revelation in the *Life Application Bible*, the author states this: "One day, God's anger toward sin will be fully and completely unleashed. Satan will be defeated with all of his agents. False religion will be destroyed. God will reward the faithful with eternal life, but all who refuse to believe in him will face eternal punishment."

Peace
Connected in Him, I stand
GHR

PSALM 59

The Strength of One

How many times were the Israelites outnumbered by their enemies? Too many to count. This psalm of David is again one of calling on God for Him to deliver David from his enemies. The verbs used in the opening verses are telling - deliver me; protect me; again, deliver me; and then save me. David's trials never seem to end.

Theologians believe this psalm may be in response to Saul's attempt to slay David in his own home. (see 1 Samuel 19). David had people who wanted him to live and often offered their protection by passing along what Saul's plans might be. This time, David's wife, Michal, warned her husband that if he didn't flee, Saul's men were going to kill him in the morning. So, Michal lowered him down through a window to escape Saul's awaiting entourage. Michal also provided deception by making David's bed appear as if he were there.

His plea to the LORD is due to his lack of understanding as to why they would want to slay him. He says, "I have done no wrong." "Arise, to help me . . .and rouse to punish."

David opens verse nine with great faith as he says, "O my Strength, I watch for you; you, O God, are my fortress, my loving God." God's name of Strength has been used on multiple occasions. In his Song, Moses praised God for His deliverance from the Egyptian army, following the crossing of the Red Sea. Listen, "The LORD is my strength and my song." (Exodus 15:2) David himself is well aware of the LORD's strength when he battled the giant, Goliath. David bragged to Goliath that his strength was not from swords and armor bearers, but he came "In the name of the LORD Almighty." (1 Samuel 17:45)

The prophets Isaiah and Jeremiah also reminded God's chosen people of God's strength. Isaiah reminded the Israelites not to fear that He was their God, and that He will strengthen them. (Isaiah 41:10) Jeremiah prophesied to Judah regarding a day of disaster (judgment) and they should remember their God as their strength and fortress and refuge in time of distress. (Jeremiah 16:19) Finally, the prophet Micah in chapter 5 reminds us of the Messiah to come and that "He will stand and shepherd His flock in the strength of the LORD." (Micah 5:4)

Like in the days of Goliath, David knew that the LORD was his shield (faith). In this psalm David recounts a similar statement saying, "God will go before me . . . our shield." We see in the St. Paul's letter to the church at Ephesus how he describes the "Armor of God." Paul compares our faith in Jesus Christ, the Messiah, as our shield from the arrows of the evil one. (Ephesians 6:13, 16) David is confident that God's shielding and deliverance will be a constant reminder to His people that indeed "God rules over Jacob." (verse 13b)

Verse 14 is a refrain from verse 6 describing how his enemies continue to return like snarling dogs seeking food. David ends with a statement of confidence, singing of His strength as his fortress and refuge. Yes, His loving (agape) God. Amen.

Peace
Connected in Him, I stand
GHR

PSALM 60

Banner Unfurled!

This psalm may imply that David has a concern over defeat by his enemies! Well, if you read about his battles in 2 Samuel 8 and 1 Chronicles 18, it would seem like David was in constant victory. But as we all know, the more victorious, the greater the temptation by the evil one.

David opens this psalm with a statement of rejection versus victory. 2 Samuel 8 tells of repeated victories over his enemies. Following his defeat of the Edomites, verse 14 says, "The LORD gave David victory everywhere he went." So, where does there seem to be any evidence of the LORD's rejection of David? The answer is that we simply are not told. The Bible only tells of David's victories. And it's important since David's armies may have been outnumbered most of the time. But with the LORD on your side, the human number advantage is minimized to nothing.

It's important here to read through the fears of David if the LORD were to reject him and even ignore the victories. Instead, concentrate on the faith of David, as he never seems to lose sight of who is in control. Without God all of creation is lost.

Verse six begins with God listing what cities and areas are His! He reminds David that Israel will be united under his rule. He reminds David that his warriors will come from Ephraim and the scepter or kingship remains with Judah. (This reflects God's promise when Jacob blesses his sons. (Genesis 49:10) Now all that remains is to take Edom and that will complete Israel's unity. Then God's flag of honor will fly unfurled in His Promised Land.

David realizes that his armies are important but without his leader, the Almighty One, all is lost. (verse 11) Yes, God's presence means victory. This psalm is not one of rejection, rather it is one in which David is ever confident of God's presence to deliver him from his enemies. We too can express our confidence that God has indeed won an everlasting victory for us on Calvary's cross. He overcame human odds that were stacked against us. Hanging on Calvary's tree, He endured the pain and suffering for our sin so that we might be reunited with the Father as we are presented blameless in His sight in the Judgment.

As you examine the Christian Flag, remember this psalm. The colors of red, white, and blue are present, each with meaning. The red cross is a symbol of Christ's blood and sacrifice for you and me. The red cross is in the middle of the blue canton which represents fidelity. And the white color of the rest of the flag represents the purity derived from Christ's bloody sacrifice and the peace that endures forever.

In conclusion, I am reminded of St. Paul's victory statement in the great Resurrection Chapter (1 Corinthians 15). Listen! "Death has been swallowed up in victory. Where, O death, is your victory? Where, O death is your sting? The sting of death is sin and the power of sin is the law. But thanks be to God! He gives us the victory through our LORD Jesus Christ!" Amen and Amen.

Peace
Connected in Him, I stand
GHR

PSALM 61

My Strong Tower

This lament psalm of David may be during the time of his son's (Absalom) attempt to take over from his father, or it could be at another time when David was away on a conquest and felt alone. David opens with a phrase, "Hear my cry!" David's crying out is similar to Jeremiah in his book of Lamentations.

Lamentations is Jeremiah's lament over the destruction of Jerusalem (circa 586 BC). Listen to Jeremiah's cry (2:18): "The hearts of the people cry out to the LORD. O wall of the Daughter of Zion, let your tears flow like a river day and night; give yourself no relief, your eyes no rest." David cry was for God to listen. David was a warrior king of Israel with many victories under his belt. But a warring nature can have its consequences. He says that "his heart grows faint." (verse 2) His request is for the LORD to lead him to the rock for refuge.

The word rock in Hebrew (*tsur*) used in this psalm is defined as a cliff, boulder, strong rock, or refuge. This Hebrew word is similar to the feminine form of the Greek word for rock *petra*. Petra means a massive rock and immovable. The word "Rock" is also a name for our LORD. "Lead me to the rock," says David. His statement of faith follows, as he states that his rock has been his refuge and a strong tower. (verse 3)

A strong tower is previously mentioned in Judges 9:51 concerning the evil ruler Abimelech. Abimelech had previously burned the tower at Shechem with all the thousand-some people perishing. But later, Abimelech attempted to kill the people in their strong tower at Thebez.

A woman dropped a boulder and struck Abimelech on his head cracking his skull. At his bequest, his aide ran a sword through him so that the people could not say a woman killed him. Thus, Judges continues, "God repaid the wickedness that Abimelech had done to his father by murdering his 70 brothers." (Judges 9:56)

David knew that his God was his "rock" and "strong tower" to provide divine protection. We too have a Rock who is our strong tower and protector. Jesus Christ is the Rock eternal. The prophet Isaiah reminds you and me today, "Trust in the LORD forever, for the LORD, the LORD, is the Rock eternal." (Isaiah 26:4)

David's tone changes from that of a lament (i.e. crying out) to one of confidence in the rock and strong tower. He states that he longs to live "in Your tent forever!" Verse six then begins his prayer for his kingship over Israel. "Increase my days," says David. The final three verses are somewhat Messianic as they look to the long living king enthroned in God's presence forever. David says, "I will ever sing praise to Your name."

The famous hymn, *Rock of Ages*, was written by Augustus Toplady in 1776. The story is told that while he was traveling through a rugged countryside near England's Cheddar Gorge, the clouds burst, and torrential sheets of rain pummeled the earth. He (a young minister) was able to find shelter standing under a rocky overhang, thus buffeting him from the wind and rain. Toplady published his hymn in *The Gospel Magazine*. In his article he stated, "Just as England could never pay her national debt, so man could never by his own merits satisfy the justice of God." The hymn described Jesus Christ as the Rock of Ages, as a remedy for our sin.

With the hymnist, we too can boldly sing:

> Rock of Ages, cleft for me,
> Let me hide myself in Thee;
> Let the water and the blood,
> From Thy riven side which flowed,
> Be of sin the double cure:

Cleanse me from its guilt and pow'r.
(LSB 761, v. 1)

Peace
Connected in Him, I stand
GHR

PSALM 62

Rest Assured!

Is this really David? Psalm 62 departs from the previous ones, where the main subject is lament. In this psalm, David exudes with confidence and reliance on God versus man. His opening words are indeed comforting as he brings in the word "rest." The Hebrew word for rest used here is *dumiyyah* which means: a silence, a quiet waiting, or repose. "My soul finds rest in God alone." The term "rest" is used throughout Scripture and even by Jesus himself. In Matthew's Gospel (11:28), Jesus says, "Come unto me, all you who are weary and burdened, and I will give you rest."

Jesus' words open with that great Gospel word of invitation, "Come." The Greek word for rest is *anapauo* which means give rest; take my ease or give interruption from labor. Jesus has indeed given us rest as He has lifted the weight of sin off our shoulders and placed it upon Himself. David is also confident in his salvation that is available only from Him - and Him alone!

Verse two is repetitive from the previous psalm where David speaks of God as his "rock" and "fortress." But here he adds, "I will never be shaken." (verse 2b). The next two verses (3-4) are galling (Dr. H. C. Leupold's word) to David. David's detractors take delight in lies and with their mouths they bless but in their hearts they curse. So, we see where David relies solely on God's strength and salvation for his eternal rest - and the opposite of those whose tongues spews lies, and whose hearts are blackened by sinful desires.

David begins the next section (verse 5) with similar language as in his opening verses. But in verse 7, he uses the term "mighty" to modify rock. As such, David places his entire trust in the God of his fathers and reminds his constituents that they too should do so. And if you trust Him without question, then you can pour out your hearts to Him. This act of pouring out is a sign of true trust.

St. Paul uses a theme from David in his epistle to the Romans. Listen to Paul's doxology in Romans 15: "May the God of hope fill you with all joy and peace as you trust in Him, so that you may overflow with hope by the power of the Holy Spirit." (15:13)

The final verses remind its readers that all else is futile. Whether lowborn or highborn, they are nothing, says David. "Together they are only a breath." (verse 9) Don't trust in what you can steal or extort, rather rely on your strong and loving (two things, v. 11-12) God. David concludes with his faith that God will judge in an absolute manner. St. Paul also comments to his readers on God's judgment in Romans 2:6, "God will give to each person according to what he has done." Thankfully, we are not saved by works, but by grace. But, in faith, we serve God by serving others, that is, works follow faith.

In conclusion, David uses immensely powerful words in this psalm of trust. Remember the following: rock, fortress, salvation, never shaken, hope, trust, strength, and love. May we experience the true joy and peace that comes from God himself and trust in Him always.

Peace
Connected in Him, I stand
GHR

PSALM 63

Living Water

Water is life-giving. It is no more evident than in this psalm of David. Here David is in the desert of Judah in flight from Absalom. 2 Samuel records his flight in various chapters and verses. David is moving about in the deserts in the Kidron Valley of Judah. It's like he is a prisoner in his own country, moving about without a bed to sleep in as he flees his enemies. David opens this psalm reminding himself, and others, that God is his God and he continues to seek Him! Even in the desert, David is expressing his faith in God. (verse 1) The second part of that verse describes his spiritual (and perhaps physical) need for water (soul and body). NOTE: Psalm 42, the opening chapter in Book II of Psalms, also talks about spiritual water ("my soul pants for you, O God").

He says, "In this dry and weary land, there is no water." The absence of water reminds us of the Israelites in their flight from the Egyptians in the Sinai Desert. Exodus 17 tells the story of Moses' request to God because of the Israelites complaint of no water. In verse six, God says to Moses, "Strike the rock and water will come out of it for the people to drink." This is another miracle of water. First, God divides the sea for the Israelites to cross then causes it to return to its original state thus drowning the pursuers. Now, in the absence of water, God supplies it from a foreign source – in abundance! God is the constant supplier of all our needs

The preincarnate Christ provided the water from the rock in the desert in the O. T. and is the "living water" described in His earthly days. John records the story of Jesus meeting the Samaritan woman at the well. Jesus asks this "no name" person from Samaria for a drink of water. She is astonished that a Jew would ask an "outcast" for water. Jesus answered her, "If you knew the gift of God and who it is that asks for a drink, you would have asked Him, and He would have given you living water." (John 4:10)

Regardless of David's physical needs, he is confident in his spiritual condition and that his God will supply all he needs for this life and the life to come. "My soul is satisfied as with the richest foods," says David. (verse 5) Just as God supplied water to the Israelites in the Sinai desert, He also supplied David's every need in the Judean desert. But of the most importance was David's spiritual needs, which he reports as "satisfied."

David says he will stay close to God, as His right hand (strength) upholds him. His pursuers will never succeed! David swears by God's name and continues to offer his love and praise and confidence that his pursuers will be silenced.

Yes, God miraculously supplied water to the millions of escapees in Sinai's desert. Similarly, He supplied his servant, David, with all he needed regardless of his situation. And then, the Christ tells the outcast woman (Samaritan) at the well that He and He alone is "The Water" of life. May you never thirst again!

Peace
Connected in Him, I stand
GHR

PSALM 64

Boomerang of Malicious Speech

(Title originated by: Elmer A. Leslie)

Theologians are unsure as to what, if any, particular situation led to the penning of this psalm by David. But as the title from Elmer Leslie's work implies, his enemy's malicious speech and threats boomerang. Later we'll see this counteraction by God in tabular form as prepared by Artur Weiser and quoted by C. Hassell Bullock in his commentary, *Psalms, Volume 1*.

How often does the Bible refer to the "tongue" from a negative perspective? The concordance I reviewed listed too many to count, but here are a few.

Location	Negative "Tongue" Reference
Psalm 5:9	tongue speaks deceit
Psalm 39:1	keep my tongue from sin
Psalm 52:4	O you deceitful tongue
Proverbs 6:17	a lying tongue
Isaiah 59:3	tongue mutters evil things
James 1:26	failure to keep tight rein on tongue
James 3:8	no man can tame the tongue

David's lament here converts words into weapons. The first six verses refer to the conspiracy of his enemies and their snare of words. Their tongues are sharpened like swords and they aim their words like arrows. (verse 3) They conspire among themselves with their evil plans, plotting injustice. Their conspiracy is perfect, they thought, but later verses show how God intervenes, returning their attacks like boomerangs.

In his commentarwy, C. Hassell Bullock quotes Artur Weiser in his beautiful comparison of the evildoer's conspiracy and God's retort.

Evildoers	God
cruel words as deadly arrows (64:3b)	God will shoot them with His arrows (64:7a)
shoot suddenly, without fear (64:4b)	They will suddenly be struck down (64:7a)
lay their traps (plots) (64:2a)	God will cause their tongues to trap them (64:8a)
plan secret ambush (64:4a)	God will expose publicly (64:8c)
unscrupulous work with no fear (64:4b)	God does his work so that people fear him (64:9a)

Psalms, Volume 1 by C. Hassell Bullock, Psalm 64 table by Weiser

So what does this psalm teach you and me today in the 21st century? First, we have seen numerous references to the evil nature of the tongue speaking deceit and lies. Secondly, James, in his epistle, warns about taming the tongue (controlling). Man by himself is unable to tame the tongue, but with God's help we can control it. Fortunately, even when we sin by saying hurtful things, God forgives our shortcomings through Christ.

Just as the evil people in this psalm conspired to hurt with sword-sharpened words, so as Christians we can confess, as St. Paul reminds the church at Philippi, "That at the name of Jesus every knee should bow, in heaven and on earth and under the earth, and every tongue confess that Jesus Christ is LORD, to the glory of God the Father." (Philippians 2:10-11)

In closing, let us all remember this beautiful prayer in Psalms: "May the words of my mouth and the meditation of my heart be pleasing in your sight O LORD, my Rock and my Redeemer." (Psalm19:14)

Peace
Connected in Him, I stand
GHR

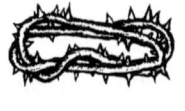

PSALM 65

Praiseworthy, Always!

Psalm 65 is the first of three psalms of praise (trilogy). The first of this trilogy is of David while the other two are "author unknown," but likely written by David. This psalm in particular is very poetic and encircles around God's abundant blessings on His people and their land. The psalm begins with the word "praise." This word in Hebrew occurs 57 times in Scripture (*tehillah*). The praise offered is a result of God's blessings and a fulfillment of their vows- as may be made by farmers (per H. C. Leupold's *Exposition of the Psalms*).

Verse three reminds us of the Law and Gospel. The first part reminds us of the overwhelming circumstances of sin, but then comes the Good News that God provides atonement. Wow! David speaks about those who are blessed as chosen and brought close to their LORD. They have been blessed by good things (verse 4) implied as both physical and spiritual. David ascribes God's deeds as "awesome." These awesome deeds are not due to our righteousness, but rather to God's, as our Creator and Savior.

This section shifts into poetic form to describe God's great creating power over all things, especially setting the mountains and calming the great seas. (NOTE: Remember God's control over the Red Sea with safe crossing by His people.) People from around the world (from morning's dawn to evening's fade) will sing for joy! God not only created but also maintains His creation by providing sustenance to the earth to bring forth its fruit in due season. Just listen to this beautiful poetry!

You care for the land and water it;
You enrich it abundantly.
The streams of God are filled with water
To provide the people with grain,
For so you have ordained it.
You drench the furrows and level its ridges;
You soften it with showers and bless its crops,
You crown the year with bounty, and your
carts overflow with abundance.
The hills are clothed with gladness.
The meadows are covered with flocks and
the valleys are mantled with grain;
They shout for joy and sing. (Psalm 65:9-13)

This is Hebrew poetry unlike our rhyming verse that we are accustomed to in modern times. David provides a great description of this "Land of Milk and Honey" that He promised to the Israelites. Water was indeed a precious resource in this area of the world, but God filled their streams and drenched its furrows.

If you examine the Jewish calendar and its agricultural activity, it is astounding how God created this year-round blessing to His people.

Month (Jewish)	Agriculture
Aviv (March/April)	Barley and Flax (spring rains)
Ziv (April/May)	No harvest
Sivan (May/June)	Figs ripen/wheat harvest
Tamuz (June/July)	Grapes
Av (July/August)	Olive
Elul (August/Sept)	Dates/summer figs
Ethanim (Sept/Oct)	no harvest (early rains)
Bul (Oct/Nov)	winter figs
Kislev (Nov/Dec)	Sowing
Tevet (Dec/Jan)	no harvest (rain/snow)
Shevat (Jan/Feb)	Almonds
Adar (Feb/Mar)	Citrus fruit

Verse 11 is the culmination of God's blessing. David uses the word "crown" to describe their year of bounty. Yes, the grasslands of the deserts overflow to provide for the livestock and the valleys are mantled with grain. God created (past tense) and God creates (present tense) every day.

Let us not forget that God causes rain to fall on the just and the unjust. But He is pleased to "bring us near" (verse 4) to live in his courts (faith). God plants faith by His Holy Spirit and then waters it with His Word and Sacrament. Praiseworthy, Always!

Peace
Connected in Him, I stand
GHR

PSALM 66

Loving Kindness: Praise God!

This psalm is the second of the "praise trilogy" (65-67) amid this great book in God's Word. The author of this psalm is unknown but is thought to have been written to observe the Israelites' deliverance from the Assyrians during the time of Hezekiah the king. (see 2 Kings 18-19). Some theologians have pointed to a possible use during one of the Festivals of Yahweh. (See table below for list). Of interesting note is the change in pronouns from "we" to "I" beginning in verse 13. As such, an argument can be made to reflect Hezekiah himself offering his personal praise to God for deliverance.

The psalm begins with jubilation as the author says, "Shout with joy to God, all the earth! Sing to the glory of His name; offer Him glory and praise." This beginning gets your blood stirring and creates a desire to join in with all God's people. The word "glory" is a powerful word, and one which is difficult to understand. A human offering of glory is virtually impossible as He is Glory Himself! Listen to a definition from Paul Tripp: "Glory encompasses the greatness, beauty, and perfection of all that He is." In other words, it's all that God is.

Verse three reminds you and me that God's deeds are awe-inspiring (*nora*) and demonstrate the greatness of His power. And all the earth bows down! The Gospel word "Come" leads off verse five, inviting all the earth to witness His works. The author reminds his readers of the miraculous water separation for the Israelites to cross over on dry land. Immediately we think of the Red Sea as they were fleeing from Egypt, but also remember God's parting of the Jordan River when the Israelites entered the Promised Land under Joshua's leadership. And it was no small feat as it was during the flood season during harvest. Joshua tells us, "The water from up-stream stopped flowing. It piled up in a heap a great distance away." (Joshua 3:16)

Indeed if this psalm refers to the LORD's deliverance from the Assyrians, then verse seven, "Let not the rebellious rise up against Him," makes sense. Remember, the angel of the LORD slayed 185,000 Assyrians! Praise God for his loving kindness. The word "love" as used in many psalms is frequently from the Hebrew (*chesed*) which is often translated as loving kindness in English. It's a measure of God's love (in mercy) to His people. The author reminds you and me that God has refined (tested) us like the refining of silver (argentum: Ag). Silver refining in ancient times was performed using heat in repeated fashion to remove the dross. The impurities float to the top and are skimmed off with the process repeated with increasing heat. Each time we go to God in prayer asking for forgiveness, He removes our sin (impurities) based on His Son's perfect sacrifice on Calvary.

Verse 13 begins the final section in which the pronoun changes to "I" from plural forms. This person not only worships his God in the temple along with his offerings, but also is an example to all who fear God to "Come and listen." The author is confident that God has heard his ardent plea for forgiveness for his sin(s) as he acknowledged that God listened to his prayer and answered. Yes, "Praise be to God" is the author's final statement in verse 20. God's love far surpasses our human understanding and His glory is indescribable!

Peace
Connected in Him, I stand
GHR

Festivals of Yahweh (7)

Festival Name	Occurrence
Passover	Spring
Unleavened Bread	Spring
First Fruits	Spring
Weeks (Pentecost)	Spring (harvest)
Trumpets	Fall
Atonement	Fall
Tabernacles (Booths)	Fall

Spring Festivals foreshadow Christ's first coming and the Fall Festivals his second coming.

PSALM 67
Praising God Yields Blessings

More years ago than I can remember (or noted), I wrote this title in my Bible from a pastor's sermon dealing with praise. His sermon title was, "When Praise is Lacking, so is our Life."

C. S. Lewis was brought up in the Protestant Church in Ireland, he said he lost his faith – turned off by boring church services and the evil in the world. He returned from World War I (injured) and then returned to Oxford University. He was perplexed by the existence of God and Christianity. It was through contacts with various individuals, including Tolkien, that he finally expressed his belief in God and renewed his faith in Christianity in 1931. His writings are many, but in his essay *"Why Does God Always Demand Praise?"* he walks through his struggles.

Psalm 67 is the final chapter of this praise trilogy (Psalms 65-67). The author is unknown but is written in a manner similar to a reasoning process: "May, then." His first of seven uses of the word may start out, "May God . . . bless us . . . make His face to shine upon us." The first two examples refer to God. The remainder all talk to all peoples and nations. The table below may help to organize the verses and the uses of the word may.

Verse	May:
67:1	God be gracious; bless; face shine upon us
67:2	Your ways and salvation be known
67:3a	Peoples praise you

67:3b	Repeat 3a
67:4	Nations be glad and sing for joy
67:5a	Peoples praise you
67:5b	Repeat 5a

As we can see from the table, God indeed is gracious to us and provides us knowledge of His ways and salvation. Indeed, all peoples and nations praise Him, for He rules justly and provides guidance to all on earth.

As my former pastor (retired) and mentor would say, "When you see the word THEN, watch out because something big follows." Verse six begins with that word that should make you sit up and take notice. The author clearly indicates the result of our praise is true blessing from God including the crops in our field. Yes, and all the ends of the earth will fear Him.

C. S. Lewis had it right. Our worship and praise to God is His way and channel to communicate to us. God communicates to us via His Word and Sacrament so that we receive the forgiveness of sins and are renewed for service to Him.

In closing, I am reminded of the Aaronic Blessing recorded for us in Numbers 6:24-26: "The LORD bless you and keep you; the LORD make His face shine upon you and be gracious to you; the LORD turn His face toward you and give you peace." Amen.

Peace
Connected in Him, I stand
GHR

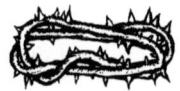

PSALM 68

Quintessential Hymn!

This psalm of David has been referred to as "A superb hymn that is unsurpassed, if not unequalled, in grandeur, lyric fire, and sustained rush of triumphant praise." H. C. Leupold, in his *Exposition of the Psalms*, quotes MacLaren in his opening statement regarding Psalm 68. Alexander MacLaren was an English minister of Scottish origin and an eminent Hebrew scholar. The psalm contains 35 verses. Leupold divides the verses into eight sections that cover everything from God overthrowing enemies to the final section referencing God's mighty power, deserving of all praise.

Authorship has been questioned by some theologians, as well as a time in the life of the king when it might have been written. Regardless, as MacLaren says, "it's a sustained rush of triumphant praise." Let's see what he's talking about. In the first six verses, David prays for God to arise and literally blow away the enemies of His people as smoke is blown by the wind. Then the righteous will rejoice before God their deliverer and extol Him who rides in the clouds (heavens KJV). In verse four, David even calls Him by His holy name, YAHWEH. In some versions, the abbreviation of YAH is used.

Beginning in verse seven, David reminds his readers how God delivered His people through the wilderness. He begins with a statement that God was in the lead as the *shekinah* cloud by day and the pillar of fire by night. This Hebrew word *shekinah* is a visible manifestation of God on earth or portrayal in a natural occurrence. He reminds His people of His divine presence on Sinai. Exodus 20 says, "When the people saw the thunder and lightning and heard the trumpet and saw the mountain in smoke, they trembled with fear." (Exodus 20:18) Finally, David reminds all that God indeed delivered them to the Promised Land. Verse 14 says that the "Almighty (*Shaddai*) scattered kings (enemies)."

God indeed chose Jerusalem as His sanctuary (described in verse 17 as from Sinai into His sanctuary"). His presence as holy as ever continues to dwell with His people. Verse 18 refers to God's residence "on high" which likely refers to His holy mount of Zion. (See Jeremiah 31:12.) The phrase, "led captives in your train," (verse 18) is a type of preincarnate Christ as the LORD entered victoriously into Jerusalem. St. Paul refers to this very verse in Ephesians 4:8 as Christ entered heaven victoriously after his death and resurrection, having conquered the ultimate enemies of sin, death, and the devil.

God subdues all enemies. David is confident that the LORD will crush the heads of his enemies from as far as Bashan (now in Syria) to the depths of the sea. You cannot escape God's divine judgment. God has humbled even the great leaders. Yes, the kings will bring gifts and the humbled bring bars of silver. Even envoys from far away Egypt and Cush (upper Nile region) will submit to God

The final section is the quintessential praise of the God who had done all things – from delivering his people from captivity to protecting them in the wilderness and finally delivering to them their Promised Land, having destroyed all their enemies. "Sing to God, O kingdoms of the earth, sing praise to the LORD." "You are awesome, O God, in your sanctuary; the God of Israel gives power and strength to His people." Praise be to God!"

God is omnipresent! His all-presence is cause for us to give Him all thanks and praise, just as the psalmist portrays in this hymn of praise.

Peace
Connected in Him, I stand
GHR

PSALM 69

Suffering Servant

My title for this psalm of David is like the section in the prophet Isaiah's book (Chapter 52-53) referring to the Christ as the "Suffering Servant." David is clearly suffering and even drowning, as shame covers his face. David opens this deep lamenting psalm with the familiar phrase, "Save me!" This phrase (*yasha*) appears 206 times in the O. T.. How many times are we in trouble and cry out to our God to save us? David's plea is no different from ours today in modern times.

This psalm is very Messianic and perhaps third most used in the N. T. following Psalms 22 and 110. Various references will be given later. According to my references, this psalm has acrostic properties (not alphabetic). The psalm consists of two sets of 22 lines: verses 1-15 and 16-36. Each of the two sections consists of bicolas (pairs) of adjacent lines in poetry and then a tricola (triple) in the final verse of each acrostic section! Whew! That analogy took smarter people than I to decipher. A bicola type verse is important. Why? The first verse says, "Save me, O God." Then the second section describes why, "For the waters have come up to my neck."

This explanation helped me as I read and re-read David's psalm. Save me . . . waters up to my neck; sink in the miry depths . . . no foothold. David is very detailed in his lament. His prayer for deliverance in the first section is followed by the cause of his suffering, a repeated plea and prayer to overthrow his enemies, then his assurance that his prayers have been answered leading to the future.

If you think about this plea from David and couple it with its

Messianic references, it tends to add more light to its N. T. references and how the Holy Spirit endowed the writer of this psalm pointing, to the future. Jesus reminds his disciples in John 15 that they "hated me without reason," from Psalm 69:4.

David's shame is in defense of God's house. Verse seven says, "For I endure scorn for your sake, and shame covers my face." (Psalm 69:7) Jesus felt the same way. John 2:17 relates how Jesus overturned the money changes in the Temple for turning it into a marketplace. David continues to pray for God's favor (verse 13) because of God's great love for His people. He also says, "Answer me with your **sure** salvation." (emphasis added – Psalm 69:13).

David continues to add his intense feelings to God. "Scorn has broken my heart." "They have put gall in my food and vinegar for my thirst." (Messianic). David desires retribution for God to "pour out" His wrath with His fierce anger.

David's confidence builds and he is sure of God's love for him and His people. "I will praise God's name in song and glorify Him with thanksgiving." (verse 30). All creation should praise Him (verse 34). Then David focuses on Zion as he is sure of His involvement in rebuilding cities in Judah.

David was indeed God's servant King and perhaps the most loved. While he was a warrior king, the kingdom of Israel was never more powerful (under God's leadership), as the country and its leader continued to endure hardship and attacks. This suffering servant is a foretaste of **The Suffering Servant** prophesied by Isaiah.

Let us be ever mindful, that while we suffer on this earth, Jesus' advice to His disciples applies to you and me today. The world may hate us without reason, but we are not OF this world but IN this world as we are citizens of heaven! (Philippians 3:20-21).

Peace
Connected in Him, I stand
GHR

PSALM 70
Never Failing

Well, repetition never hurts! This psalm is similar to the last half of Psalm 40. The words have changed slightly but they are essentially the same. One theologian (Ernst Wilhelm Hengstenberg) suggests that David himself may have prepared the second half of Psalm 40 as a separate piece, and that the minor changes noted in Psalm 70 are merely author's freedom in choice of words.

The psalm opens with David's plea for God to act quickly to save him from those who seek his life. His pursuers are attempting to put David to shame and ruin him! David quotes his pursuers as using the interjection of derision, "Aha! Aha!" This interjection is used 12 different times in Scripture but mostly in the O.T. The prophet Ezekiel uses this term on multiple occasions in his book. Ezekiel himself was a prophet during the time of the Babylonian captivity. Ezekiel was taken into captivity in 597 BC and remained there until 570 BC. Beginning in chapter 25, Ezekiel prophesies revenge to various peoples who scorned the Israelites. And during his prophesy, he uses this term of derision, "Aha!" It is sort of a modern day, "Take that!"

David's prayer is quite short, compared to his other psalms of lament. He prays that those "who seek You" continue to rejoice and not be dismayed. I am particularly taken by David's words in conclusion. Like the humble Publican in his prayer, David too is admitting his poor and needy condition. He asks God to come quickly and address his needs – as He is his deliverer. And don't delay!

We know that God indeed keeps His every promise to us. He

has never totally ignored His chosen. In fact, in Ezekiel's time, he prophesies that God's glory will return to Jerusalem and will "fill the temple of the LORD." (Ezekiel 43:4-5) Just as God returned his people from Babylon after a total of 70 years in captivity, we too have become blameless because of the blood of the Lamb of God who died for us on Calvary's cross.

David's words are certainly worth repeating from an earlier psalm. We all need to be reminded that even though the world may seem to be seeking our demise, we can count our LORD to deliver us from the snares of the Evil One. The devil cannot penetrate our shield of faith.

Peace
Connected in Him, I stand
GHR

PSALM 71

An Old Man's Confidence

Psalm 71 was written by a man of long-standing belief in the Almighty. Who he was is not known, but the authorship is not as important as what he says? Perhaps it's sage advice to the world's youth. Many theologians have suggested it is of David in his elder years, while some have even suggested the prophet Jeremiah. But regardless, the author is a man of faith from his youth. This psalm also has remnants of other psalms according to many theologians (Psalms 22 various; 31; 35; 38; 40 and 109).

I have a long-standing note in my Bible's margin, referring to hope in Paul's letter to the Romans. Why? The first verses of this psalm are this old man's hope for ultimate deliverance, because God is his rock and refuge to whom he can always go! St. Paul reminds his readers, "For everything that was written in the past was written to teach us, so that through endurance and the encouragement of the Scriptures we might have hope." (Romans 15:4) Reading through this psalm as a life-long Christian and an old man, I can be rest assured that God continues to have faith in the old to tell the young of God's continued protection of those whom He loves.

The author states that he has relied on God from his mother's womb. (verse 6b) As such, now in his elder years, he is honored to be a portent (sign) of God's continued strength and refuge to those whom He has called. The author has some fear that God will forsake him in his advancing years when his strength has been zapped from his body. But the author is confident that God will not forsake him as his enemies might presume. In fact, the author uses the phrase, "as for me," which reminds me of the elder leader of the Israelites. His name was Joshua. When he was 110 years old, he said, "But as for me and my house, we will serve the LORD." (Josh 24:15) Yes, in his waning years, his confidence was as strong as a waxing moon.

Regardless of our physical strength, we continue to have a mouth that can offer praises to the Almighty and remind the youth that God has saved him and will save them too. God's righteousness is immeasurable. The author states, "His righteousness reaches to the skies." (verse 19) The youth must stay strong and endure the world's trials and tribulations as the elder has done!

The elder's lips continue to sing His praises and His faithfulness. May God continue to empower the nation's elders to proclaim the Savior and His unfailing promises. Do not fall from His grace. Rather trust in the promises versus resting on the premises.

Remember Paul's benediction in Romans 15: "May the God of hope fill you with all joy and peace as you trust in Him, so that you may overflow with hope by the power of the Holy Spirit."

Peace
Connected in Him, I stand
GHR

PSALM 72

Endow with Your Righteousness

This chapter concludes the second book of Psalms. As we remember, this section of Psalms also reminds us of its parallel in the Pentateuch. The second section of Psalms refers to Moses' second book, Exodus, whose theme is "ruin and rescue." While many theologians believe this psalm was authored by Solomon, it also is clear that it is a prayer offered by his father, David, as he desires that the wisdom of God may be with his son during his rule.

David's plea in verse one is for God to endow his son with righteousness. While David's prayer is for his physical son, Solomon, one can easily see that it refers to the Son of David, the LORD Jesus Christ, in a spiritual sense. Solomon would reign for 40 years as did his father, David. David's prayer is for a just, righteous, compassionate and yes, glorious reign. We know that young Solomon was a little child (1 Kings 3:7) and acknowledged to God his ignorance. Thus, he asked for a discerning heart to govern. And God gave it to him!

David's reign was successful as God provided victories over his enemies despite the adverse odds. David acknowledged God's hand in all the victories and now prays for his son to continue to walk in the God's light – especially as a just king including the afflicted ones. (verse 2)

The next few verses (verses 5-8) are more about our LORD Jesus Christ as the King versus Solomon as the earthly king. Why? The enduring rule is referred to as "as long as the sun . . .and the moon."

Later, the author says, "He will rule from sea to sea and from the River (Euphrates) to the ends of the earth." (verse 8).

The rule of a king must also be one of compassion in his just rule. The psalmist says, "For he will deliver the needy who cry out, the afflicted who have no one to help. (verse 12) Words like, "take pity, save, rescue," are important signs of a wise and compassionate king. Jesus, the Christ, (and King) was all these and more.

The king's reign is prosperous as gifts and prayers are offered for him and to him. God's blessing abounds not only in a spiritual sense but a physical one. "Let the grain abound throughout the land . . .and its fruit flourish." (verse 16). And again, the psalmist refers to the endless reign of the King (verse 17) and that all nations will praise him.

The final verses of this psalm (and Book II) are doxological. "Praise be to the LORD God, the God of Israel, who alone does marvelous deeds. Praise be to his glorious name forever; may the whole earth be filled with His glory. Amen and Amen." (verses 18-19).

God indeed did rescue His people from all their adversaries and delivered them to the Land of Milk and Honey as He promised. He provided for a united kingdom of Israel for a time under just and compassionate rule of David and his son just as God's son as King of kings and LORD of lords rules the universe. God indeed blessed Israel during David and Solomon's rule. David's prayer in this psalm penned by his son is also relevant for you and me today. We pray that all peoples will look to God Almighty for deliverance from the Evil One. We pray that he will provide for our physical needs to sustain this life. And finally, that He will provide us His Spirit of wisdom that we may see Him as our Savior with our spiritual eyes.

Peace
Connected in Him, I stand
GHR

PSALMS, BOOK III PROLOGUE

Psalm 73 begins the third book in the Psalter, running through Psalm 89. Along with Book IV, it is tied for the shortest of the five books. The five-book division mirrors that of the Pentateuch, the books of Moses. Book III places an emphasis on the sanctuary, or the church. The book of Leviticus corresponds to this book, as it deals with the Tabernacle and God's holiness and the tribe of Levi. (Indiana Wesleyan University – course note).

Book III consists chiefly of Asaph's psalms with two collections (Asaphite and Korahitic). The Asaphites were of the tribe of Levi and served as temple musicians. Theologians place these psalms during the time of King Hezekiah and extending into the reign of Manasseh. It may have been compiled following the Israelite's return from captivity in Babylon.

According to *Structuring the Psalms* (esv.org), Book II closed with the high point of royal aspirations and Book III concludes in Psalm 89 with these expectations badly threatened.

The book of Leviticus relates to the Levites, one of the 12 tribes of Israel. One clan or family of the Levites, Aaron, was set apart to be priests. The remaining Levites were to be assistants to the priests. Their duties were the care of the tabernacle, and later the care of the temple; and to be teachers, scribes, musicians, officers, and judges. (Source: *Halley's Bible Handbook*, Introduction to Leviticus).

PSALM 73

Pride . . . The Strangling Necklace

Psalm 73 begins the third book of Psalms and is authored by Asaph or one of the Asaphites. If written by Asaph himself, the words could also be those of David. Regardless, the psalm would seem as though the author was questioning whether God was good to the Israelites. The reason for his concern relates to the apparent success of the wicked. The author even states his envy for those who seem to be so successful and trouble-free.

I have entitled these notes as *Pride: The Strangling Necklace* which is taken from verse six. Following his statement of envy, the author elaborates on the wicked's struggle-free life. "Their bodies are healthy and strong . . . free from burdens . . . not plagued by human ills." (verses 4-5) Then verse six says, "Therefore, pride is their necklace." Perhaps their earthly necks are adorned with the jewelry of success?

The author goes into detail to show how the wicked succeed in this life. I have prepared a table that summarizes verses 6b-9.

Body	Yield
Clothes (clothe)	Violence
Hearts	Iniquity
Minds	Limitless evil
Speech	Arrogance→evil and oppression
Mouth (tongues)	Claim ownership heaven and earth

With no fear of the unknown (verse 11), they lap up water in abundance. My Bible footnote suggests the Hebrew meaning of this verse is unknown but H. C. Leupold in his *Exposition of the Psalms* quotes *Koenig*: "(the) scene might have been observed in an oasis, where a thirsty camel gulp down water in endless amounts." The wicked (scoffers) say, "How can God know?" The prophet Job also reflects on the apparent success of the wicked that is similar to Psalm 73. (See Job 21:7-15)

Verses 13-14 contrast his life with that of the scoffers. He had kept his heart clean and his hands washed in innocence. The washing of hands in innocence is repeated in Matthew 27:24 when Pilot claimed total innocence over Jesus' eventual death by washing his hands in front of all Jesus' accusers. Yet, Asaph claims that his ills or troubles continue all the day long (verse 14). His earthly attempt to understand how the scoffers succeeded and avoided troubles eluded him, but once he consulted the Almighty (entered the sanctuary of God) did he **understand their final destiny.** (a strangling necklace).

The sin of pride of the scoffers will only lead to their earthly success strangling them in the final chapter of life. They are completely swept away (verse 19) with no earthly asset to save them.

Asaph's tone builds to one of confidence in the LORD and His control over all things. "Yes, I am always with you . . . You hold me with Your right hand . . . Guide me with Your counsel→take me into glory." (verses 23-24). The omnipresence confessed here by Asaph is repeated by Jesus the Messiah himself at His ascension in the Great Commission. (See Matt. 28:18-20). He concludes that his earthly condition is nothing compared to his promised inheritance of heaven. (verse 25) The Christian has a citizenship in heaven (see Philippians 3:20-21) - a passport to eternity with I AM!

The final verses are very poetic (26-28) where Asaph states his never-dying confidence in God's strength and his portion forever. He concludes that God will destroy the unfaithful! "**But as for me**" (Psalm 73:8) says Asaph is thankful that he is near God, his Sovereign and refuge.

Peace
Connected in Him, I stand
GHR

P. S. In Joshua's final farewell, he states to all the people of Israel, "Now fear the LORD and serve Him with all faithfulness. . . **But as for me** and my household, we will serve the LORD." (Joshua 24:14-15)

PSALM 74

Spiritual Poverty

For 70 years, the Jews were in captivity in Babylon. The temple has been destroyed and there was a feeling of spiritual poverty. The author opens with a question, "Why have you rejected us forever, O God?" The timing of this psalm is somewhat in question. Some would suggest that it was during the Maccabean period while most are of the opinion that it occurs during or shortly after the destruction of the temple in Jerusalem in 586 BC. If the latter is true, it would not be David's Asaph who wrote the psalm rather one of his descendants who continued to serve in the temple. (a family name rather than personal name).

The prophet Isaiah reminds His people that there will always be a remnant. Isaiah 11:10 says, "In that day the Root of Jesse will stand as a banner for the peoples. . .In that day, the LORD will reach out His hand a second time to reclaim the remnant left from . . . Babylon." The author is concerned that their God has totally ignored their plight as His anger smolders against the sheep of His pasture. (verse1b). Isaiah also reminds us that the "Holy and glorious temple, where our fathers praised you, has been burned with fire and all that we treasured lies in ruins." (Isaiah 64:11) Asaph recalls how God purchased His people of old and how He redeemed them for His inheritance - Mt. Zion (now and forever).

The author is concerned about the ruins in His holy city and especially God's sanctuary. The destruction was far wielding with their axes and hatchets. (verse 6) The total destruction defiled not only the dwelling, but His name! The author is now of the mind that they have no prophets left to provide a communication from God to His people. That would mean that Jeremiah is now gone, and Ezekiel remains in captivity. The prophet Jeremiah did prophesy that He will "bring health and healing to it." (Jeremiah 33:6) God's people are crying out, "How long?" The enemy continues to mock the God of Israel, the author requests their destruction at God's hand.

Verse 12 begins the author's remembrance of God's power and dominion in the past. He split the sea (Red Sea and Jordan); created everything (sun, moon, etc). The author reminds God that He cannot hand over His doves to the wild beasts. Remember Your covenant! Your oppressed, including the poor and needy, are in need of Your response and saving grace. Rise up! Do not ignore!

God's people were never in total poverty, just as you and I are never without our loving God. He has promised to be with us until the very end of the age. The solution is not anything that we can do. Rather we need only to accept His loving, graceful gift of salvation by the blood of His Son, Jesus. May the remnant of Israel continue to believe and then accept this atoning grace.

In conclusion, God's Holy Spirit resides in all His believers. We are His living temple in service to the One who saved us. Just as God never left His people in captivity, He has and never will ignore His believers in faith.

Peace
Connected in Him, I stand
GHR

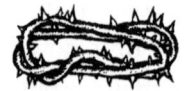

PSALM 75
A Cup of Wrath

This psalm is attributed to Asaph once again, but which Asaph is another question. Some theologians have placed the timing of this psalm in the time of Sennacherib, King of Assyria, and his attempt to take Jerusalem. This would be around 701 BC. Of course, we know the story where the angel of the LORD destroyed 185,000 Assyrians and Sennacherib returned to Assyria without having accomplished his goal.

This psalm is sort of a sandwich opening and closing of praise and thanksgiving with the middle a judgment of the proud and arrogant. Asaph opens with a glorious statement of praise suggesting his God is continually present! The NIV capitalizes the word "Name," indicating God. Recognizing that God is never very far away is more warming than a winter parka in sub-zero weather.

Verse two begins with God saying that all is His time(ing), including His judging. His statement of strength is shown as a picture of God saving strength over the Assyrian's attempt to conquer Jerusalem. While the earth may quake, our God holds up the building pillars that support but also each of us during times of tremors in our lives. So, the arrogant can boast no more! Their human "horn" (suggesting strength) is flaccid compared to the Horn of Strength that is God Himself.

The "horn of strength" is very prominent in the wonderful prayer of Hannah in 1 Samuel 2. Listen to the opening words in her prayer: "My heart rejoices in the LORD; in the LORD my horn is lifted high."

The author reminds us that God is the righteous judge. Some will be exalted, and others will drink the cup of wrath. The cup is full of foaming (potent) wine mixed with spices. While it appears pleasant, the cup of wrath is one that is "so intoxicating that it causes him to stagger about, that is a cup of God's anger." (Leupold's Commentary). The prophet Isaiah proclaims Zion's restoration from captivity and announces the LORD's wrath on its enemies. Isaiah 51:23 says, "I will put it (cup of wrath) into the hands of your tormentors."

Asaph's concluding sentences are again praiseworthy. First, the author states his everlasting praise to the God of Jacob. Second, he is confident in His strength versus that of his enemies.

In summary, let us remember the righteous judge and the One whose strength is unequaled. Listen to the prophet Zechariah and his song (also called Benedictus): "Praise be to the LORD, the God of Israel, because He has come and has redeemed His people. He has raised up a horn of salvation for us in the house of his servant David." (Luke 1:68-69)

Peace
Connected in Him, I stand
GHR

PSALM 76

The Character of God

Asaph writes a most beautiful psalm referring to the God of Israel. He states, "In Judah God is known; His name is great in Israel."

The word "name," used again here refers to all that God is and was and is to be. It also speaks to His attributes. When I examined the "character" of God on the internet, I found a very interesting reference to the "30-Names and Attributes of God," (To download a copy go to: navlink.org/names-of-God) All the names and/or attributes are certainly on point. But the link adds a description that is also very poignant. The most significant to me was the attribute of "infinite:" The God who is beyond measurement . . . He has no beginning no end, and no limits."

Let's go back to Asaph's psalm. His opening is not only acknowledging God and His presence (his tent in Salem—see Genesis and Melchizedek) but that He has protected His people by averting the enemy's arrows and other weapons.

The timing of this psalm remains in question, but some have suggested a similar situation to the previous one, vis-à-vis the Assyrian attack on Jerusalem. Jerusalem was a fortified city but it could be penetrated . . . but with God and His protection, the City of Salem (Jerusalem) was impenetrable! Asaph says, "At your rebuke, O God of Jacob; both horse and chariot lie still." (verse 6)

God's judgment is final and just. He has saved the afflicted of the land (Israel). The author says, "Surely Your wrath against men brings your praise." "Therefore," make vows to your LORD your God and fulfill them," says the author. These acts of superiority have not gone unnoticed, as neighboring lands noticed and have brought gifts to "the One to be feared." What comfort!

The character of God continues to shine on His people. Never has any hurdle or threat ever confronted them or encamped on their boundaries without God's knowledge. If allowed, He always had a plan of protecting the remnant of Israel. God's people need to remember His character/attributes. God is victorious! To God alone be praise!

The character of God is manifested in the Messiah. His is the One who was promised in Genesis 3:15, then born of the virgin Mary to be sin for us and crucified on Calvary's cross for our sins. That character, while both God and man, cannot be denied. His infinite nature is awe-inspiring and leads us to the Bethlehem cradle to worship Him, the Word made flesh. (Logos: is Greek for "Word of God")

May God's total character continue to live and breathe in your life as He has in mine. May your character continue to reflect His presence and to serve Him as He served us.

Peace
Connected in Him, I stand
GHR

PSALM 77

Perplexed

This psalm is attributed to Asaph, but its time is uncertain. H. C. Leupold offers a suggestion that it was written in the time of Josiah (641-609 BC), but prior to the Chaldean invasion (597 BC). (Note: Chaldea is often associated with Babylonia.) Chaldea is located in the northeast portion of Babylonia between the Rivers (Tigris and Euphrates). It is reported that Babylonia took total control of Chaldea in 572 BC, during the time of Nebuchadnezzar II.

H. C. Leupold, in his *Exposition of the Psalms,* suggests this psalm has some relationship to Habakkuk 3. Habakkuk was a prophet to Judah during the time of Babylonian captivity during which he died. Chapter three in the minor prophet's book is a psalm-like prayer defined with the term *shigionoth* which is interpreted as a lyrical poem composed under strong mental emotion. With that said, let's examine the author's words. He opens with a similar lament, "I cried out to God for help; I cried out to God to hear me." If you continue to read through verse nine, the author seems to believe that God has totally ignored His people, never to restore them.

His moaning affects his whole being. "My soul refused to be comforted . . . my spirit grew faint . . . my eyes would not close . . . too troubled to speak." (verses 2-5) But verse 10 begins to show his perplexed attitude is changing. "Then I thought . . . I will remember the deeds and miracles . . . and meditate on all Your works and deeds." (verses 10-12) He now realizes that God's ways are holy and unchanging, He remembers how God never lost sight of the remnant of Israel in

Egypt and, regardless of the conditions, God's power and control were unequaled.

The poetry is beautifully written as the author recounts God's actions of old. "The waters writhed . . . the depths convulsed . . . skies resounded with thunder . . . earth trembled and quaked." (verses16-18) Even as perplexed as Asaph appears to be in the opening verses, once he turns to God in prayer, he recounts how God has never failed to save His people. Yes, God created a path in the Red Sea for the millions to cross and shepherded the flock with His servants Moses and Aaron, by His Glory.

Perplexed? Our lesson today is that we, like Asaph, can find ourselves questioning God's presence in our lives. Has He ignored us? Has He in anger withheld His compassion? (verse 9) If you read Habakkuk's prayer, you may get comforted in the prophet's words. Listen: "I will wait patiently for the day of calamity to come on the nation invading us (or trouble in our day)." "The Sovereign LORD is my strength; He makes my feet like the feet of a deer; it enables me to go on the heights (to push onward; to be uplifted)."

Listen to the hymnist *What a Friend We Have in Jesus*.

> Are we weak and heavy laden,
> Cumbered with a load of care?
> Precious Savior still our refuge—
> Take it to the LORD in prayer.
> Do thy friends despise, forsake thee?
> Take it to the LORD in prayer.
> In His arms He'll take and shield thee;
> Thou wilt find a solace there.
> (LSB 770, verse 3)

Peace
Connected in Him, I stand
GHR

PSALM 78

From Generation to Generation

This psalm of Asaph is one of instruction (didactic). The time is uncertain, but many believe it is the same Asaph that served King David as a musician. As I read through this psalm initially, I was reminded of the "oral" history passed down from my father to me and from his father to him, etc. This is also particularly important when it comes to our faith life. Why? As verse seven tells us, "Then they would put their trust in God and would not forget His deeds but would keep His commands." In addition, this generational passing of information also suggests that the children will not repeat the errors of the past. Ergo, "They would not be like their forefathers—a stubborn and rebellious generation." (verse 8a)

Psalm 78 is almost Janus-like. Who was Janus? He was the Roman god in mythology with two faces, one looking back and one looking forward. The name January was taken from the word Janus as the month looks forward to a new year and back to the one just passed. In modern times, a Janus word has taken on opposite meaning. It is called a contronym (contranym), literally, having two opposite meanings. In the case of this psalm, we have God who is perfect and looking out for His own, providing all that is needed to sustain us. On the other hand, we have the recipients of God's provisions who are grumbling (stubborn and rebellious).

Asaph goes into great detail regarding the wonderful deeds of God Most High (*El Elyon*). Remember the great plagues that Moses and Aaron brought down on Egypt from God himself? And the final plague was the death of the first born of all living things, except for the blood of the lamb was painted over the doorposts of the Israelites. His miracles in their departure were nothing less than miraculous, from splitting the Red Sea to providing food and water in the desert. Yet, the people continued to grumble. Numbers 14 tells of their even considering a new leader to take them back to Egypt so that they would not die in the desert. Verse 32 says, "In spite of all this, they kept on sinning." Verse 34 reminds us that they returned to God when subjected to His divine judgment. It was a vicious cycle. **Sin→Judgment→Repentance (shallow, per H. C. Leupold Commentary)→Forgiveness→Sin . . .repeat**

Sometime the past acts can influence the acts of the future generations. The author reminds us that they remembered that God was their Rock (v. 35) and their Redeemer. Again, we see a Janus-like action. With one face they are saying God is all-in-all and the other face a lying tongue. (verse 36)

As they approached the land of Canaan, the 12 spies were sent out to scout the land. Ten returned with a dismal report, while Joshua and Caleb were bullish on the "land of milk and honey." It's ours for the taking! But the people grumbled. The land of Israel became disjointed over time, as the ten northern tribes split from the Kingdom of Judah (two southern tribes). They Kingdom of Israel (also known as Kingdom of Ephraim) fell away. Eventually, they were taken captive by the Assyrians, never to return. The southern tribes were prosperous under King David, the shepherd of God's people and a foretaste of the promised Shepherd who was the Bread of Life and the Living Water.

It is the attitude and serving nature of David that God desires. Sin and its consequences are deadly, unless there is repentance and forgiveness through Jesus, the Lamb of God. It behooves the older generation to tell the younger generation of God's grace and mercy. He is *El Elyon*, God Most High. He is the Rock and Redeemer for all who believe and accept Him as LORD and Savior. May the lessons of the past teach the present and future generations that God is Love. Perhaps a lesson for us is to read this psalm to our children to remind them of God's everlasting care for His flock.

Peace
Connected in Him, I stand
GHR

PSALM 79

City Defiled

This psalm opens with a statement from its author that God's city and its Temple has been invaded, with the future of generations in doubt. The prophet Jeremiah served His LORD through 40 terrible years. (*Halley's Bible Handbook*). He was called to be a prophet in 626 BC. According to theologians, Jerusalem was first invaded in 605 BC and partially destroyed. Then again in 597 and its final destruction in 586 BC.

Here, the author (Asaph) cries out for God to hear him. The exact timing of this psalm is in question but as the first paragraph describes it was likely during the time of Jeremiah the prophet. The northern ten tribes of Israel have already been taken into captivity. The tiny Kingdom of Judah is now in peril, with Jerusalem reduced to rubble. (verse 1)

The author says, "We are objects of reproach to our neighbors, of scorn and derision to those around us." (verse 4) How long? Will not Your jealous nature burn like fire? Verse six begins with a frequently used verb in the O. T. The verb "pour out" is used here (115 times in the O. T. *shaphak*). The object of the verb is not good! Yes, pour out Your wrath, O God! The pouring out process is like that of a molten metal during the separation of impurities. That's what is needed for those who "do not call on Your name." Verses 6-7 are virtually a carbon copies of Jeremiah 10:25.

Asaph prayerfully requests that God would not hold the sins of their fathers against them. Mercy is the attribute of God that he seeks. Mercy will turn the face of God to one of compassion in desperate times. He acknowledges God as his Savior for "glory" is His name. This word "glory" is well known to the O. T. Israelites, as it was, He (Glory), that was omnipresent in the desert and led them to the land of milk and honey. The Babylonians (Chaldeans) are ridiculing God's people as they say, "Where is your God?"

Asaph pleas that God would rescue those who are destined to die at the hands of their enemies, as their groans have reached the heavenly realms. He even asks God to pay them back to the "max," that is seven times. (the number of completeness).

"Then, we (your) people" will praise you forever . . . from generation to generation. Praise the LORD! Amen.

Peace
Connected in Him, I stand
GHR

PSALM 80

Song of the Vineyard

This psalm brings tears to your eyes just as it did to the people of Israel. Tears brought on by their own sin and total denial of The Shepherd who had delivered His flock from captivity in Egypt to the Promised Land. But then what? They continually disobeyed their Shepherd and now they are no longer in control of their own destiny.

The psalmist opens with a tearful plea: "Hear us, O Shepherd of Israel." The author acknowledges that God is enthroned between the cherubim, which could be a reference to the Tabernacle or to heaven itself. God was thought to be enthroned above the cherubim that stood over the Mercy Seat (See Exodus 25:22). A N. T. reference to the throne in heaven is mentioned in Revelation 4:6. Regardless, God is enthroned on high and shines forth as the only true God and Jesus Christ whom He has sent. But God's presence is perhaps veiled, as the author pleads for God to "shine forth."

The author mentions several tribes of Israel here including both the northern and southern tribes which may suggest that all are reminded of how they have ignored the God Most High. "Awaken Your might; come and save us." What more can they say? God's anger has been long-standing, and their tears are their diet, as they drink them by the bowlful. (verse 5). The final verse in this section (verse 7) summarizes the author's plea: "Restore us, O God Almighty, make your face shine upon us that we may be saved."

The next section begins talking in the metaphor of a vine and vineyard. Israel here is called a vine that God brought out of Egypt. The prophet Isaiah writes "The Song of the Vineyard." (Isaiah 5:1-7) The vine was dug up from its previous location and then replanted in the land that God had promised. Isaiah is pronouncing judgment as can be seen in verse two where the crop was bad. The psalmist recounts how the land of Israel was once fruitful but now its walls are broken down and its enemies have ravaged the land.

Jesus the Messiah reminds us in John's Gospel that He is the True Vine and we are the branches. (John 15:5) Unless we are attached to the vine, we cannot bear good fruit. This is one of the seven I AM's in the N. T., showing the character of the LORD God and His Son, Jesus. The heavenly father is the gardener in this dialogue of Jesus. The gardener's duty is to prune the vine of branches that are not fruitful.

Is it too late for Israel? The author closes in verses 17-18 asking God's favor on them, including their king. A promise is made that we won't turn away from You again! And finally, the author repeats verse seven with the "Restore and Save" prayer.

May we be reminded that Jesus Christ is the True Vine and that, apart from Him, we can do nothing. Our prayer continues to be for God to shine forth on us and be gracious and merciful to us as sinner/saints.

Peace
Connected in Him, I stand
GHR

PSALM 81

The Desires of God

Psalm 81 is well-known to Jewish worshippers, as a "Passover Psalm." Some might suggest that it may also refer to the Feast of Tabernacles. Theologians cannot determine which festival this may be referencing. Regardless, the author states that God's people were to worship their LORD God! Verse three reminds the people of Israel to sound the ram's horn at the new moon and when it is full. The "Feast," capitalized in NIV, likely refers to either the Passover or the Tabernacles. However, H. C. Leupold, in his *Exposition of the Psalms,* suggests that the distinction between a particular feast or festival is futile. The new moon was a signal of a new cycle and thus new beginnings.

The author reminds his readers that God removed their burden, as He rescued them from their bondage. Remember from Exodus that hard labor in brick and mortar that made their lives bitter. (Exodus 1:14) God's response to their need is summarized in two events. First, God answered them out of a thundercloud, which likely refers to His presence on Sinai when He delivered the Laws to Moses and made His covenant to the people of Israel. Secondly, He provided daily needs, especially water from the rock at Meribah (where Israel grumbled).

A new section begins in verse eight, where God issues a warning to "listen!" God's desires are made perfectly clear to His people. His first commandment is repeated, "You shall have no foreign god among you . . . nor bow down to any alien god." His covenant relationship with Israel is made manifest in His delivering them out of bondage to the Promised Land. What does God require? Well, in part, the first commandment is clear: no other gods, period! Second, He requires obedience with the promise to subdue their enemies. (verses 13-14) Go back to Exodus 23:22: "If you listen carefully to what He (God) says and do all that I say, I will be an enemy to your enemies and will oppose those who oppose you."

God's presence is known as His Glory – the Shekinah cloud and the pillar of fire. His presence and promises are genuine. In verse 10b, God promises to fill their mouths signaling His generous gifts.

But, says verse 11, "You would not listen . . . and would not submit!" God repeats His promise from Exodus here, "If Israel would follow My ways, how quickly would I subdue their enemies." It sounds like there's not a happy ending (Gospel). Well, the author reminds us all that those who have (or will) trust in the LORD their God will be fed with the finest wheat and with honey from the rock . . . and be totally satisfied." The sweetness of the Gospel is such that the Genesis protevangel ("First Gospel" 3:15) message has been delivered as promised. Now, the sweet salvation is totally ours if we only believe in the Messiah and His saving sacrifice and glorious resurrection. So just as the new moon brought new beginnings, so our Savior's sacrificial offering on Calvary brings new beginnings and life everlasting with Him in eternity.

Peace
Connected in Him, I stand
GHR

PSALM 82

Indictment and Verdict

God is Love, but God is also the Divine Judge! Asaph writes this psalm that indicts the judges of his day regarding their injustice. Following his indictment, the verdict follows that will subject them to the divine Judge himself. The Asaph spoken of here as the author is likely David's Asaph per many theologians.

Let's examine how God and his spokesmen speak to His people related to their obedience to the laws and guidelines that God instructed them prior to their entry into the Promised Land. Deuteronomy 4:6-7 says, "Observe them (laws) carefully, for this will show your wisdom and understanding to the nations, who will hear about all these decrees and say, 'Surely this great nation is a wise and understanding people.'" Later, during Jehoshaphat's rule (873-848 BC per Rose's *Book of Bible Charts & Time Lines*), He appointed judges in Judah. (See 2 Chronicles 19:5-7) Listen to His instructions: "Consider carefully what you do, because you are not judging for man but for the LORD, who is with you whenever you give a verdict."

Asaph begins his psalm as he echoes the previous thought from 2 Chronicles: "God presides in the great assembly; He gives judgment among the gods (rulers, judges)." Verse two begins an indictment of the unjust judges or rulers. "How long will You defend unjust . . . show impartiality (failure to) . . . defend the weak and fatherless (failure to) . . . rights of poor and oppressed (failure to)." (verses 3-4) Jesus quotes this psalm in John 10 as He is dealing with the Jewish leaders during the Feast of Dedication (Hanukkah). The leaders attempted to stone

Jesus for claiming to be God. Jesus retorts with this statement, "Is it not written in your law, 'I have said you are gods'" to whom the word of God came – and the Scripture cannot be broken." (John 10:34-35)

Asaph then moves into the verdict phase of this psalm. He reminds the unjust rulers (judges) that they are mere men and will die! As sons of the Most High, we too will be subject to the Righteous Judge on the Day of the LORD.

The final verse calls for God to "Rise up and judge the earth." As H. C. Leupold states in his *Exposition of the Psalms,* that, "God is the guardian of justice." He requires those in a position of authority as rulers and judges to be fair, impartial, and to seek justice. Remember the words of Moses from Deuteronomy, "Observe them (laws) carefully, for this will show your wisdom and understanding." (Deuteronomy 4:6) Following David's 40-year rule, his son Solomon assumed the throne of his father. I Chronicles 29 reminds us that Solomon "Sat on the throne of the LORD." (1 Chronicles 29:23) The text also reminds us that Solomon prospered, and all Israel obeyed him. God was pleased and highly exalted Solomon in the sight of Israel.

The true God is known for His mighty acts, protection of His people, and perfect justice. May we continue to walk in His ways, worshipping our Creator, Redeemer, and Sanctifier of our lives as we await the Day of the LORD and the reunion with Him in eternity.

Peace
Connected in Him, I stand
GHR

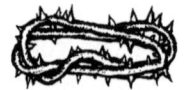

PSALM 83

The Enemies of God

This psalm is an urgent plea by Asaph for God to awaken and save His people from their many enemies. This chapter identifies 10 different peoples or areas surrounding God's people.

Area of Enemies	Distinction
Edom	Edomites and Esau's descendants
Ishmaelites	a/k/a Midianites; Arabs
Moab	Lot's descendants (See Gen 19:34: Moabites
Hagar's Descendants	See Ishmaelites
Gebal (Byblos)	Seaport in Phoenicia
Ammon	Lot's descendants (See Gen 19:38); Ammonites
Amalek	Grandson of Esau; Amalekites
Philistia	Philistines
Tyre	Lebanon
Assyria	Assyrians (Neo Assyrian period 911-609BC)

Who else could be against God's people? The timing of this psalm is not known, but many suggest it was during the time of Jehoshaphat (873-848 BC). After Asaph opens with his urgent plea, he says, "See how your enemies are astir." (verse 2) The Hebrew word for astir is *hamah* which means to growl, roar, or be boisterous. The KJV uses the word uproar. Regardless of the word used, the meaning is the same. We have a picture here of a mass of evil doers and haters of God's people. They are "rearing their heads," in preparation for attacking.

They are ever so desirous of erasing God's people so that they will no longer be remembered. That sounds like the 21st century! Their purpose is unified (of one mind).

The author requests God's action similar, to His acts that are recorded in the Book of Judges (4-5 and 7-8). Asaph requests God to make them like the tumbleweed and chaff that the wind blows away. (verse 13) Asaph doesn't ask God to make them like fire, as you say. Rather, he asks God to pursue them like a fire or a flame (tempest). And if that is not terrifying enough, the author requests God to terrify them with your storm (wind implied) and to cover their faces with shame that they may perish in disgrace.

So what happens? 2 Chronicles 20 records Jehoshaphat's defeat of his enemies. "A vast army is coming against you," said the king's advisers. What did the king do? He went to the LORD in prayer including all the people of Judah. He said, "O our God, will You not judge them? For we have no power to face this vast army." (2 Chronicles 20:11-12) God answered his prayer and told them "Do not be afraid or discouraged." (2 Chronicles 20:15) And the people of God sang His praises saying, "Give thanks to the LORD for his love endures forever." (2 Chronicles 20:21) God indeed went ahead of Judah's army and caused their enemies to destroy one another.

Asaph's concluding verse shows his confidence in the LORD, the God Most High and ruler of all the earth. Yes, God delivers us from Satan's attacks that would separate us from the love of God, just as God's people's enemies desired for Israel's name to be erased forever. Thankfully, God sent His Son to destroy our enemies, included death itself and to write our name in the Book of Life.

Peace
Connected in Him, I stand
GHR

PSALM 84

A Pilgrimage to His Sanctuary

The author of this psalm in Book III shifts from Asaph to the Sons of Korah. Theologians are generally unsure as to the author's name or even the timing of its writing, but the Sons of Korah are given authorship per the heading. These Korahites were Levitical servants at the Temple. In David's time, the sons were set over the service of song in the house of Yahweh, after the Ark had been returned. In other places, their task was mentioned as "Keepers of the threshold of the Tent." The opening sentences of this psalm lead one to believe that this author(s) might have been absent from the House of the LORD for reasons not totally clear. His words, "My soul yearns, even faints for the courts of the LORD." (verse 2)

The opening words are most inspiring! "How lovely is Your dwelling place." Can you and I say that today? Is it important that we're in the House of the LORD on His day? If true about his absence, then this statement is more impressive as he has desperately missed being in God's House. The author comments that even the birds of the air find the House of God to be home for their nests. (verse 3) Verse four begins with "Blessed" are those who dwell in His house and are ever praising Him. The next verse continues this thought of blessings for those who set their hearts on the pilgrimage to God's House – possibly a spiritual journey in search of God.

Under what circumstances did God's people make a pilgrimage to Jerusalem? Required travel was for each of three festivals: Passover, Tabernacles, and Weeks. H. C. Leupold in his commentary, *Exposition of the Psalms*, reminds us today that "Pilgrimages were long, dusty, and tiresome." Thus, these trips, per se, took much energy and fortitude to visit God's House. The author reminds us that they had to travel through the Valley of Baca (which means weeping). But the author also reminds us that God blesses (pools) the valley with the autumn rains. God indeed creates and provides sustenance to His creation.

The next two verses (8-9) are a prayer for their shield or sovereign (king). The author requests God to look with favor on the anointed one of Israel (Judah). Indeed King David was committed to his God Almighty and His house of worship. David's primary source of strength was the LORD of Hosts as he battled his enemies. I am reminded of David's first prayer to God requesting His assistance over the Philistines. God said, "Go, for I will surely hand the Philistines over to you." (2 Sam 5:19-20) Again, David inquires of God regarding the Philistines. God again gave David instructions as to how He himself would go out in front and deliver the enemy to David. (2 Sam 5:22-28)

The author, a doorkeeper in God's House, expresses his thankfulness in a way that seems unusual: "Better is ONE day in YOUR courts, than ONE THOUSAND elsewhere." (Emphasis added) Yes, to dwell in God's house is much better than to dwell in the house of the earthly and seemingly successful (referred to as wicked) individuals. Why is that? Well, the author indicates that his LORD God is his sun and shield. This shield is One and the same as the One who spoke to Abram in Genesis 15:1! The final verses give promise to you and me today. The LORD bestows favor and honor, nor does He withhold any good thing for those who walk blameless before the LORD. Amen to "Blessed is the man who trusts in You!" (verse 12)

How is your pilgrimage to God's house? Do you travel through the valley of dryness? Or is your travel without hindrance? Regardless, remember the author: one in a 1,000 is far superior to the alternative. Worship Him regularly!

Peace
Connected in Him, I stand
GHR

Note: *Essential Bible Comparison to the Psalms* remarks about the use of the word, LORD, God, and Lord Almighty. The Psalm opens and closes with LORD Almighty. The term LORD and God are used seven (7) times – the number associated with completeness and perfection.

PSALM 85

Past, Present & Future

The Sons of Korah are again the author(s) of this psalm. Theologians are unsure as to the exact timing of this psalm but shortly after Judah's return from exile may be a good guesstimate. Let's look back at the Babylonian captivity. The siege on Jerusalem began in 605 BC and concluded in 586 BC with the destruction of the Temple. The return from exile did not begin until the fall of the Babylonians to Persia and Cyrus the Great in 539-538 BC. Cyrus granted the Jews' release, which did not occur all at once, but rather over a period of time.

Ezra records the early return and the beginning restoration process of the Temple in Jerusalem (circa 538-7 BC). The construction period lasted until 516 BC. It was then that some theologians believe this psalm was written approximately some 20 years after the exile (H. C. Leupold's *Exposition of the Psalms*). That having been said, let's look at the psalm itself. I have titled this psalm as *Past, Present & Future*. Yes, they are the verb tenses and helps define the sections in the psalm. The opening three verses are all past tense verbs where the author is thankful that God showed favor, restored, forgave, covered, set aside, and turned from.

That opening is a wonderful admission of past sins and how God's grace and loving-kindness covered their guilt. But human nature being what it is, sin rears its hoary head! The author begins verse four with the present tense and asks God to "Restore us again." He pleads with God not to hold his anger forever nor to forget His unfailing love for His people.

Verse eight begins with the future tense, where the author indicates that they will listen this time and asks that God would keep them faithful, not returning to their old ways. The balance of this psalm (verse 9) is beautiful poetry. Listen to the psalmist: "Love and faithfulness meet together; righteousness and peace kiss each other. Faithfulness springs forth from the earth, and righteousness looks down from heaven." (verses 10-11). The reward for faithfulness to the LORD Almighty is indeed "good." He promises that the land will yield its harvest.

The application from this psalm is true for us today. We were dead to sin (past tense). But God, in His loving kindness, promised to provide a way out. His Son was born to die for our sins and unfaithfulness. Our present condition is salvation for those who believe in the Messiah and His gift of forgiveness. Yet, as sin continues to pervade the earth, He continues to rescue us from sin, when we confess the errors of our way and beg forgiveness with the hope to do better in the future. Remember the words of St. Paul in the famous Resurrection Chapter (I Corinthians 15): "Thanks be to God! He gives us the victory through our LORD Jesus Christ." (1 Corinthians 15:57)

My closing words are from the hymnist Sigismund von Birken (1626-81) in *Let Us Ever Walk with Jesus.*

Let us ever walk with Jesus,
Follow His example pure,
Through a world that would deceive us
And to sin our spirits lure.
Onward in His footsteps treading,
Pilgrims here, our home above,
Full of faith and hope and love,
Let us do the Father's bidding.
Faithful Lord, with me abide;
I shall follow where Your guide.
(LSB 685, v. 1)

Peace
Connected in Him, I stand
GHR

PSALM 86

Slow to Anger; Abounding in Love

Book III departs from its usual authors and returns to David, the great leader of Israel and Judah. No particular time is associated with this psalm. In fact, some have questioned David's authorship. But since this psalm is a mosaic (H. C. Leupold's proposition) of previous psalms of David, one could assume that this too is one of David's. Theologians have even suggested that certain verses in this psalm mirror those of Psalms 25-28 and 54-57. The psalm is definitely a lament - also typical of David's style.

The first seven verses lead off with a definite plea or cry for help. This table lists each plea and then his request and/or the reason for his cry for help.

Cry (Plea) Help	Request or Reason
Hear . . . Answer	I am poor and needy
Guard my life	I am devoted to You
Save your servant	Who trusts in You
Have mercy	I call to You all day long
Bring joy	I lift up my soul
Hear . . . listen	For mercy
I call	You answer

Verse eight begins David's profession of God's singular greatness. He states, "There is none like You, O LORD." I am reminded of the story of Elijah and the 450 Baal prophets. (1 Kings 18:19-39) Here

Elijah baits the prophets to call on their god to light the fire for the sacrifice. He began to taunt them at noon, saying, "Shout louder!" Their pleas increased in intensity without success. Midday passed and it was time for the evening sacrifice, but still no response. Then Elijah said to all those gathered, "Come here to me." Elijah then rebuilt the altar of the LORD encircled it with a trench. He prepared the sacrifice and proceeded to have them pour water from four large jars over the offering of wood. He had them pour water a second and a third time, until everything was drenched; and even the trench was filled with water. Then Elijah lifted his voice to God saying, "O LORD, God of Abraham, Isaac and Israel, let it be known today that You are God." (verse 36) "Then, the fire of the LORD fell and burned up the sacrifice, the wood, the stones and the soil; and also licked up the water in the trenches." There's more to the story, but the point is very clear just as David professes in his psalm that there is ONE GOD. (Emphasis added)

Verse 12 begins with David's praise to the LORD who has taught him the truth and the way. David requests that God would always give him an undivided heart (true loyalty). His praise to God Almighty glorifying His name responds to God's great deliverance even from the depths of the grave (Sheol). Even as David gives praise, his enemies continue to attack him seeking his life.

"But You O LORD, are a compassionate and gracious God, slow to anger, abounding in love and faithfulness." (verse 15) David chose words from Moses in Exodus 34, when Moses returned to Yahweh after he broke God's Law tablets in anger, following the Israelites' golden calf worship. Moses returned and God wrote on the chiseled stone the words that were on the first tablets. He appears to Moses in the cloud and said, "The LORD, The LORD, the compassionate and gracious God, **slow to anger, abounding in love and faithfulness**." (Exodus 34:6 – emphasis added)

David concludes again with a shortened version of the first verses asking for God to help him in his troubles. The psalm opens with a lengthy cry for help. Then David singles out God as **The God** versus other earthy gods. (verse 8) Then he praises the Almighty for His deliverance noting his slowness to anger and unfailing love. Finally, he repeats his plea for help.

Our application today is to focus on the true nature of God and His superiority to the world and how it purports to be "all we need." I am reminded of the story of Jesus' healing of the boy with an evil spirit (Mark 9). The father of the boy with seizures came to Jesus. The evil spirit caused convulsions, throwing him to the ground, robbing him of speech, and causing foaming from the mouth. The father responded to Jesus' question about how long this had been going on and said, "If you can do anything, take pity on us and help us." (Mark 9:22) Then he said, "I believe, help my unbelief." (paraphrased, verse 24). An immediate healing was the result of the man's faith.

Like David, we too can cry out for help to rescue us from the worldly gods that tend to offer but can't deliver. Only God can deliver, just as He promised, our eternal deliverance through the perfect sacrifice of His Son on Calvary. "Help my unbelief."

Peace
Connected in Him, I stand
GHR

PSALM 87

Adoption: Born Again!

The Sons of Korah write a rather unusual psalm. Can you imagine Israel's enemies as fellow citizens? Almost unthinkable! Before we make any judgment, let's sit back and examine what the author(s) have to say.

The psalmist opens with a powerful statement about God's relationship to His holy mountain, the city of God. Yes, "the LORD loves the gates of Zion," says verse two. Zion is Jerusalem, also known as the City of David. If we review Israel's history, we see that once David was anointed over all Israel, his home was moved from Hebron to Jerusalem, thus the city of David. And God's home was there. The Ark of the Covenant was moved to Jerusalem and resided in a Tent until David's son became king and built a house for the LORD. In verse three, the psalmist says, "Glorious things are said of you, O city of God." In verse four, we see the psalmist relate to Israel's neighboring countries.

Yes, glorious things are indeed said of God! God was pleased with His home on the Holy Mountain. And in 2 Samuel 7, we see Nathan telling David that it will be his son who will build a permanent house for the LORD. "He (David's son) is the one who will build a house for my Name, and I will establish the throne of his kingdom forever." (verse 13) David accepted the prophet's message and he offered up his praise saying, "With Your blessing the house of Your servant will be blessed forever." (verse 29b)

God's blessings on His people were noticeable and even acknowledged by the neighbors. The psalmist begins to list several names, many of which were historical enemies. But now, they acknowledge God! How about Rahab (Egypt) and Babylon? Egypt and its Pharaohs were arrogant and mistreated God' people. Babylon attacked, destroyed, and took His people into captivity for decades. And now they're adopted? How can this be?

Then he adds to his list Philistia, a long-time enemy of Israel; Tyre, a sophisticated seaport just north of Israel; and finally Cush (Ethiopia). Collectively, the psalmist indicates "This one was born in Zion." They were all adopted into the family of God, so to speak.

Born again! I am reminded of our LORD's conversation with a great Jewish leader, Nicodemus. His nighttime meeting was clandestine in nature for fear of his status and relationship with his peers on the ruling council. Jesus replied to his query about who Jesus was, saying, "Unless a man is born again, he cannot see the kingdom of God." (John 3:3). St. Paul also reminds Titus in his epistle that we are saved, not because of our righteousness, but because of His mercy. "He saved us through the washing of rebirth and renewal by the Holy Spirit." (Titus 3:5)

Regardless of these neighbors' past misdeeds, they too can become members of the Kingdom of God by rebirth in the Holy Spirit of Christ himself. And the psalmist says, "The LORD will write in the register . . . this one was born in Zion." As I am preparing my book on missions and missionaries, I am confident that God does want all to be saved and to come to the knowledge of Truth. Yes, even the Babylonians and Egyptians.

Peace
Connected in Him, I stand
GHR

P. S. As I was preparing these notes on Psalm 87, I was listening to my office TV in the background. The Golf Channel was playing an interview with Bernhard Langer. The interviewer asked him about a time when he had a void in his life. Bernhard spoke of a time when he was invited to a Bible Study while on tour. He and his wife attended that night and the speaker quoted John 3:3 about being born again. I stopped in my tracks! I had already titled my notes and was about to reference the same story. My body reacted with a tingling sensation in amazement, as God speaks to me in ways that only He understands.

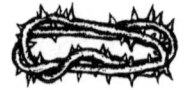

PSALM 88

Total Darkness: The Pit!

"Life is the pits," as the saying goes. I have found that a Dr. Gerry Lewis authored a book entitled "*When Life is the Pits.*" As I reviewed the website promoting the book, the author quotes Jeremiah in his book of Lamentations. To set the stage, Jeremiah penned Lamentations as his lament like multiple psalms. Jeremiah's lament is over his inability to save Jerusalem, yet he also expresses his faith that God will raise it up out of the ruins. Chapter three seems to be complaining that God has ignored him and his prayers. (*Halley's Bible Handbook*). Listen now to Jeremiah's lament: "I called on your name, O LORD, from the depths of the pit. You heard my plea: 'Do not close your ears to my cry for relief.'" (Lamentations 3:55-56)

If you examine the word "pit" in Hebrew, the word is *bowr*. It is defined as dark places, darkness, or the lowest dark. It is in this context that Psalm 88 is written. The chapter is authored by Heman the Ezrahite, who was a temple singer with the Sons of Korah. If you look back in, 1 Chronicles, you see that Heman was the grandson of Samuel, the prophet and was listed as a temple musician. (1 Chronicles 6:33)

With that background, let's take a look at the psalmist's message. The psalm is definitely a lament as he opens with a plea "Day and night I cry out before You." (verse 1b) His concern is that God has turned (His ear) from his plea. The author continues to describe his plea as one of a "soul full of trouble" and his "life draws near the grave." (verse 3) If we look back to Psalm 22, the great Messianic psalm that basically refers to Good Friday, and then compare it to this psalm, one theologian compares this psalm to Holy Saturday. (*Essential Bible Comparisons to the Psalms*)

As verses three and four suggest, his despair is so great that he fears that as his life draws near to the grave (*Sheol*), he is counted with those who go down to the pit. The darkest of dark! He compares his situation to a man without strength and cut off from God's care.

Verse six suggests he is now assigned to the "lowest" pit. This term is similar to the "lowest dark" definition from the Hebrew. If the previous reference to Holy Saturday is true, then we can certainly see the resemblance to our LORD's walk to Calvary and knowing full well that He is destined for the deepest, dark pit for His sacrifice for your sins and mine. Further. consistent with our LORD's journey, the psalmist says, "You have taken me from my closest friends." (verse 8) As we know from the N. T., the disciples fled when times got rough! The author feels confined (to the grave) and cannot escape.

We all know full well that our LORD did, in fact, overcome the pit and that He rose victorious from the grave. The psalmist continues to offer prayers daily (in the morning) as he seeks relief from his dark abode. "Why O LORD, do You reject me and hide Your face?" (verse 14) He states his condition has existed from his youth even to the point of destruction. His feelings are that total darkness is his closest friend. How dire!

Regardless of the author's despair, we can rejoice in the total salvation from the pit of darkness by the work of Jesus Christ and His perfect sacrifice for our sins and separation (pit) from God. May God shine his LIGHT on your DARKNESS to raise you up from your pit of total darkness to His everlasting light. Amen! (Emphasis added)

Peace
Connected in Him, I stand
GHR

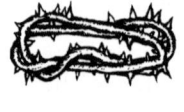

PSALM 89

The Firm Covenant

This psalm concludes Book III of Psalms. The author of this psalm is Ethan the Ezrahite. Ethan is mentioned eight times in the O. T. He was likely a musician in David's court (or Solomon's). His name means *strong, optimistic.* This psalm repeats the covenant God made to David that his throne would remain forever. Let's look back to 2 Samuel 7:16 to see His promise: "Your house and Your kingdom will endure forever before Me; Your throne will be established forever." This promise is Davidic and Messianic. It is repeated in Luke 1, when the angel Gabriel appears to Mary and tells her she is favored and will be with child. Not just any child, but the Son of God and Son of David. "The LORD God will give Him the throne of his father David, and He will reign over the house of Jacob forever; his kingdom will never end." (Luke 1:32b-33)

If we turn to Matthew's account of Jesus' genealogy, we see in the opening sentence, "Jesus Christ, the son of David, the Son of Abraham." (Matthew 1:1) Why does Matthew list both David and Abraham? With David it shows Jesus' royalty as The King and with Abraham it shows He is an Israelite and the promised Messiah promised in Genesis 3:15.

The psalmist uses the first four verses as an introduction that talks about God's love and faithfulness and His covenant with King David. His throne will endure forever. Verse five begins with God's creation, praising His name. "Heavens praise Your wonders . . ." Ethan then uses a rhetorical question to lead off subsequent verses. "Who is like the LORD among the heavenly beings?" "He is greatly feared . . . He is more awesome . . . Your faithfulness surrounds you . . . You rule the surging sea . . . You crushed Rahab (refers to Egypt) . . . with Your strong arm You founded the world . . . Your arm is endued with power." Each of these qualities and characteristics can only belong to the LORD God Almighty, the LORD Most High. (*El Elyon*)

H. C. Leupold in his *Exposition of the Psalms,* says, "More marvelous are God's moral attributes. Two of these may in a beautiful figure be compared to the bases on which His regal throne is erected." (verses 14-15) Yes, righteousness and justice are His throne's foundation. Blessed are those who walk in the light of His presence. God indeed is the strength of His people (horn = strength).

Verse 19 begins a section where God is represented as the speaker. It is sort of a Messianic look forward through David, His chosen one. He said, "I found David . . . My hand will sustain him . . . No wicked will oppress him . . . through My name his horn will be exalted." God's covenant with man cannot be invalidated, says Dr. H. C. Leupold. The Gospel writers tell of Jesus' lineage and connection to David. Luke 2 reminds us that Joseph and Mary traveled up from Nazareth to Judea, to Bethlehem, the town of David, because **he (Joseph) belonged to the house and line of David.**

Unfortunately, the unfaithfulness of God's people rears its ugly head. "You have renounced the covenant with your servant . . . defiled his crown . . . broken his walls . . . reduced his stronghold to ruins." (verses 39-40) The author again is lamenting God's hidden face. "How long, O LORD?" How many times have we heard that cry of loneliness in these psalms?! Ethan asks God, "What man can live and not see death?" (verse 48) The answer of course is no one! So, he asks God to show his great love just as He did in His covenant with David.

What a way to end Book III. God's covenant for His son David is fulfilled and projected forward to the King of Kings and Lord of Lords, Jesus, the Son of David. The psalmist's plea is for God in His great mercy to remember His faithfulness – The Firm Covenant.

Peace
Connected in Him, I stand
GHR

PSALMS: BOOK IV PROLOGUE

Book IV is a distinct departure from the first three books, in that the section was added to the Psalms some 200-300 years following the first three books. Many theologians think that Book IV was added to the Psalms during the time of Ezra and Nehemiah and the return from captivity in Babylon. (458-445 BC).

Book IV is sometimes compared to Numbers, the fourth book of the Pentateuch. Numbers highlights Israel's failures and its time spent in the wilderness. It also depicts its relationship to other nations, as well as God's kingdom in relationship to other nations. One theologian said, "It's an unfolding drama." This section shows the brokenness of the world and human morality.

Most of this section's psalms are anonymous. One Jewish source suggested that Psalms 90-92 are attributed to Moses along with Psalms 104-106. Psalms 101-103 are Davidic with the remainder unknown. The legend in my NIV Bible ascribes one to Moses (90) and two to David (101, 103) with the remaining unknown. Some theologians have compared this book IV to the prophet Isaiah, chapters 40-55. (a/k/a Book of Consolation)

Sue Gillingham (see biography below) in her excerpt from one of her publications, describes the Psalms as a "Five-Part Drama." She said, "Not only are the books different in lengths, but the interest in the figure of David differs greatly within each of them." The most frequently used name for God is Jehovah according to many sources. Regardless, of the brokenness of the world, including morality, God is still in charge.

Note: Dr. Susan Gillingham: She is a British theologian, academic and Anglican deacon. She specializes in the Hebrew Bible, including Psalms. She is a fellow and tutor in theology at Worcester College, Oxford. She has authored multiple publications on the Book of Psalms and other topics.

PSALM 90

Everlasting God!

Halley's Bible Handbook considers this psalm of Moses to be one of the first written since he lived some 400 years prior to David. This psalm is sometimes referred to as a "Song of Moses." Other songs of this "man of God," are recorded in Exodus 15 and Deuteronomy 32. The title of this psalm refers to "Moses the man of God." This ascribed title is repeated from Deuteronomy 33:1 and Joshua 14:6. He was chosen by God, the I AM, himself in the burning bush. "So now, Go, I AM sending you," says the LORD himself. (Exodus 3:10) And go he did!

After 10 plagues were sent to the Egyptians, the Israelites left Egypt and headed toward the Promised Land, a land flowing with milk and honey. But what happened? Well, they did evil in the sight of the LORD and were destined to wandering in the wilderness for 40 years. Remembering these events, let's now take a look at Moses' psalm. He begins his psalm with a proper salute to the LORD's having been their dwelling place for generations – the God of Abraham, Isaac, and Jacob (Israel). Moses acknowledges the everlasting nature of God. He was before the creation of the mountains!

While God's nature has no beginning and no ending, man's life is finite. The next verses acknowledge the futility of man, as our days are numbered. He compares our brevity (a day) to God's time (a thousand years). Even shorter, as Moses compares our life to a watch in the night (4 hours). The lives of men are like new grass in the morning and by evening it is dry and withered. Dr. H. C. Leupold in his *Exposition of the Psalms,* uses the word "evanescent" which is like a vanishing vapor.

God's anger with His chosen people is characterized as "consuming" and "terrifying." All our days pass away under Your wrath; "we finish our years with a moan (whisper)." (verse 9) Life is transient — here compared to 70 or even 80 years - and then we fly away. (Moses lived to be 120 years old (Deut. 34:7). The language of Moses in verse 12 is a little more tempered. He asks God to teach them to number their days and prays for wisdom. Wisdom that is not earthly, but wisdom that comes with faith and trust in God. If we look at Solomon's book of Proverbs, "The fear of the LORD is the beginning of wisdom; and knowledge of the Holy One is understanding." (Proverbs 9:10) And later in Proverbs, Solomon says, "Understanding is a fountain of life to those who have it." (Proverbs 16:22)

"Relent," says Moses and "have compassion." His request is to shower them with His unfailing love in the morning, just as he refreshes the grass, however unlike the daily refreshing of grass, Moses asks that His unfailing love last all of our days. Forty years in the wilderness with the former generation dying off must have been a rough time in Moses' life. This Song of Moses in Psalm 90 concludes with Moses' request for the LORD's favor to rest upon them.

Moses himself did not enter the Promised Land; but God took him by the hand, and led him to Mt. Nebo, and there He showed him the whole land. And there, God himself buried him! Yes, God's everlasting nature and never-failing promises were fulfilled as He delivered the land to His people. Moses' prayer can be ours today. May God's favor rest upon us and bless the labor of our hands as we serve Him, the everlasting God.

Peace
Connected in Him, I stand
GHR

PSALM 91

Call→Response

This psalm is identified as anonymous in most Bibles; however, some Jewish authorities attribute its authorship to Moses. In the previous psalm, Moses reflects on man's frailty and the shortness of their life compared to the daily grasses growing and fading. Here, we see the tenor of this psalm as one in which God is the Divine protector. In the psalmist's opening verse, he refers to God as the "Almighty." In the Hebrew it's *Shaddai*. The KJV version uses *Shaddai* as an adjective for God. (that is, Almighty God)

The opening verses are similar to Psalm 46, where the author there says, "God is our refuge and strength, an ever-present help in trouble." (Psalm 46:1) Is it Worth repeating? Let's see!

The language used by the psalmist in the opening verse is "residential." He says, "He who dwells in the shelter of the Most High (*El Elyon*) will rest in the shadow of the Almighty." Does this mean we only are at rest if we're in the House of God? No, as Christians we know that we are a temple of the indwelling Holy Spirit. Thus we have the great comfort of knowing that He will be our refuge.

In the first few verses we see a dual pronoun use of "I" and "you" which suggests the conversation is between two individuals. The *Essential Bible Companion to the Psalms* suggests it's between a king and a priest and/or a prophet. The first person says, "I will say, He is my refuge and my fortress . . . in whom I trust." (verse 2) Then the personal pronoun changes to "you" in verse five. The author compares God's divine protection to the birds of the air where he says, "Cover you with his feathers . . . (place) you under His wings." Implied here perhaps is that, if God can indeed protect his feathered creation, can He not protect us?

The psalmist proclaims that no danger is too great for God's protection – whether terror at night or arrows by day. The greatness of His protection is fully described in verse seven: "A thousand may fall at your side; ten thousand at your right hand." But . . . here it comes . . . "It will not come near you!" Yes, God shelters all of us under faith's umbrella (shield) to provide divine protection. Remember the divine protection of His people in captivity during the final plague? Yes, the angel of the LORD passed over the homes where the blood of the lamb was painted over the doorpost. It's the shield of faith that is evident!

The psalmist is confident regarding God, the Most High, as their dwelling place. (verse 9) His refuge will repel all of Satan's arrows and no disaster will come near their tent. Then comes this famous verse 11 that is repeated by divine inspiration of the Most High himself in the N. T. after His baptism when He is tempted by Satan. "For He will command His angels concerning you to guard you in all your ways; they will lift you up in their hands, so that You will not strike Your foot against a stone." (Go to Matthew 4:6 and Luke 4:10 for the Devil's quote of this psalm).

God's promise of divine protection is reiterated in verse 14: "Because He loves me . . . I will protect him." (Psalm 91:14) It also reminds you and me that we need to be in God's presence in prayer, as the psalmist says, "Call upon Me. . . I will answer." (verse 15) Yes, we have God's divine promise that He will answer our prayers. Remember Jesus' words, "Ask and it will be given . . . seek and you shall find . . . knock and the door opens." (Matthew 7:7) Finally, I would leave you with these words. If you feel alone and abandoned, not knowing if God even knows, remember this! Jesus promises rest for our soul and extends an invitation to you and me, "Come unto me, all you who are weary and burdened, and I will give you rest." (Matthew 11:28) Rest here is compared to a burden of a yoke (working frame on an oxen)→Jesus' yoke is easy, and His burden is light. Yes, in faith we can endure the troubles of today.

And as the author says, "I will satisfy him . . . with my long life and show him my salvation." Amen.

Peace
Connected in Him, I stand
GHR

PSALM 92
Flourishing

This psalm is identified as anonymous but regardless of its authorship, it is indeed one in which we give thanks for the works of the LORD. As an offering of praise, we "make music to the Most High." Our music is from a 10-stringed lyre and a harp as we proclaim his love and faithfulness. Amen!

Some theologians suggest this psalm was written about the time of the Persian's victory over the Babylonians and the Israelites' release. Regardless, it is a statement of victory as we progress through the psalm. Beginning in verse four, the author describes the righteous are cognizant of the LORD's deeds and the profoundness of His thoughts. As such, they sing for joy. To the contrary, the senseless man is clueless and will be forever destroyed. (verse 7)

Verse eight is the center piece of this psalm, "But You, O LORD, are exalted forever." This single line amid two sections is praiseworthy. It first acknowledges the statements in the first section and then leads into the concluding verses. As opposed to the first verses, this section begins with the enemies of God. "Surely, they will perish . . . and evildoers will be scattered" says the psalmist. (verse 9)

Verse 10 begins with the laudatory psalm that, according to theologians, was for the Sabbath. The definition of the Sabbath differs from Jewish to Christian tradition. In the Jewish tradition, the Sabbath is from sunset on Friday until Saturday sunset. In many Christian traditions, the fulfillment of the Sabbath is based on Christ's resurrection on Easter Sunday. If we examine the language of the psalmist here, we see two phenomenon (1) exalting the horn; (2) pouring fine oils. Next we see how the righteous are compared to God's creation, where He compares the "righteous" to a flourishing palm tree and the cedars of Lebanon.

Like the flourishing palm and cedars of Lebanon, God has "planted" the righteous in the house of the LORD. And they will bear fruit even into their old age! Don't mind creations dogma about old age. The LORD reigns over creation just as He designated Sarah to bear in a very old age and Elizabeth to bear the last O. T. prophet John, to proclaim the coming of the LORD.

The author concludes with a profession of faith that his LORD is his Rock. This Rock is a name for the Almighty and he states, "There is no wickedness in Him." (verse 14) This God of ours is One who rested on the seventh day of creation, signifying perfection or completeness, as the number implies. Yet, God does not now rest any day nor time of the day as we can count on Him to be ever vigilant to our daily needs. Regardless of our station in life, we constantly need to remind ourselves that God is the LORD of our life and controls not only creation but also the destruction of our earthly enemies.

In conclusion, let's listen to the hymnist and his words.
Praise to the LORD, the Almighty, the King of creation!
O my soul praise Him for He is your health and salvation!
Let all who hear Now to His temple draw near,
Joining in glad adoration!

Praise to the LORD! O let all that is in me adore Him!
All that has life and breath, come now with praises before Him!
Let the Amen
Sound from His people again;
Gladly forever adore Him!
(LSB 790, verses 1 and 5)

Yes, as we daily enter the gates of the Almighty's presence, let us always remember He is the One who has delivered and continues to deliver us from the enemies of sin, death, and the Evil One. Amen.

Peace
Connected in Him, I stand
GHR

PSALM 93

Royal Robe of the King

This psalm is "short and to the point!" This phrase best describes this anonymous psalm. It contains only five short verses but reminds us of the royalty of our God and His Kingship over all creation. When you think of royalty, what color comes to mind? I referred to a website (http://color-meanings.com/biblical-meaning-colors) for guidance.

The table below list the primary and secondary colors and their biblical meaning. There are multiple other colors mentioned but they are too numerous to list here.

Color	Meaning
Yellow, primary	Trials
Blue, primary	Word of God/Healing power of God
Red, primary	Flesh/blood of the Lamb/atonement
Green, secondary	Immortality/resurrection
Purple, secondary	Royalty/priesthood
Orange, secondary	Fire of God/deliverance

Color Meaning, by Jacob Olesen

The psalmist opens this psalm with a proclamation that the LORD reigns! And He is robed in majesty (repeated for emphasis)! Not only is the King robed in majesty but is armed with strength. This same King is Creator God, Who has established the world and Whose rule is from all eternity. All creation praises God as the author describes how the seas of the world lift up their voice with their pounding waves in total adoration of their creator. As powerful as the seas and the mighty thunder are, the Most High God is mightier.

The psalmist concludes this brief psalm by saying that His holiness and statutes are perfect. God's testimonies and house will endure forever. A later psalm (Psalm 111) amplifies the enduring qualities of God. "Glorious and majestic are His deeds," says the psalmist (Psalm 111:3). Later, "The works of His hands are faithful and just; all His precepts are trustworthy." (verse 7) And steadfast forever and ever!

May we be in awe of this King and LORD over all creation. He is mighty and righteous, ever faithful to all who follow His precepts.

Peace
Connected in Him, I stand
GHR

PSALM 94

The Scales of Justice

The tone quickly changes from the previous psalm to this one. The opening is clearly a plea for God to avenge the oppressors of His people. Some theologians believe that this injustice was from within the kingdom of Israel versus outside oppressors. The timing is also unclear, as some would place its writing earlier, while others in the time of the Babylonian exile or shortly after their return.

The scales of justice should be balanced as on the one hand we have evil deeds, and on the other, counterbalancing, is the punishment for crimes committed. In the first seven verses we see a description of the wickedness. The psalmist pleads for God to "shine forth" and to "rise up" to repay the unjust with justice. The author is at an apparent wit's end as he asks, "How long will the wicked be jubilant?" (verse 3b)

Injustice is not atypical in the O. T., or the N. T. for that matter. The period of the Judges in the O. T. was approximately 300 years (1350 BC – 1050 BC), ending with the first king of Israel. The judges were 12 in number and served in a variety of capacities, but most prominent was their rescue of God's people from its enemies and establishing justice. In some instances, the judges were delivering a cry for their sin and apostasy. In Judges 10, they said, "We have sinned . . . please rescue us now."

Verse seven suggests that this oppression may be internal, as the oppressors said, "The LORD does not see," implying that since He didn't respond, He must have been "asleep at the switch." The author now begins a litany of warnings to those miscreants (villains, per H.

C. Leupold's *Exposition of the Psalms*). The author is confident that the LORD is omniscient and knows the thoughts of man regardless of their futility.

"Blessed," begins the next section, where the psalmist shifts to show that he is well aware that God will act in His time. "You grant him relief from the days of trouble." (verse 13) His confidence in God's everlasting promise to His people to protect them is never lost in this world of sin. "Judgment will again be founded on righteousness and the upright in heart will follow." (verse 15) His conclusion is that, unless God had not assisted, he would have ended up in the silence of death.

Verses (18-19) are beautifully poetic. "My foot slipped and You supported me . . My anxiety was great, and you consoled me with joy." (paraphrased) These statements lead into his rhetorical question, "Can a corrupt throne be allied with You?" (verse 20) The answer is obvious as the psalmist reiterates his confidence that the LORD is his fortress, his rock and his refuge. (verse 23). Yes, the LORD will destroy the wicked. Remember the prophet Jeremiah saying, "For the LORD is a God of retribution; He will repay in full." (Jeremiah 51:56b)

The oppression of God's people is also present in the N. T., during Jesus' time. The Jewish leaders were in great fear of Jesus' detracting from their prominence. They plotted against Him to destroy Him but their attempts were futile even though they were successful in crucifying Him. Jesus reminded His disciples that in two days the Passover would begin and that He would be delivered over to his oppressors to be crucified. God did not intervene with the final judgment of the Jews and Roman rulers; but He did overcome and provide retribution to Satan himself, so that we might have life and have it abundantly.

Peace
Connected in Him, I stand
GHR

PSALM 95

Venite!

This psalm is a beautiful hymn of praise, followed by a plea for Israel not to regress, similar to their forefathers in the desert prior to entry into the Promised Land. *Venite* is a Latin term for "come ye" and is commonly used during Matins. Matins means morning prayer and is generally the first of seven canonical hours (matins, prime, terce, sext, nones, vespers, and compline - Roman Catholic and many Western Churches). The Venite is an invitational prayer. and some also conclude with the *Gloria Patri*. (Glory be to the Father)

This Venite is contained in the first seven verses of this psalm by an unknown author. For more years than I can remember, I have sung this Venite during one of our church's liturgical services. I cannot embellish the author's words as he invites all who worship to come to the LORD in song and shout to the Rock of their salvation, giving Him thanks for saving them from death's dark portal. Yes, the author continues to sing to the LORD for His great creation and how He is King above all gods!

At the conclusion of verse seven, the psalmist says, "Today"! Yes, those who read this psalm are reminded not to repeat the sins of the prior generation(s), like those in the wilderness who complained at Meribah for water and at Massah (means testing) in the desert. God's anger was manifest in 40 years of wandering, with those over the age of 20 being prohibited from entering the Promised Land. God said, "They shall never enter my rest." The term "rest" is an earthly metaphor of the heavenly homeland. (*Halley's Bible Handbook*).

The author of the Hebrews uses this "rest" language in chapters 3 and 4. In chapter 3, the author repeats the psalmist in verse 7b, saying, "Today . . . do not harden your hearts." Then in Hebrews 4:3, he quotes Psalm 95:11 referring to God's Promised Land in eternity versus the Promised Land that was promised long ago to Moses. Yes, God invites you and me in faith to enjoy His rest (salvation in Jesus Christ).

In closing, let us remember the words of Jesus himself in Matthew 11:28, "Come to me, all you who are weary and burdened, and I will give you rest." The gospel message invites us and promises to lift the heavy baggage of sin to yield a rest that knows no earthly definition. It's a heavenly or spiritual rest through the blood of the Lamb of God, based on His work of redemption on Calvary.

Peace
Connected in Him, I stand
GHR

PSALM 96
The Joyful Advent

Psalm 96 is in the middle of a series of psalms in Book IV that are often referred to as "Theocratic Psalms." A theocracy is a form of government in which God is the supreme ruler. This series begins with Psalm 93 and concludes with 100. Some theologians refer to them in pairs - 93 paired with 94 and so on. Like many psalms in this book, the author's identity is left to the imagination. Some suspect David, due to the similarity with 1 Chronicles 16 and his "Psalm of Thanks." Others refer to this psalm as a "mosaic" that takes bits and pieces from other portions of Scripture, particularly other Psalms and Isaiah. Regardless, this psalm is one of thanksgiving. H. C. Leupold notes a broad eschatological outlook . . . with the hope of the LORD's coming. (*Leupold's Exposition of the Psalms*).

In the opening verses, the psalmist praises the Almighty, giving Him thanks (day after day) for His gift of salvation. This phrase reminds me of the book of Acts of the Apostles, where the apostles are rejoicing following their chastisement by the ruling council for preaching and healing. "Day after day . . . proclaiming the good news that Jesus is the Christ." (Acts 5:42) From the O. T. hymnbook to the N. T. Apostles, together they continue to sing His praise day after day.

Verse four begins with a statement that the LORD is great and worthy of our praise. That profound statement is followed up with reasons why! First, He is feared above all gods, real or imagined. Secondly, He is the creator of the heavens and earth and their splendor and majesty give credit to His name. And finally, His glory and strength are ever before Him in His sanctuary. The LORD is king, as the entire earth trembles at His name!

The psalmist calls out, "Let the heavens rejoice, let the earth be glad." Everything in and of the world rejoices at His greatness. The psalmist concludes his verse with the joyful expectation of the LORD's return (Advent) as He comes to judge the earth in all righteousness and truth.

Listen to the words of the hymnist as he sings of God's Advent as Judge.

> As judge, on clouds of light,
> He soon will come again
> And His true members all unite
> With Him in heav'n to reign.
> (LSB 331 v. 4)

May we all with gladsome voice sing praises to His name, as day after day we are reminded of His great work of salvation, so that on the Day of Judgment we will reign with Him in eternity. Joyous!

Peace
Connected in Him, I stand
GHR

PSALM 97

The LORD Reigns!

Psalm 97 continues in this "theocratic" theme. In this psalm, the psalmist portrays the LORD's reign and how the entire creation responds to His glory, His righteousness, and His justice. This table describes the various elements listed in verses two through six, but it cannot compare to the beautiful poetic verse.

Description	Response
Clouds and thick darkness	Surround Him
Righteousness & Justice	Foundation of His throne
Fire	Consumes His foes, everywhere
His Lightning	Lights up the world; earth trembles
Mountains	Melt like wax before Him
Heavens	Proclaim His righteousness
All people	Witness His glory

The psalmist reminds us that God is veiled in the familiar cloud that defined His presence as He led His people out of captivity. His majestic glory is compared to lightning that lights up the world and all creation trembles! His fire consumes all enemies, even the final enemy of death. His marvelous mountains are like putty and melt as if made up of wax. The heavens proclaim His righteousness; and all people witness His glory as the LORD reigns.

Verse seven describes the shame of those who have sought to find solace in graven images (idols). God commands us in the decalogue that we are not to have any graven image (idol), as our God is a jealous God and deserving of all praise and worship. (Exodus 20:4 KJV)

The final section describes the joy of God's people. Especially the psalmist reminisces over His past deeds and how He delivered them from their enemies (hands of the wicked). Yes, the True Light shines in the lives of all who know Him and accept Him as their LORD and Savior from sin. Because He has saved us from eternal damnation and the all-encompassing fire, we can rejoice in the LORD and praise His holy name.

Some have compared this section of psalms (96 through 98) to Isaiah chapters 40 through 55. These chapters have been summarized as a "Book of Consolation." The prophet Isaiah opens chapter 40 with "Comfort, comfort my people." The prophet announces forgiveness to Israel and reminds them that God's Word lasts forever and that a Shepherd will guide them to the Promised Land. The latter portion of this Book of Consolation contains the great "Suffering Servant" chapters, where Isaiah describes the Shepherd's work of salvation, using verbs in the past tense (800 years before Christ).

May the Light of the world shine in your life now and forevermore.

Peace
Connected in Him, I stand
GHR

PSALM 98
Just & Fair

Many of the psalms in this Book IV are psalms of praise that were part and parcel of various enthronement ceremonies of YHWH the King. Yahweh himself was Israel's deliverer from the travesties of slavery under Pharaoh's Egypt. This Yahweh was indeed the first, and certainly the only perfect king of Israel. Multiple earthly kings would follow but Yahweh was their King! His throne will rule forever and ever. Matthew, in his gospel, goes into much detail to show the Kingship of our LORD, the Messiah and deliverer. He shows in his genealogy how Jesus was the Son of David and the Son of Abraham. His kingship however was not what the Israelites were expecting. They were looking for a David-like king.

The Messiah was enthroned on high following his Messianic duties on Calvary's cross. Several references to the enthronement of Jesus Christ the Messiah are found in the epistles of St. Paul and the author of Hebrews. (Philippians 2:9, 1 Timothy 3:16, and Hebrews 1:5)

Psalm 98 is one of these enthronement types of psalms, celebrating their King. The timing of this psalm is thought to be following their freedom, under Babylonian captivity. The first verse gives praise for His marvelous deeds and His strength (right arm) that worked salvation (freedom) for them. "He has remembered His love and faithfulness," says the psalmist. (verse 3) The celebration of this historical enthronement of Yahweh echoes with shouts of joy, jubilant song, music from the harp, the lyre, the trumpets, and the ram's horn. Creation gives its praise as the sea and its inhabitants give praise. The rivers and mountains add to the song as the LORD, the King, comes as judge in all righteousness and equity (just and fair).

Let's read Paul's message to the Church at Philippi in chapter two. "He humbled himself and became obedient to death – even death on a cross! Therefore, God exalted Him to the highest place and gave him the name that is above every name, that at the name of Jesus every knee should bow, in heaven and on earth and under the earth, and every tongue confess that Jesus Christ is LORD, to the glory of God the Father." (Philippians 2:8-11)

Yes, Jesus is the King eternal, enthroned on high at the right hand of the Father. He will come again as the **Just and Fair** judge, claiming those who have been baptized into His death and raised to life again by virtue of His glorious resurrection and victory over sin, death and the Evil One. Amen!

Peace
Connected in Him, I stand
GHR

PSALM 99

Exalted! The LORD our God

This psalm is not redundant (to Psalm 98) as it continues to give praise to the LORD, the God of Israel. As Dr. H. C. Leupold says in his commentary, *Exposition of the Psalms*, "But it has a distinctive character all of its own . . . more of awe than of joy." The psalmist begins with similar language of the reign of the LORD. Then he refers to the Ark of the Covenant where He sits between the cherubim on the Mercy Seat (atonement). In awe, the "nations tremble."

The word "exalt(ed)" is used three times in this psalm. The first is in verse two as He is elevated over all the nations of the world. "Let them praise your great and awesome name! The second use is in verse five and, it is repeated in verse nine. The psalmist refers to the worshippers at His footstool. The footstool reference could be to the earth or to Zion but may also be one where the worshipper is in humble adoration of the King, the LORD God.

References to several of God's servants are made here, first dating back to Moses and Aaron, His priests, and to the prophet Samuel who anointed David as king. Samuel also was the last judge and ushered the way into the kingly period in Israel's history. The psalmist is clear to note that these men were submissive to the LORD and He answered them. They are given credit for having followed His statutes and decrees. Whether spoken to from the cloud or in a nighttime appearance, these men were in awe of the LORD. Samuel's response to the LORD's calling is a very personal one. 1 Samuel 3 records the event. "The

LORD came and stood there, calling. Samuel responded, "Speak, for your servant is listening."

The psalmist simply says, "You answered them." (verse 8) He was and continues to be a forgiving God. While there are consequences to sin, the blood of the Lamb of God has made us blameless before the Mercy Seat of God. The psalmist concludes his short psalm with the final use of exaltation saying, "Exalt the LORD our God and worship at His holy mountain, for the LORD our God is holy."

Yes, Moses was the Christ-like deliverer of His people from captivity. Aaron was the first of a priestly line, serving the LORD in His Tabernacle and Temple. Samuel was the judge and prophet who led Israel into its kingly period and ultimately to the King of Israel, Jesus Christ, the promised Messiah.

Peace
Connected in Him, I stand
GHR

PSALM 100

Worship the LORD with Gladness

There was no doubt as to my title for this psalm. It has a personal meaning, dating back to one of my grandchildren's memory verse in first grade. My wife and I were overnighting at my daughter's house. I offered to take the kids to school that day. As we left the house, my daughter said, "Help Sam with his memory." She handed me the printed slip of paper with his memory verse. The trip to school was a matter of a few minutes; but given the brevity of the memory, it would be a breeze. To give the verse some meaning, I set the verse (title) to song adding the book, chapter, and verse at the end. As a result of that day some years ago, I find myself singing that again and again.

Psalm 100 is also a Venite (Come), as verse 2b says, "Come before Him with joyful songs." (verse 2b) This very short, unauthored psalm has more words of wisdom than would fill the Grand Canyon. "Know that the LORD is God." First and foremost, our God is the only True God. Secondly, "It is He who made us." Yes, we are the works of His creation. Thirdly, "We are His people, the sheep of His pasture." He has indeed shepherded us out of the wrath of sin to His everlasting righteousness through His perfect, atoning sacrifice. So this trilogy identifies God the True God, then gives Him credit for having made us, and finally identifies Him our Savior from sin's wrath.

As saved people of God, we can enter into His gates with thanksgiving and His courts with praise. (verse 4) Verses 4b and 5 provide the basis for a mealtime prayer that I learned at an early age: "O give thanks unto the LORD, for He is good, and His mercy endures forever. Amen."

This prayer was typically said at the conclusion of every family meal. Not only did we give thanks for His blessings of food, but also for His everlasting mercy for the people of God.

I am reminded of the epiphany hymn, *As with Gladness Men of Old*, as the title emphasizes the word gladness. Let us remember the words of this hymnist.

> Holy Jesus, every day Keep us in the narrow way;
> And when earthly things are past,
> Bring our ransomed souls at last
> Where they need no star to guide,
> Where no clouds Thy glory hide.
> (LSB 397, v. 4)

Let us remember to continue to worship Him with all gladness each and every day. He is and was and is to come. (P. S. Sam's memory verse: "Worship the LORD with gladness. Psalm 100 verse 2.")

Peace
Connected in Him, I stand
GHR

PSALM 101
Walk the Walk

David's name comes up once again as the author of this psalm. The timing remains in question but could be shortly after his assumption of the throne from Saul or following the combined rule of Israel and Judah. Regardless, the psalmist is clearly stating his personal goals and promises. The number of times (10) he says, "I will" points to a pledge-like affirmation for his rule over God's people. Dr. H. C. Leupold suggests that some theologians of old have described this psalm of David as "A Mirror for Magistrates."

As a catechumen, I learned about a mirror as an object lesson to remember the Law and the Gospel. A mirror shows us our sin (Law) and it also shows us our Savior (Gospel). As former theologians have suggested, David is pledging his service to His LORD and the people that he serves. The psalmist opens with words of praise to the Almighty for His love and justice. (the first two uses of "I will"). The next "I will" in verse 2 is perhaps most revealing of his character. He pledges, with God's help, to lead a blameless life. This is the first of three uses of the word "blameless."

What does it mean to be blameless? Is it synonymous with sinless? The dictionary defines it as "free from guilt or blame." If you examine various Bible translations, words used range from faultless to perfect to integrity. Perhaps a more meaningful definition of "blameless" is "beyond reproach." Blameless is certainly not sinless, as all have sinned and fallen short of the glory of God. God's Son performed his perfect (one and done) atonement for sin so that we can appear blameless before the Mercy Seat of God. David is attempting to "walk the walk" that is expected of a just ruler.

David's kingly walk is not only to rule justly but to walk blamelessly in his own house. (verse 2b-3) He continues to pledge to avoid faithless men and those with perverse hearts. He states he will protect the integrity of his people (neighbors) from slander.

David indeed is focused as he says, "My eyes will be. . ." A ruler must stay focused in order to be effective. He cannot be deceitful or speak falsely and still stand in the presence of the LORD. David was true to His LORD and leader. He was careful to walk blamelessly before his LORD which is true of a great leader. His eyes were focused on his duties and he speaks of protecting his constituents from slander and will avoid those (put to silence) who are wicked.

The uses of the word "blameless" in God's Holy Word are many. Perhaps the first use was to describe Noah as a "righteous and blameless" man (Gen 6:9). St. Paul says it this way in 1 Corinthians 1:8: "He will keep you strong to the end, so that you will be blameless on the day of our LORD Jesus Christ." As Christians, we should make every effort to walk blamelessly so that our witness shows a life consistent with our calling as God's own!

Peace
Connected in Him, I stand
GHR

PSALM 102

A Faint Heart

The prologue of this psalm is curious: "A prayer of an afflicted man. When he is faint and pours out his lament before the LORD." Who this man is or when it took place is somewhat a mystery. Some would suggest it occurred at the time of the Exile or shortly before the time of the rebuilding of Jerusalem. Is it a physical or emotional affliction? Is it personal or communal?

I have entitled my notes for this psalm, "A Faint Heart" as it covers both physical and emotional stress and distress that bemoan and cry out to the LORD for help. "Hear my prayer. . . my cry for help comes to you. . . do not hide Your face from me." The psalmist's opening plea for help is one that causes your innermost being to anguish in pain. The phrase "hide your face" is particularly troublesome as one thinks about God is turning His back on us! The prophet Isaiah talks about Israel's exile period. Listen! "I will wait for the LORD, who is hiding His face from the house of Jacob." (Isaiah 8:17) The psalmist pleas for God to turn His ear to him and answer quickly!

The words of the psalmist are poetic in nature: "For my days vanish like smoke; my bones burn like glowing embers; my heart is blighted and withered like grass." (verses 3-4) The result is that he is "skin and bones," which we would call emaciated today – or even cachectic! He compares himself to an owl (tawny owl, desert owl) who hunts at night for large insects, mice, and voles. His food is meager at best, described as ashes and tears for drink. Why? Because God's blessings have been withdrawn! He is withering like the evening grass. (verse 11)

Now the tone changes. Verse 12 starts with "But You, O LORD." Yes as faint of heart as he might be, he remembers God. First, He exclaims that God is enthroned forever. Secondly, he states that His renown has endured; and finally, You will arise for Zion! (verses 12-13) The psalmist remembers the Temple of the LORD and how the stones are dear. The dust of their history moves God's people to pity for the loss of His house.

The tenor of this psalm picks up as a crescendo in music. Listen: "The nations will fear the name of the LORD, all the kings will revere His glory. . . He will rebuild Zion." (verses 15-16) God indeed does not have a deaf ear, as his early plea suggests. "He will respond to the prayers of the destitute." The psalmist is now telling future generations that they too must praise the LORD! The LORD has indeed heard the pleas (groans) of the prisoners and releases those condemned to death (wages of sin). So the name of the LORD will be declared in Zion (notice future tense) . . .when the peoples and the kingdoms assembled to worship the LORD.

The author now concludes that, in the course of his life, his strength was broken and his days were shortened. He then recounts God's creation of the world, in which He set the foundations of everything that exists. While the earth and all that is in it will perish, YOU (emphasis added) remain the same, and "Your years will never end." (verse 27) The eternity of God in this section is manifested in Hebrews 1:10-12, where the author quotes the psalmist. The O. T. prophet Malachi also reminds us that "I the LORD do not change. So you, O descendants of Jacob, are not destroyed." (Malachi 3:6) Yes, God never forgets His promises to rescue those who are faithful.

Listen to the words of the hymnist, Thomas Kelly, in *Stricken, Smitten, and Afflicted.*

> Here we have a firm foundation,
> Here the refuge of the lost:
> Christ, the Rock of our salvation,
> Is the name of which we boast;
> Lamb of God, for sinners wounded,

Sacrifice to cancel guilt!
None shall ever be confounded
Who on Him their hope have built.
(LSB 451, v. 4)

The faint of heart seek His refuge in the Good News of the One promised long ago. Keep heart!

Peace
Connected in Him, I stand
GHR

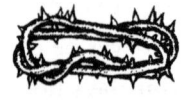

PSALM 103
Outburst of Thankfulness

Once you read this beautiful psalm of praise, you are likely to agree with me that this is perhaps David's best! While we're not sure when during David's life it was written, some have proposed that it could have been in his latter days, as he looked back at God's impact on his life.

First, this psalm contains 22 lines but is not an alphabetic acrostic psalm – where each line begins with a letter of the Hebrew alphabet. Second, the word "praise" is used seven times in this psalm, which is a number this is associated with completeness or perfection.

The first five verses list the benefits of the LORD not only to David the author but to you and me and those who have come to faith. The table below summarizes the benefits

The LORD	Result
Forgives	All my sins
Heals	All your diseases
Redeems	Your life
Crowns	You with love & compassion
Satisfies	Your desires with good things

Psalm 103:3-5

As the opening suggests we should, "Praise the LORD, O my soul, and forget not all His benefits." Yes indeed! The five items in the table above conclude with how God satisfies our every need and desire with good things. I am reminded of a common prayer used that is from one of David's psalms (145). Pray with me; "The eyes of all look to you, and you give them their food at the proper time. You open your hand and satisfy the desires of every living thing." Amen. (Psalm 145:15)

With all those benefits, what else can David say? Verse six begins with a statement of the LORD's work of righteousness and justice for all the oppressed. The I AM appeared to Moses and told him He had seen the oppression of His people. Here David reminds us that Moses was His mouthpiece repeating the deeds of the LORD. He is compassionate, He is gracious, slow to anger, and abounding in love. These words of David are taken from Exodus 34:6ff as God passed in front of Moses and said, "The LORD is a compassionate and gracious God, slow to anger, abounding in love and faithfulness. . ."

David points out that the anger of God is temporary, and He will not harbor it forever just as He dealt with and then forgave the Israelites in their desert wanderings. Verse 11 summarizes how His love for those who fear Him is great - so much so, that our sin has been removed as far as the east if from the west! While life is temporary, God's love for us and His plan of salvation is from everlasting to everlasting. (verse 17) David recounts that God's love extends to future generations for those who keep His covenant and remember His precepts.

The final section is the quintessential praise for all the above reasons. The LORD's throne in heaven is established forever and rules overall. David begins his list of groups giving praise with angels, then heavenly host (an organized body of angels from Hebrew *tsaba*), and finally everybody everywhere in His dominion. Praise the Lord!

Peace
Connected in Him, I stand
GHR

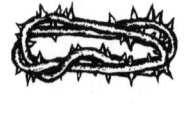

PSALM 104

The Majesty of Creation

This psalm presents something of an enigma. While the author is not listed in the NIV, the Septuagint (Greek O. T.) lists the author as David. I have entitled these notes "The Majesty of Creation," based on a note in my aged (30+ years and multiple bindings) Bible from either a prior Bible study and/or a possible sermon note. Regardless, as we read through these 35 verses (5 groups of 7), it is clear that our God is truly the world's ONLY true God.

There are multiple stories regarding creation, but as Christians we can only rely on God's Word as our source of the truth. Some would call creation a "myth;" but we can see in the Bible how God's great wisdom of creation was not a myth but indeed real by His "Word." The Hebrew word *Elohim* means created. And in **six** days!

While this psalm extends beyond the six-day event, it is noteworthy to look back to the Six-Day Creation by The Word.

Creation Day	Result
Day 1	Divides darkness from light (day and night)
Day 2	Expanse (sky) between waters
Day 3	Sea and Land; vegetation
Day 4	Sun, moon and stars; seasons
Day 5	Sea and sky creatures
Day 6	Land creatures and man

And God said, "It was good." That was His observation at the conclusion of each creating day. At the conclusion of the sixth day, God said, "it was very good." And the seventh day, He rested.

If we examine the verses in chapters 1-2 of Genesis, we see several variances of the number "7." These examples are taken from the Hebrew Bible.

- Chapter 1:1- consists of seven words
- Chapter 1:2 consists of 14 words
- Chapter 2:1-3 consists of 35 words
- Elohim is mentioned 35 times
- Heaven and earth are mentions 21 times
- Variation of "It was good" occur 7 times.

(Source: The "Sevens" of Genesis 1:1 – 2:3, by William D. Ramey, http://inthebeginning.org)

The psalmist begins his chapter with "You are very great." What else can we say? Then he says, "You are clothed with splendor and majesty." With those opening remarks, what can we expect but a perfect creation in the Glory of God himself?

The psalm is poetic and was not necessarily for a ceremonial event according to many theologians. The author takes a broad, visual perspective of God's creation and in his mind's eye describes what he sees. The psalmist refers to God's destruction via the rain over the earth (verse 6) and His promise to Noah in Genesis chapter nine. His creation rebounds from disaster! In poetic fashion, the author describes how the earth responds.

The author continues to refer to the Six Day Creation in his dialogue. Several examples are the moon marks off the seasons; Darkness is night; and Sun rises. (verses 19-20a) The author issues a rhetorical question: "How many are your works?" The answer is manifold in his quick reply, beginning with "The earth is full of your creatures." Just look at God's creation and all that is therein, and you can't help but worship Him.

The creation continues to look to its Creator for food (sustenance). Verse 28 reminds us that when God provides our daily needs, we gather it up and are then satisfied. Creation is not only a "six-day event" but ongoing as He always provides for our daily needs.

The psalmist tells us that the people were terrified when God hides His face but rejoices when God's grace restores us to a new life. (verses 29-30) The psalmist then gives his praise to God Almighty, that His glory will endure forever!

Therefore, "I will sing to the LORD all my life; I will sing to my God as long as I live." (verse 33) The concluding verses are repetitive, as the psalmist says, "Praise the LORD, O my soul. Praise the LORD."

May the God of all Glory continue to create in you a new heart each and every day as you walk in His path of righteousness and serve Him as He directs. Amen!

Peace
Connected in Him, I stand
GHR

PSALM 105

Hallelujah!

Reading this psalm from an unknown author is like reading a biblical history book. The timing of this psalm is questioned by some; but many would agree that it was in the post-exilic period (return from Babylon) to offer encouragement to a discouraged people. (H. C. Leupold's *Exposition on the Psalms*). This psalm and the concluding psalm in Book IV (106) are considered complementary. There are also similarities with Psalm 78 and this psalm. Finally, the first 15 verses of Psalm 105 are almost identical to David's "Psalm of Thanks" in 1 Chronicles 16:8ff, which reflects David's praise for the return of the Ark of the Covenant to Jerusalem.

The opening verse is powerfully worded, in that we give thanks first, call on Him, and then tell everyone what He has done. This phrase is repeated by the prophet Isaiah in his chapter 12:4.

The first five verses are packed with praise and thanksgiving to the LORD. The first trilogy is three verbs: look, seek, and remember. The second trilogy lifts His acts of wonders, miracles, and judgments. The psalmist reminds us always to look to the LORD for His strength; then, to seek His face (presence) always and finally; and finally, to remember His deeds. (verses 4-5)

If theologians are correct in their assumption of the post-exilic period, then the repeated history lesson (verses 7-45) is important to offer encouragement to the returning Israelites that God indeed has not forgotten them. The author begins with the patriarchs (Abraham,

Isaac, and Jacob) and how He has always remembered His covenant. He indeed delivered them to the land of Canaan.

The psalmist refers to the time of famine in the land and how Joseph, who was sold off by his brothers, was indeed in God's plan to save His people from starvation. Joseph found favor with the Egyptian leaders and managed assets in the time of plenty to prepare for the famine. The need for food brought Jacob and his family to Egypt and they and all Israel flourished so much so that the Egyptians feared and enslaved them. Moses was then called by God Himself to lead His people from captivity to Canaan, the Promised Land. The process took signs and wonders sent by God through Moses and Aaron to get Pharaoh to release them. The psalmist reminds the current readers of God's signs and wonders (plagues recorded in Exodus 7-12). The final straw was the death of all living Egyptian firstborn!

Verse 39 reminds its readers that God not only saved them from Egypt's tyranny, but He was visibly present with them in their journey, as the cloud and pillar of fire. He provided every need of food and water in miraculous manner. The result was their inheritance of the Promised Land (verse 44).

The psalmist concludes with "Praise the LORD" (Hallelujah). The two Hebrew words, *halal* (praise) and *Yah* (shortened form of YHWH), make up Hallelujah.

This psalm would have certainly brought encouragement to the returning exiles and it also reminds us today that God promised us a way out of captivity (sin) by the blood of the Lamb who made us blameless before God's throne.

Peace
Connected in Him, I stand
GHR

PSALM 106

From Cheerful to Somber

While the pair of Psalms 105 and 106 are linked somewhat, the tone changes from one of a cheerful nature to one of a more somber mood. This psalm is similar in length to the previous one, and again there is no known author. The timing again is likely in the exilic or post-exilic period. I was intrigued by H. C. Leupold's opening statement and quote from MacLaren, "The history of God's past is a record of continuous mercies, the history of man's one as of continuous sin." As I thought about MacLaren's statement, I then added a caveat, saying, "But with a contrite heart, the mercies of God yield forgiveness and a rightness with God."

The author opens (and closes) with "Praise the LORD" (Hallelujah). The following sentence is much like an ancient common table prayer, "Give thanks to the LORD, for He is good; His love endures forever." He shifts to a question perhaps even rhetorical: "Who can proclaim the mighty acts of the LORD?" For one who does right, the favor of the LORD provides blessings. The psalmist is ever mindful of the nation and those in need of His mercy that they may share in the joy and eternal inheritance. He admits sinning just as the fathers of old did! The psalmist elaborates on multiple transgressions, anger, and eventual mercy/deliverance.

Examples of Moses and Phinehas (grandson of Aaron and High Priest) are given to show their intervention of the wrath of God. Listening to instructions about their inheritance of the land of Canaan was an issue. They did not do as the LORD required (verse 34). Rather they intermarried, worshipped idols, and sacrificed inappropriately. Therefore, the LORD was angry and eventually they were led off into captivity.

But God's mercy and His covenant with His people shines through. The psalmist says, "He took note of their distress when He heard their cry. . .and He relented." (verse 45-46) Verse 47 begins their plea of "Save us." Their captors made them mindful of how they had sinned and deserved God's wrath but now they are weary and ask to be saved. They promise to give thanks for God's delivering them from their enemies to the praise of His Holy Name.

"Praise be to the LORD, the God of Israel, from everlasting to everlasting. Let the people say Amen! Praise the LORD." Amen.

As with the previous books in Psalms, the conclusion is similar, and in this case the same as the concluding verse in Book I.

The plight of God's people is not dissimilar to our predicament. We daily sin much and need God's mercy and forgiveness. Our prayer is that we ask God to begin our day in His service and to keep us on the narrow path, in line with His will.

Peace
Connected in Him, I stand
GHR

PSALMS: BOOK V PROLOGUE

This final book in the Book of Songs (Psalms) is the largest by number (44). According to one commentary, it has less of a common theme than other books in Psalms. The numbering system of the psalms varies, including the Septuagint used by the Eastern Orthodox churches which has Psalm 151. A Hebrew version of this psalm was found in the Psalms scroll in the Dead Sea Scrolls. Others also claim numbers 152 through 156 (Pershitta which means "Simple Version" Syriac churches).

Authorship of the various 44 psalms include David with 15, his son Solomon with one, and the other remaining psalms are unknown or anonymous. Categorically, Book V is generally associated with the fifth book of the Pentateuch (Deuteronomy). The last book of Moses generally refers to God and His Word. This section in Psalms has a general theme of praising God and His Word.

One commentary suggests this book is divided into three sections. The first section (107-119) was written for Passover or Unleavened Bread. The middle section (120-134) is called "Hallel," or praise psalms. The final section (135-150) was written for the Feast of Tabernacles. (Source: thegospelcoalition.org) According to *Halley's Bible Handbook*, these songs of ascent (also called songs of degrees or pilgrim songs) were to be sung (a capella) while pilgrims were traveling up to the religious feasts at Jerusalem. The word "ascents" is derived from the fact that all roads leading to Jerusalem were up hill.

A unique feature noted in this final book is the section called *Hallel* (meaning praise) where Jewish families would sing these psalms (113-118) on the night of Passover at the beginning of a meal (113-114), and then at the end (115-118) of the meal. The other unique feature is Psalm

119 which is the longest chapter in the Bible (176 verses). It is divided into 22 sections, each beginning with a letter of the Hebrew alphabet (acrostic). Every verse mentions the Word of God under one or another of these names: law, statutes, righteous laws, decrees, commands, precepts, words, and ways. (*Halley's Bible Handbook*) – with few minor exceptions (verses 90, 121, 122, and 132) Each stanza contains eight lines.

The final psalms (146-150) are called *Hallelujah* psalms, as each begins with that word. Psalm 150 is especially praiseworthy (See the chapter *From Beginning to End* in this book).

Overall, these 150 most beautiful songs were written over a period of 900+ years, beginning with the time of Moses through the exilic period, following their Babylonian captivity.

May God bless your reading and study of these various chapters as He has done for me in my hours, days, and weeks of study.

Peace
Connected in Him, I stand
GHR

PSALM 107

Crying Out . . .Giving Thanks

While this psalm is the beginning of the final book, there are some similarities to the two previous psalms at the conclusion of Book IV, namely, the opening verse(s), "Giving thanks to the LORD." More important, is the second part of the opening which states that our God's love (agape) endures forever.

This long chapter embodies several figurative examples of deliverance. H. C. Leupold points out in his *Exposition of the Psalms* that the Israelites' predicament is like the following:

- Exile: like a caravan lost in the wilderness
- Imprisonment
- Recovery from a severe illness
- Ship at sea in a great storm

During each of the four sections that follow the thanksgiving, the psalmist lays out their predicament, followed by repeated episodes of them crying out and then giving thanks to the LORD for His unfailing love (deliverance). Verses 6, 13, 19, and 28 are all essentially the same, "They cried out to the LORD in their trouble," and then He delivered them. Following, in verses 8, 15, 21, and 31, again we see essentially the same phrases of praise and thanksgiving for His unfailing love: "Let them give thanks to the LORD for His unfailing love."

The verses in between their crying out and giving thanks are equally important. Listen to the verbs: "He led them . . .He brought them out . . .He rescued them. . .He stilled the storm." In all cases, regardless of the calamity, God indeed saw their pain and delivered them after they cried out for mercy. His unfailing love endures forever, as the opening verse reminds us.

The final section of this psalm points out the ups and downs from prosperity to the pits and pits to prosperity. But in the end, the upright sees and rejoice! The needy were indeed lifted out of their affliction. Thanks be to God that He continues to watch over those who follow Him and His ways.

Regardless of the storm in our lives, we need to wholly lean on Jesus for His agape love and promised deliverance. Listen to the hymnist as he writes:

> While life's dark maze I tread
> And griefs around me spread, Be Thou my guide;
> Bid darkness turn to day,
> Wipe sorrow's tears away,
> Nor let me ever stray From Thee aside.
> (LSB 702, v. 3)

Peace
Connected in Him, I stand
GHR

PSALM 108

Triumph Over Enemies:
Take Comfort!

Book V returns with a psalm of David. This psalm is a compilation of two previous psalms (57 and 60). The first five verses are similar to Psalm 57:7-11 and the final verses are similar to Psalm 60:5-12. Theologians cannot really determine if one draws on the others. Regardless, sometimes repeating is not bad at all! David opens this psalm with words of a steadfast spirit for his God Almighty. With his musical instruments, he continues to sing His praises about God's great love for His people and His faithfulness. David describes God's faithfulness as reaching from the ground to the skies and His glory extending over all the earth.

I am reminded of the various instruments played to give praise to God that are listed in the final chapter of Psalms – trumpet, harp, lyre, tambourine, strings, flute, and cymbals. God's orchestra is never without assets to sing His praise. From his opening statement of praise, David shifts to a plea to save them, and help them with his strength (right hand).

Matthew Henry's Commentary reminds us that we need, in prayer, to take comfort of what God has secured for us. God had promised David to give him "the hearts of his subjects." *Matthew Henry's Commentary* comments on several parts of the country (verses 7-9) as God's own! Among them are, Shechem, the first capital of Israel, and Edom who was a long-term adversary of the Jews. David remarks about Edom, the descendants of Esau (Red) and the adversary of Jacob, his brother. The prophet Obadiah prophesies of Edom's total obliteration. The last hurrah for the Edomites (Idumeans) was the Herod clan. Herod the Great's father (Antipater) was an Edomite, and, due to his relationship with the Romans, was instrumental in his son's position in Judea. The Edomites were minimalized via the Nabateans and then destroyed in 70 A.D. when Jerusalem was destroyed.

David is confident that God will indeed deliver Israel from all of their enemies and will center His relationship with His people in the "Fortified City." He repeats his request to assist him and his armies to deliver them from their enemies for without God, David is helpless. And without God's aid, they will trample down the enemies.

God has indeed delivered us from all enemies including death that have separated us from the love of God which is in Christ Jesus. King David gives us confidence that regardless of our size and human capabilities, with His guidance all things are possible. May you and I continue to go to God in prayer, as Matthew Henry suggested, and "Take comfort in what God has secured for us." Amen!

Peace
Connected in Him, I stand
GHR

PSALM 109

A Garment of Cursing and Disgrace

David opens this psalm with a plea for God to "speak up!" "Do not remain silent for the wicked have opened their mouths against me," says David.

Let's return to God's creation when Adam and Eve were in the Garden of Eden, sinless and in the image of God. Garments were never needed until they sinned and fell short of the Glory of God. Their curse was elimination from God's perfect garden and their disgrace was being aware of their nakedness and total separation from God's holiness. Perhaps, it's in this mindset that David is penning this beautiful psalm.

David opens with a plea for God to return from silence. David feels surrounded by evil and deceitful men who have lying tongues. He attempted to befriend them, but they "returned evil for good." (verse 5) He asks that the accuser be found guilty and his days be numbered. If possible, do not allow him to succeed in expanding his kingdom (fatherless and children as beggars). In German, the word is *aufschnitten* which means "cut off." David says, "May their sins always remain before the LORD, that He may cut off the memory of them from the earth." (verse 15)

David reminds us that the Evil One's wardrobe is nothing more than lies and that his cloak surrounds his evil ideals. What are you wearing? The psalmist (David) describes his enemies in terms of their clothing. He describes the evil man ("Evil One" per footnote, NIV) as being clothed in cursing (verse18) and disgrace and shame (verse 29). But David is not dismayed as he states, "But You, O LORD deal with me for Your name's sake; and out of the goodness of Your love, deliver me." (verse 21) David's confidence in the LORD is magnificent. He admits he may fade like a shadow or his knees may give way, but the Evil One knows that it is God's hand that has delivered him. As such, the oppressors will be clothed in disgrace and with his mouth David will greatly extol the name of the LORD. (verses 29-30) Yes, the LORD sits at the right hand of God in victory over sin, death, and the Evil One to save the lives of those who have faith in Him.

Our LORD was mocked, berated, smitten, and otherwise hated for the sake of you and me, because of our separation from God, due to our sin. The Father remained silent as His one and only Son hung on Calvary's tree for the sins of the world. And we can remain confident that just as He raised His Son from the grave, that we will be raised to be with Him in eternity.

Peace
Connected in Him, I stand
GHR

PSALM 110

Prophet, Priest & King

Did you know that this psalm is quoted in the N. T. more often than any other psalm? David offers beautiful gospel words in this prophetic psalm. Some have referred to this psalm as "David's Creed." *Matthew Henry's Commentary* states that almost all of the articles of the Christian faith are found in this psalm.

This gospel-based psalm is purely Messianic as had been promised long before. The Messiah has a three-fold function as a prophet, a priest, and a king. David touches on each of these functions in this short psalm. David opens with that famous and oft-quoted statement: "The LORD says to my LORD; 'Sit at my right hand until I make your enemies a footstool for your feet.'" This opening verse became a stumbling block to the Jewish leaders of Jesus' day. Matthew 22:41-46 records dialogue between Jesus and the Pharisees. Jesus asked them, "What do you think about the Christ? Whose son is He?" They replied, "The Son of David." Jesus then remarked, "How is it then that David, speaking by the Spirit, calls him LORD? (Psalm110:1 KJV) The stumbling block was Jesus' question, "If then David calls him "LORD," how can He be his son?" Silence!

Verse one describes the LORD as king over all, sitting at the place of honor at the right hand of God. Verse two is prophetic where the Messiah will extend His kingdom from Zion. The word "extend" is important as we think about how God's Son came to save all, and here, we see the message of the Messiah extending out from Zion. Verse four lists the third function of the Messiah which is the unending priesthood similar to the order of Melchizedek. Melchizedek was a priest-king of (Jeru)Salem (The City of Peace) long before the Levitical priestly line. Several N. T. references come from the "priest" section (verse 4). There are multiple references in the book of Hebrews (5:6,10; 6:20 and 7:3) call Jesus a "priest forever" or a "priest in the order of Melchizedek."

The author to the Hebrews takes multiple chapters to expound on this "Great High Priest" role and how He is superior to any and all other Levitical High Priests. Beginning with chapter four, the Hebrews author begins his litany concerning the Messiah's high-priestly function. He says, "We have a great high priest who has gone through the heavens, Jesus the Son of God." In chapter seven, he further states, "Jesus lives forever, He has a permanent priesthood. Therefore, He is able to save completely those who come to God through Him, because He always lives to intercede for them." Finally, he states how Jesus is far superior to other high priests. Listen: "(He) is holy, blameless, pure, set apart, and exalted above the heavens." (Hebrews 7:26)

Verses five and beyond describe successful warfare where the LORD sitting at the right hand, will "crush kings on the day of His wrath." His judgment of the nations will be over all the earth and no one can escape the judgment of the Almighty. This short psalm ends on a positive note. When Jesus died, He bowed his head (John 19:30) but he soon lifted up His head by His own power in His resurrection and was raised in glory as "The Conqueror" over sin, death, and the devil.

(Source: www.biblestudytools.com/commentaries)

Peace
Connected in Him, I stand
GHR

PSALM 111
Eternal Praise

Psalm 111 is a partner with the subsequent psalm. They are both alphabetic acrostic with the same number of syllables (Hebrew) and identical line structure. (*Essential Bible Companion to the Psalms*) After the opening Hallelujah, there are 22-line segments (111 and 112). The authorship is anonymous for both.

One commentary suggested reading this psalm from the aspect of what He is and what He does. I made a list under each title. Listen how the psalmist describes who God is: righteous, gracious, compassionate, powerful, faithful, just, trustworthy, holy, awesome, and wise (wisdom). As to what He does: great are His works; glorious and majestic are His deeds; His wonders are remembered, Provider of food; and above all The Redeemer.

Many theologians would agree that this psalm was written in the post-exilic period, following their Babylonian captivity. Following the opening "Hallelujah", the psalmist says, "I will extol (praise highly) the LORD with all my heart." He offers an eternal praise to the One who has delivered them from their enemies. He continues by attributing greatness to the LORD's works and deeds. And yes, His righteousness endures forever. This phrase is certainly not uncommon, as we have heard it repeated on several occasions in previous psalms.

His graciousness and compassion are noted and are reminders of the words of Moses in Exodus 34:6: "The LORD, the LORD, the compassionate and gracious God, slow to anger, abounding in love and faithfulness. . ." Then the psalmist comments on these attributes saying,

"The works of His hands are faithful and just. . .and trustworthy." (verse 7)

All of whom God is and what He does are culminated in His work of redemption. Not only did He redeem His people from their captors, but He redeems all who trust in His name, His holy and awesome name. (verse 9b) The concluding verse is familiar and is repeated in Solomon's Book of Proverbs. In the opening chapter, Solomon says, "The fear of the LORD is the beginning of knowledge," (Proverbs 1:7) and then in chapter nine, "The fear of the LORD is the beginning of wisdom, and knowledge of the Holy One is understanding." (Proverbs 9:10)

The psalmist has written a beautiful hymn of praise, perhaps in observance of a festival, even the Passover. Regardless of when and why it was written, the precepts (principles) of this psalm of eternal praise is just as valuable today, in the 21st century.

In closing, listen to the words of the hymnist in this hymn of praise and adoration:

Praise to the LORD! O let all that is in me adore Him!
All that has life and breath, come now with praises before Him!
Let the Amen
Sound from His people again;
Gladly forever adore Him!
(LSB 790, v. 5)

Peace
Connected in Him, I stand
GHR

PSALM 112
Eternal Praise, Phase II

This psalm is a twin so to speak of the previous psalm. (Refer to Ps 111 Notes). The previous psalm concentrated on the LORD and who He is and what He does. While this psalm has some duplicate or similar verses, it has a minor shift and appears to be focused on the man who "fears the LORD." The psalmist opens with the same Hallelujah statement.

We have seen in the prior psalm that the "Fear of the LORD is the beginning of wisdom." Wisdom is another name for the LORD Jesus Christ. (See Eccl.7:12b) Now we see the attributes of a man of God who fears the One and only God of the universe. I have taken the liberty of reviewing this psalm from that standpoint and have created a table that summarizes the psalmist's list.

Man who fears the LORD is (will):
Find great delight in His commands
Will be blessed (generations)
Light the darkness
Generous and lends freely
Conducts his affairs justly
Has a steadfast heart
Charitable

First, the man who fears the LORD will always listen to His commands. Why? Because they are just and righteous. The man who fears the LORD will also teach his offspring about the LORD and His righteousness, and thus the blessing will continue. The psalmist says they will enjoy wealth and riches. In the 21st century one could easily assume that we have a God that will endow everyone with more money than can be counted. But I would suggest that God indeed supplies our everyday needs in abundance, so that we know from whom they came! All that we have is God's and we are merely stewards of His gifts. Thus, I taught my children we were not rich in money, but in blessings!

The psalmist implies that the man who fears the LORD may - and in fact will at some time - see times of trouble. But God will indeed shine through the darkness (troubles) with His marvelous light. The rest of the attributes is consistent with a man who listens to the LORD. He is generous and charitable with the assets that God has given to him. His heart is right with God (steadfast) and does not waver. Finally, he conducts his life's affairs justly.

Like the previous psalm, the psalmist ends the 3rd verse with "His righteousness endures forever." This is a phrase that should never be forgotten as the God we know is consistent and never failing with His promises.

In summary, we see that Psalm 111 elaborates on the attributes of God and then how He acts for and with His people. In the current psalm we see the results of the man (person) who fears and trusts the LORD. He is a great steward of the grace and mercy that God extends to His kingdom, and He acts in accordance His good and gracious will.

Peace
Connected in Him, I stand
GHR

PSALM 113

Hallel!

This psalm is the first of several psalms (113-117) that are referred to as "Hallel," the Hebrew word for *praise*. Many theologians agree that this psalm is post-exilic and, mirrors a rather discouraging state of mind from the Israelites returning to their land. We see such words as poor, needy, and barren to describe a disparaging song; but regardless, they find great opportunity to offer praise to the LORD.

This psalm, along with 114, was sung at the beginning of a meal for each of the three major festivals, as well as the festival of New Moon (Rosh Chodesh) and Dedication (Hanukkah). The New Moon Festival was the 1st day of each Hebrew month. The remaining Hallel psalms (115-118) were sung following a meal. This practice was followed by our LORD during Passover. (See Matthew 26:30 and Mark 14:26.)

This psalm of praise uses the word "praise" or "praised" six times with the majority at the beginning of the psalm. Note that the "Hallelujah" phrase opens and closes this psalm, as bookends. H. C. Leupold, in his *Exposition of the Psalms*, describes the three-fold summons to praise the LORD. First, the psalmist refers to "servants" who praise the LORD. In this case, I like to believe he is referring to ALL who know the LORD as their Creator, Redeemer, and Sanctifier. Second, he says that praise is to be ongoing from now to evermore - in other words, unending. And third, the psalmist uses the sun of creation, from its rising to its setting to define the breadth. That includes all nations, just as the sun provides light and heat to all the world.

The next section, beginning with the 4th verse, remarks about God's greatness. His glory is above the heavens. The psalmist uses a rhetorical question: "Who is like the LORD our God?" And the answer of course is "none!" Who else can be enthroned at the right hand of God, exalted in the heavens, yet at the same time be compassionate and looking after us here on earth? Yes, He is inclusive of the poor, the needy, and the barren womb. The psalmist uses words like "raises" and "lifts" to describe how the LORD impacts those in need – described as an "ash heap." These final few verses are similar to the Song of Hannah found in 1 Samuel 2, after the LORD had opened her womb to give her Samuel, the prophet. She opens her song with "My heart rejoices." Later in her song, she remarks as to how the LORD is compassionate to the needy and "lifts them from the ash heap." (1 Samuel 2:8)

What else can we say? The name of the LORD is to be praised from the rising of the sun to its setting. As God's servants, we see His hand at work not only in our lives, but also in the world in which we live. He continues to sustain His creation. The sun has never failed to rise in the morning and set in the evening! He waters the earth in due season. He makes the grain to spring forth a new crop; but more importantly, He sent His Son to be sin for us to justify us before the throne of God. Praise the Lord!

Peace
Connected in Him, I stand
GHR

PSALM 114

Deliverance Remembered

Just as Psalm 113 was post-exilic (Babylon), this psalm is also a post-exile psalm that also records their misery in Egypt and how God provided passage from captivity to the Promised Land. The psalmist opens his song with a reminder that God delivered Jacob's descendants from the land of Egypt. Just how large was his family? I prepared a table below that shows his children and their birth mothers. The number shown in parentheses is the sequential number from oldest to youngest.

Leah	Bilhah (*)	Zilpah (**)	Rachel
Reuben (1)	Dan (5)	Gad (7)	Joseph (12)
Simeon (2)	Naphtali (6)	Asher (8)	Benjamin (13)
Levi (3)			
Judah (4)			
Issachar (9)			
Zebulun (10)			
Dinah (11)			

Source: American Bible Society; * Rachel's handmaid **Leah's handmaid

Interestingly, the 12 tribes of Jacob (Israel) are his sons, however, the division of land was not to his 12 sons, rather, only 10 of his sons received an allotment with the remaining two going to Joseph's two sons. The Levites, as the priestly line, did not receive an allotment, rather, were granted "priestly cities" in each of the 12 divisions of land.

The psalmist describes Judah as God's sanctuary and Israel as

His dominion. These two locations are not the kingdom divided but rather Judah as the forefather of our LORD and Israel the location of His worship center. Israel was God's dominion or chosen people. The psalmist recounts God's great miracles of deliverance from the Egyptians with the parting of the Red Sea to pushing back the waters (flood season) of the Jordan River. In poetic form, the psalmist recounts how God's creation gives praise to its creator – mountains skipping like rams and the hills like lambs. The *Essential Bible Companion to the Psalms* makes a note in its Reflection: "Is there anything the Lord cannot do? Tremble indeed at his presence." The final miracle of water (besides the Red Sea and Jordan River) is that of providing drinking water to His people in a miraculous way. Just as God divided and controlled the waters of the sea and river, he also made water gush forth from rocks, providing springs of water for their drink.

These two Hallel psalms (113-114) for the beginning of the meal, describe praise to the God of deliverance both from Babylon and from Egypt. He, too, continues to deliver you and me from the bondage of sin by His sacrificial death, His glorious resurrection, and His ascension to the throne on high. Soli Deo Gloria!

Peace
Connected in Him, I stand
GHR

PSALM 115

He is Their Help & Shield

This psalm begins the last section of the Hallel psalms for the end of the various festival meals. The psalmist is anonymous but very poetic as he compares the God of Israel to all other gods whose origin are nebulous. The psalmist begins by leaving no doubt as to where his allegiance lies – it's the LORD where Glory dwells. His love and faithfulness have no beginning and no ending.

While our God is in the heavens (alive and well), the idols made of argentum (Ag: Silver) and auric (Au: Gold) are merely man-made. They have no mouths to speak, no ears that hear, no noses that smell, no hands that feel, or feet that walk, and they are without a sound from their throats. The idols are senseless!

Verse nine begins a trilogy of repeated praise. Here the author begins with the house of Israel, then shifts to the house of the priests (Aaron), and finally all those who place their trust in Him. Yes, **He is their help and their shield.** (verse 9-11) The psalmist acknowledges God's promise made ages ago that He will bless Abraham and his descendants that would outnumber the grains of sand or stars in the sky.

The terms "help and shield" are important enough that the author repeats them three times. God is our Heavenly Helper Who has provided assistance necessary to redeem our sinful lives. He is our shield (our faith – see Ephesians 6:16) that extinguishes the arrows of Satan. The author then repeats the trilogy (Israel, Aaron, and those who fear God) as He blesses them.

I am reminded that the house of Aaron was ordained by God to be the priestly line for Israel. In Exodus, we're told that God designed an ephod (breastplate) for making decisions. Moses went into great detail as to its construction that included four rows of three stones, each representing the tribes of Israel. The breastplate also included two unknown stones called Urim and Thummim that were used for making decisions. This breastplate marks a sign that God indeed was present with the high priest and was paramount in making critical decisions. As such, God blessed their increase as they were to continue to extol the LORD.

As a side note, the 12 stones in the ephod are enumerated in Exodus 28:15-21. Some of the stones sound familiar, while others are vague. They are ruby, topaz, beryl, turquoise, sapphire, emerald, jacinth, agate, amethyst, chrysolite, onyx, and jasper. Eight of these 12 stones are also specifically mentioned in Revelation 21 in the "foundation of the city wall in the Heavenly Jerusalem."

The author concludes this descriptive psalm with complete confidence that the heavens are the LORD's, and that only the believers that fear Him will continue to extol His name while the worshippers of other gods will go down in silence! May we continue to go to our God who is our help and shield and avoid those man-made gods that have no life or breath. Listen to the words of the hymnist from the 17th century, *O God, Our Help in Ages Past*.

> Before the hills in order stood or earth received her frame,
> From everlasting Thou art God To endless years the same.
> O God, our help in ages past our hope for years to come,
> Be Thou our guard while troubles last and our eternal home.
> (LSB 733, v. 3, 5)

Peace
Connected in Him, I stand
GHR

PSALM 116
Two for One

Halley's Bible Handbook calls this psalm "One of the best." The Septuagint (LXX) is the Greek O. T. translation of the Hebrew text. This translation basically divides this psalm into parts, verses 1-9 and 10-19. The Septuagint is quoted more often in the N. T. than the original Hebrew Bible.

The opening of this anonymous psalm comes from the thankful heart of one that was saved from death's door (grave). The psalmist opens with his "Love for the LORD for He heard my voice; and my cry for mercy." The psalmist feels the pinch of death like entangling cords. (verse 3) In trouble, the psalmist calls on the name of the LORD for saving. Why? Because the LORD is gracious and righteous. H. C. Leupold, in his *Exposition of the Psalms*, comments on the unusual combination of these two attributes – gracious and righteous. "The first stresses the underserved character of the help while the second the energy with which God maintains His honor," says Leupold.

Verse six opens with a statement regarding how the LORD protects the simplehearted. The KJV uses the word "simple," which can be translated as silly, foolish, lack of wisdom, or open minded. "When I was in great need (low), He saved me." Here the psalmist is mindful to his troubles and calls out for help from the gracious and righteous God. His condition is secured! God has indeed provided an answer to his prayer and now the psalmist says, "Be at rest once more. . .for the LORD has been good to you." (verse 7) The LORD has delivered his soul from death (Sheol), his eyes from tears, and his feet from stumbling. The result: he now walks before the LORD in the land of the living. (verse 9)

Verse 10 begins the second part of this psalm that the Septuagint treats as a second psalm. St. Paul used the Septuagint translation when he quoted this verse in 2 Corinthians 4:13, "It is written, 'I believed therefore I have spoken.'" St. Paul goes on to say in his epistle, "With that same spirit of faith we also believe and therefore speak." (2 Corinthians 4:13b) The psalmist enters into a response language for God's graciousness. "How can I repay the LORD for all His goodness to me?" (verse 12) This verse, along with several subsequent verses, is used as an "Offertory" in many Protestant services. Here is one such Offertory:

> What shall I render to the LORD for all His benefits to me?
> I will offer the sacrifice of thanksgiving and
> will call on the name of the LORD.
> I will take the cup of salvation and will
> call on the name of the LORD.
> I will pay my vows to the LORD now in
> the presence of all His people,
> In the courts of the LORD's house, in the midst of you, O Jerusalem.
> (LSB, Divine Service, Setting One)

I am particularly drawn to verse 15 which states, "Precious in the sight of the LORD is the death of His saints." To me, victory is won when one of God's own dies in faith such that their life was precious, resulting in the believer gaining eternal life with his Savior. And that's precious! Listen to St. Paul in Romans 14:8: "If we live, we live to the LORD; and if we die, we die to the LORD. So, whether we live or die, we belong to the LORD."

The psalmist ties both sections together very well where the author sees death's reality closing in on him, yet he knows God is gracious and righteous to those who love him. And in the second section, the psalmist expresses his thanks, and offers a sacrifice to fulfill his vow to the LORD. Hallelujah!

Peace
Connected in Him, I stand
GHR

PSALM 117

Short, But Sweet!

This psalm has several characteristics apart from its message. First, it's the middle chapter in the 1,189 chapters of the Bible – yes, there are 594 before and after it. Secondly, it's the shortest chapter in the Bible. Some theologians believe it is a "fragment" or part of another psalm, while others consider it on a stand-alone basis.

Psalm 117 continues in the *Hallel* list of psalms. In particular, this one was sung after the meal of a major Jewish festival. In these 29 short words (NIV) (16 in Hebrew), the psalmist packs a punch that is sweet to one's ears. Let's take a look.

Like several of the *Hallel* psalms, which open and/or close with Praise the LORD, this psalm does both. The first verse concludes with "all you nations (Gentiles)." Israel was God's nation, but He is also the God of all nations and nationalities (peoples). This verse is quoted by St. Paul in the epistle of Romans. First, Paul makes a case that Abraham is father to all: "He is the father of us all." (Romans 4:16) Then in Romans 15:11, Paul quotes Psalm 117:1 as he encourages the Gentiles and Jews to live in the unity of the Good News of Jesus Christ, as He accepted us all in faith.

The second and final verse is a universal statement of God's great love for "us," in that His faithfulness endures forever. God is LORD of all nations, both Jew and Greek, slave and free. All are His creation, and He wants all to be saved and to come to the knowledge of the truth, says Scripture.

This psalm has been set to music by various authors and composers, including Bach. *Lobet den Herrn, alle Heiden* (Praise the LORD, all ye nations) is a motet by Bach drawn from Psalm 117:1-2. While its composition date is unknown, it was first published in 1821.

What a sweet message for all God's creation to praise His name because His love endures forever. Amen! Hallelujah

Peace
Connected in Him, I stand
GHR

PSALM 118

This is the Day the LORD has Made

This psalm is the final psalm in the *Hallel* section. This *Hallel* was sung by Jesus and His disciples following their Passover meal prior to exiting to the Garden of Gethsemane. The great reformer, The Reverend Dr. Martin Luther stated, "This is my own psalm which I specially love." There are a lot of memorable verses that are quoted in other parts of the O. T. and then by N. T. writers and Jesus himself. Perhaps the most recognizable verse (24) is the title to these notes, "This is the day that the LORD has made; let us rejoice and be glad in it."

Some theologians believe this psalm was written around the time of Nehemiah and the completion of the wall rebuilding process in Jerusalem. (See Neh. 12:27) The rebuilding process was not completed for almost 100 years after their return from Babylon.

Some theologians believe this psalm is divided into six stanzas. The psalmist repeatedly uses the word "LORD" in all but five verses. In the opening four verses we see the phrase, "His love endures forever." The psalmist is clear to include ALL people – from God's chosen people (Israel), to the priestly line (Aaron), and to all who fear the LORD. This phrase then reappears as the final words of the psalmist. This phrase also applies to us today reminding us that God's love extends forever.

The tune quickly changes in verse five, suggesting not everyone was happy. In fact, Nehemiah states in his chapter 4:7, that there was opposition to the completion of the wall. The psalmist points out that the LORD answered by setting him free. Then we see a familiar quote used in Hebrews 13:6: "The LORD is my helper; I will not be afraid.

What can man do to me?" He says, "It is better to take refuge in the LORD than to trust man." (Psalm 118:8) Yes, the balance of life should be heavily weighted to the LORD's side. For with God, all things are possible, says Scripture.

Verse 14 is also awfully familiar, with the words of praise seemingly jumping off the page. "The LORD is my strength and my song; He has become my salvation." This very same sentence is quoted by the prophet Isaiah 12:2b. This verse then leads into the next stanza which is perhaps the strongest tone of praise in this entire psalm. The psalmist praises God for his righteousness, His strength, and His saving grace (not given over to death).

The following stanza (verse 22) begins with a messianic reference to Jesus as the Cornerstone, which is quoted by St. Matthew 21:42 shortly after His triumphal entry into Jerusalem on Palm Sunday. "Just as Jesus is the cornerstone of our faith, Israel was the cornerstone of God's plan with nations," says H. C. Leupold in his *Exposition of the Psalms*. The famous verse (24) is perhaps multi-purposed. The word "day" could be a reference to each day in our lives, giving credence to the LORD who graced us with another day of service to Him and His creation. It could also refer to the divine plan of God that has dawned on Israel. God's divine plan and His covenant are always fulfilled. The "day" perhaps refers to His delivering them from bondage in Egypt, through the desert trials to the Promised Land. And finally, the "day" could also refer to the Messiah's triumphal entry into the City of David. Verse 26 was sung by the bystanders as Jesus rode into Zion on a donkey singing, "Blessed is He who comes in the name of the LORD." (Matthew 21:9)

Yes, the psalmist states that "the LORD is God and that He has made "His light" to shine upon us." This same "light" is quoted in Isaiah 60:1 then repeated in St. John's opening of his Gospel. "In Him was life, and that life was the LIGHT of men." (John 1:4 emphasis added). This beautiful psalm of praise concludes with the final two verses in which the psalmist reminds us that God is the only God, and he exalts Him; and gives thanks for His love that endures forever.

Many songs and hymns have been written using Psalm 118:24, but the one that I like the best is the one that I have heard primarily sung by children. As you arise each day, consider using this beautiful little prayer acknowledging God's grace to you.

This is the day, this is the day.
That the Lord has made, that the Lord has made.
We will rejoice, we will rejoice,
And be glad in it, and be glad in it.
This is the day that the Lord has made.
We will rejoice and be glad in it.
This is the day, this is the day
That the Lord has made.
(Author unknown)

Peace
Connected in Him, I stand
GHR

PSALM 118 ATTACHMENT: OPEN THE GATES

The psalmist says, "This is the gate of the LORD through which the righteous may enter." (verse 20) The city of Jerusalem is encircled by a wall that has multiple gates. Nehemiah carefully lists all 10 gates that we rebuilt in the wall. The psalmist compares God's gracious action of redemption to the opening of a gate to welcome the saved by His Son's righteous act. The table below identifies each gate and its significance and/or use.

Gate	Description and Notes
Sheep Gate (Nehemiah 3:1)	Gate through which sheep and lambs would enter used in sacrifice.
Fish Gate (3:3)	Fishermen of Galilee would bring their catch to be sold in the market
Old Gate (Jeshannah) (3:6)	Nehemiah is the only book in the Bible where it's called Old Gate; May have been one of the original gates made?
Valley Gate (3:13)	Opened out to the Valley of Hinnom. (Gehenna)
Dung Gate (3:14)	Southeast corner of old city and the only gate leading to the Jewish quarter. Named for the residue from the Temple and dumped into the Valley of Hinnom and burned.
Fountain Gate (3:15)	Located near the Pool of Siloam (Siloah); used by the people for cleansing before proceeding to the temple.
Water Gate (3:26)	Led to Gihon Spring located adjacent to the Kidron Valley.
Horse Gate (3:28)	Close to the King's stables; men would ride out of this gate to war.
East Gate (3:29)	Opens to and looks toward the Mt. of Olives
Inspection Gate (3:31)	A/K/A Miphkad Gate; Tradition says King David would meet his troops to inspect them.

Source: Bible Study on the Book of Nehemiah: The Gates of Jerusalem; I. Gordon.

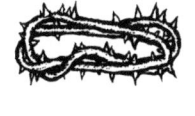

PSALM 119

Introduction to the Acrostic Psalm

This 22-stanza psalm is an alphabetic acrostic psalm by an unknown author. As stated in the Prologue to Book V, this 176-verse psalm is the longest in the Bible. Each of the 22 stanzas has eight lines and every verse mentions the Word of God under one of the following names: law, statutes, righteous laws, decrees, commands, precepts, word, ways (testimonies, ordinances), with a few exceptions. (*Halley's Bible Handbook*)

H. C. Leupold in his *Exposition of the Psalms* points out that the psalmist uses 10 synonyms for God's Word: law, word, saying, commandment, statute, ordinance, precept, testimony, way, and path. This description is similar to Halley's comment listed above.

The dating of this psalm is suggested by some theologians to be in the time of Ezra and Nehemiah. Ezra's return to Jerusalem preceded Nehemiah's time by 14 years (458-444 BC). Ezra's duty as priest was to teach religion to the people while Nehemiah was a civil servant, with authority from the King of Persia to rebuild the walls of Jerusalem. The Israelites had been back almost 100 years but made little progress beyond rebuilding the temple. Interruption came from internal and external sources regarding the wall's progress which caused multiple work stoppages.

H. C. Leupold states in his *Exposition of the Psalms*, "there was enough memory of the captivity among the returnees that they didn't want to make the same mistakes." While each section begins with a letter of the Hebrew alphabet, there does not seem to be any stanza-to-stanza connection other than a strong reference to the law and Word of God.

The table below lists each stanza and its title for the notes that follow.

Stanza No/Letter	Theme
1 (Aleph)	A Walking Joy
2 (Beth)	The Riches of Your Statutes
3 (Gimel)	Spiritual Sight
4 (Daleth)	Hold Fast!
5 (He)	The Verbs of Wisdom & Understanding
6 (Waw)	Touching the Word
7 (Zayin)	The Theme of My Song
8 (Cheth/Heth)	A Change of Direction
9 (Teth)	God's Word: Priceless!
10 (Yodh)	Comfort to the Righteous
11 (Kaph)	Hope's Building Block
12 (Lamedh)	Boundless Nature of God
13 (Mem)	The Sweetness of God's Word
14 (Nun)	A Lighted Path
15 (Samekh)	Faithfulness in Opposition
16 (Ayin)	Cling to the Word
17 (Pe)	The Gate is the Only Answer
18 (Tsadhe)	Righteousness is Everlasting
19 (Qoph)	Pray Without Ceasing
20 (Resh)	Life's Renewal
21 (Sin/Shin)	Trembling Yes; Stumbling No
22 (Taw)	Insightful

PSALM 119.1

Aleph: A Walking Joy

The psalmist opens with the word "blessed" that reminds us of the Beatitudes in the book of Matthew. The first verse says: "Blessed are those whose ways are blameless." The Beatitudes, in Matthew 5:8, uses "pure in heart" which can also be translated blameless. The blameless are those who walk in His ways. These eight verses use a variety of law-like words: law, statutes, ways, precepts, decrees, and commands.

The second blessed statement refers to those who keep His statutes and seek Him with all their heart. The Hebrew word for heart can also refers to the mind. Moses wrote, "Love the LORD your God with all your heart and will all your soul and with all your strength." (Deuteronomy 6:5) Jesus quotes the O. T. to the Pharisees when He says, "Love the LORD your God with all your heart. . .soul. . . mind. . . and strength." (Mark 12:30) Both the mind and the heart control our actions.

Those who walk in His ways are those who are blameless. God's precepts are such that we are to obey them all. But we cannot obey them without exception and the psalmist is suggesting that if we're steadfast in seeking His ways and obeying His decrees, we are exhibiting what God has commanded. "Seeking Him" means our entire being - heart, mind, soul, and strength!

The psalmist reminds us that he is always seeking to learn God's laws and pleads with God not to forsake him. This first stanza is a joyful expression of how we are to continue to study His Word and His precepts. The blood of the spotless Lamb of God renders us blameless before the His throne. By Jesus' work of redemption, we can walk in joy having been rendered blameless before His throne. Amen!

Peace
Connected in Him, I stand
GHR

PSALM 119.2

Beth: The Riches of Your Statutes

The psalmist opens with a question followed by the solution. I believe the psalmist's opening can be paraphrased, "keep your heart pure by living according to Your Word!" The term pure heart reminds me of the prayer of David in Psalm 51 after the prophet Nathan came to David following his sin with Bathsheba. Listen to David's plea: "Create in me a pure heart O God, and renew a steadfast spirit within me. . .Restore to me the joy of your salvation and grant me a willing spirit to sustain me. (Psalm 51:10,12)

The person pictured here is a young man. He seeks God with his whole heart and hides God's Word in his heart. Hidden? Not from the standpoint of losing it, rather, I believe so that no one can steal the precious laws of God from him. The psalmist is open to a continual learning process. "Teach me Your decrees," says the psalmist. And the young man rejoices at God's statutes as one would rejoice in great riches.

God's blessings surely cover every aspect of our life, but the greatest of the blessings is the knowledge of the Holy One and His plan of salvation through His Son, Jesus, the Messiah. One must meditate on God's precepts, as the psalmist reminds us. As we read and study His Word, we can reinforce our faith and maintain our walk on the narrow path that leads to eternal life.

As the young man says, "I delight in Your decrees; and I will not neglect Your Word." (verse 16) I am reminded of St. Paul's instructions to the church at Colossae, "Let the Word of Christ dwell in you richly as you teach and admonish one another with all wisdom, and as you sing psalms, hymns, and spiritual songs with gratitude in your hearts to God." (Colossians 3:16)

Peace
Connected in Him, I stand
GHR

PSALM 119.3

Gimel: Spiritual Sight

The psalmist opens this third stanza of Psalm 119: "Do good to your servant and I will live." Then, the psalmist says, "I will obey Your Word." (verse 17b) His request is to see God's wonderful things in the law. Not physical sight but spiritual sight. While he is a stranger on earth, his soul constantly longs for God's laws.

We are all strangers on this earth as St. Paul reminds us in Philippians, "Our citizenship is in heaven." (Philippians 3:20) The psalmist feels the persecution from those around him as they continue to slander him. He pleads for God to remove him from their scorn and contempt and he will meditate on God's decrees.

The final verse in this stanza provides confidence to you and me as he states, "Your statutes are my delight." (verse 24) This verse is a reminder of the very first psalm that opens with the person who fears the LORD. The psalmist says, "But his delight is in the law of the LORD, and on his law, he meditates day and night." (Psalm 1:2) What a companion verse to this verse in the third stanza.

As Christians, we receive our spiritual sight when we come to the knowledge of the truth by the Holy Spirit as the seed of faith is planted in our hearts in the waters of Holy Baptism. How fitting! Remember the disciple Thomas (often referred to as "Doubting Thomas") who refused to believe that the LORD had risen and who appeared to his fellow disciples. It was not until Jesus returned and invited Thomas to put his hand into his side that he believed. Jesus said, "Because you have seen, you have believed. Blessed are those who have not seen and yet have believed." (John 20:29) Spiritual sight dates back thousands of years as we see Abraham believed and it was counted to him for righteousness.

Spiritual sight continues to remain keen by listening to God's Word to see His glorious and good will toward those who call Him LORD and Savior.

Peace
Connected in Him, I stand
GHR

PSALM 119.4

Daleth: Hold Fast!

The psalmist opens with a "downer" mood as he states, "I am laid low in the dust." He pleads for God to preserve his life according to His Word. He then looks back to his former days and recounts his ways and how the LORD answered him. The LORD taught him His decrees, and he continues to seek understanding of God's precepts.

The psalmist continues with words of deep remorse when he says, "My soul is weary with sorrow." (verse 28) He asks God to strengthen him and to keep him from a deceitful path of destruction by His grace! Yes, God's Word is "**G**od's **R**ighteousness **a**t **C**hrist's **E**xpense (GRACE)."

The psalmist, considering all options, chose the way of truth. Remember, Jesus said, "I AM the Way, the Truth, and the Life." (emphasis added) The psalmist has set his heart on God's laws. Verse 31 says, "Hold fast" to God's statutes. This phrase is synonymous with multiple other uses dating back to Moses and the book of Deuteronomy. To summarize its use, I have prepared a table with several references.

Hold Fast Reference	Phrase
Deuteronomy 10:20	Fear the LORD your God and serve Him. Hold fast to Him
Deuteronomy 11:22	Love the LORD your God, to walk in His ways and to hold fast to Him.
Deuteronomy 30:20	That you may love the LORD your God, listen to His voice, and hold fast to Him

2 Thessalonians 2:15	So then, brothers, stand firm and hold to the teachings
Revelation 3:11	Hold on to what you have, so that no one can take your crown.

The O. T. commonly talks about holding fast to God's statutes, especially in Moses' book of Deuteronomy. Moses said, "And now, O Israel, what does the LORD your God require of you? (Deuteronomy 10:12) Moses says: "Fear (LORD), Walk in His ways, Love Him, and to serve Him." (Deuteronomy 10:12, paraphrased) The N. T. apostle Paul tells the church at Thessalonica to stand firm and hold (fast) to the LORD's teachings.

The reference to hold fast is a lesson for you and me today. Just as the LORD instructed Moses to tell the Israelites, we are to fear the LORD, serve Him, and hold fast to His Word, these same words apply to you and me. The psalmist ends with a great gospel message. "I run in the path of Your commands, for You have set my heart free." (verse 32)

Yes, the gospel **sets us apart** from the sin that separates us from the love of God. We received salvation from the Lamb who was sinless and was sin for us so that we might have life and have it abundantly, says scripture. So, hold fast to your faith and walk with Him in the Light of Life to avoid sin's path of destruction.

Peace
Connected in Him, I stand
GHR

PSALM 119.5

He: The Verbs of Wisdom & Understanding

This psalm is one of a prayer for understanding the precepts of the LORD. The verbs used here are numerous and often repeated. I have prepared a table of the verbs used along with the verse where they are located.

Verse	Verbs
33	Teach me (decrees)
34	Give me (understanding)
35	Direct (my path)
36	Turn (my heart)
37	Turn (my eyes)
	Preserve (my life)
38	Fulfill (your promise)
39	Take away (disgrace)
40	Preserve (my life)

The psalmist opens with a clear request for the LORD to teach him His decrees so that he can keep them to the end. Once he is taught, he begs for understanding of the decrees and precepts; and to obey what God demands of us. Once we have the first two requests to teach him decrees and give him understanding, the balance of the verbs is more of a directional type request. The psalmist is eager for the LORD to keep him on the straight and narrow path.

He is desirous for God to turn his heart and eyes in the right direction to avoid worthless things. As such, he is confident that God will preserve his life according to His Holy Word. The next part of that verse is key, beginning with the phrase, "So that You may be feared." (verse 38b)

The psalmist digresses slightly as sort of an afterthought when he requests that God take away the disgrace (sin) that is shown by the law and its mirror. "How I long for your precepts," says the psalmist. (verse 40) Finally, the psalmist repeats the verb "preserve" in verse 40: "Preserve my life in your righteousness." (Psalm 119:40b) Yes, if we follow God's Word and His precepts, and look only to Him and His Son's redemption on Calvary, then we too will be righteous in the sight of God as our sin is covered by the blood of the Lamb.

May your spiritual eyes and heart see and obey the precepts of God that He might renew our life in all righteousness. May He take away the disgrace of our sin and fulfill His eternal promise for those who are faithful.

Peace
Connected in Him, I stand
GHR

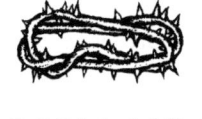

PSALM 119.6

Waw: Touching the Word

This sixth stanza is an interesting one where the psalmist is praying for grace based on God's unfailing love and the courage to continue in the precepts of the LORD despite his suffering. I have entitled this note as "Touching the Word," based on the final verse in this section. The psalmist says, "I lift up my hands to Your commands which I love." (verse 48) This "lifting up" is a process as if to touch something. In this case, the psalmist refers to God's commandments and His Word.

In the opening verse, the author prays for God's unfailing love through which he receives the salvation of promise. His particular suffering appears to be from people who taunt him because of his belief and trust. Belief comes from faith and faith by hearing of the Word of God, says scripture. He pleads that God's Word will not be removed from his possession and his promise to obey forever. The jailer at Philippi comments in Acts 16, "What must I do to be saved?" And Paul responded, "Believe!"

The psalmist then rejoices (verse 45-46) that he walks about in freedom as he offers up testimony to kings about God's goodness as he is confident, he will not be put to shame. The psalmist "delights" in God's commands which is similar to the first psalm (Psalm 1:2 – delight in the law of the LORD).

The psalmist closes with a verse that reminds you and me of the closeness of God to all of us. He says, "I lift up my hands." For what? God's commandments and His Word. God's Word is not some ethereal concept but a real living and continuing covenant that God promised so long ago. God's presence was first noted in Genesis in the Garden of Eden with His creation. His presence continues with His people from Abraham, Isaac, Jacob, and beyond! His Word was touchable in the tablets of stone that Moses delivered to the Israelites, and His Word was mouthed by His spokesmen – both prophet and priest alike.

The touch of the Word is ever present throughout the Bible but perhaps the most prominent to me is in the Gospel of Luke where Jesus (The Word) was traveling through Galilee preaching and teaching. As Jesus was enroute to the home of Jairus for his daughter's situation, a woman approached Jesus among the crowds. She had some sort of a bleeding disorder for some time that no one could solve. She was able to reach out and touch Jesus's cloak (in faith). In a crowd of many, Jesus immediately noticed her touch and said, "Who touched me?" The woman than fell at His feet and acknowledged her touch to which Jesus said, "Your faith has healed you." (Luke 8:48)

Yes, the Word touched and healed! The psalmist too was confident that his delight in God's decrees and laws meant that God had touched him also! The psalmist prayed for grace and eventually noted he had reached out to "touch the Word." This touching is possible for you and me today as we read and study the Word and receive God's grace and mercy in His Word and Sacrament.

Peace
Connected in Him, I stand
GHR

PSALM 119.7

Zayin: The Theme of My Song

The psalmist continues in his state of affliction. What is his salvation? The first two verses are very telling. First, he notes that God's Word has given him hope. Secondly, his hope (in suffering) is God's promise to preserve his life.

The psalmist admits that the arrogant mock him, but he remains faithful (verse 51). He recounts God's everlasting covenant with His people and promise to be their God in all circumstances. The psalmist says, "I do not turn from Your law." (verse 51) The author recounts the ancient laws of the LORD dating back to Mt. Sinai and the desert wanderings. He states his ongoing comfort in God's laws.

What else can happen? The wicked are indignant! They have forsaken Your laws and decrees. But the psalmist says, "Your decrees are the theme of my song." St. Paul recounts in his epistle to the Romans, "For everything that was written in the past was written to teach us, so that through endurance and the encouragement of the Scriptures we might have hope." (Romans 15:4) The psalmist says that God's decrees are his "theme," regardless of his dwelling place. The psalmist's tone may have likely been an inspiration to St. Paul in his encouragement to the church at Corinth.

The psalmist promises to keep God's laws/precepts. His theme is consistent despite his afflictions. The theme of his song is that he will obey God's precepts. May God grant you His grace and mercy so that, like the psalmist, we can obey his precepts as our song of thanks.

Peace
Connected in Him, I Stand
GHR

PSALM 119.8

(C)heth: A Change of Direction

The psalmist opens with an affirmation of faith. He says, "You are my portion (inheritance, legacy or reward), O LORD." And he has promised to obey His Word. Verse 58 reminds us that he has "sought the face" of the LORD. This phrase is used in other parts of Scripture including David's Psalm of Thanks in 1 Chronicle 16:11. David says, "Look to the LORD and His strength; seek His face always." (Repeated in Psalm 105). Seeking God is not like He is far away. St. Paul reminded the people in Athens (Acts 17), "Men would seek Him and perhaps reach out for him and find him, though He is not far away." Jesus taught His disciples about prayer in Luke 11. In that section, He reminds them to "Ask and it will be given; seek and you will find; knock and the door will be opened." (Luke 11:9)

The psalmist then considers his current ways in verse 59. What he concludes is that he needs to change his direction towards God's statutes. And in a hurry: "hasten and not delay." (verse 60) The prayer life of the psalmist is fervent as he even arises at midnight to give thanks for God's righteousness and His statutes. He promises to keep good company by befriending all those who fear God and follow His precepts.

The concluding verse in this stanza shows the vast nature of God's love. The psalmist says, "The earth is filled with Your love." God is never far away as we heard from St. Paul. And His love is everywhere for those who love Him.

If you are in a direction in life that is going away from the face of the LORD, then turn around and right your steps. Seek His Face!

Peace
Connected in Him, I stand
GHR

PSALM 119.9

Teth: God's Word: Priceless!

Have you ever considered the value of God's love for you? Well, the psalmist has in this ninth stanza of Psalm 119. Here we see a picture of a man who previously went astray and then suffered some affliction which made him sit up; and take note of who he was and where he was going. His opening words are a plea for God to do good (blessings) to him. What is the source of God's blessings? The answer the psalmist found is that God must teach him so that he has knowledge, understanding, and good judgment. Solomon said very succinctly in Proverbs 9:10, "The knowledge of the Holy One is understanding."

Affliction and suffering drove the psalmist to God. He admits changing his ways to obeying God's commands. Even though the arrogant lie about me, I maintain my faithfulness to God and keep Your precepts. The unrighteous have calloused hearts and are without feeling. But the righteous delight in Your law.

The prophet Job was challenged by the Evil One, with God's permission. Job's life was changed with the loss of everything except his faith. He says, "Blessed is the man whom God corrects; so, do not despise the discipline of the Almighty." (Shaddai). The dialogue following reminds you and me that when troubles come, God does not forsake us rather He binds our wounds and ransoms us from death, says Job. (Job 5:18-20)

The psalmist looks back and sees the value of his affliction in that he learned of God's decrees and held them as a precious asset. He compares the value of God's Word to silver and gold. "The law from

Your mouth is more precious to me than thousands of pieces of silver and gold." By today's standards, 1,000 pieces (if 1 ounce each) of gold is worth $1.9 million and $28,510 in silver. (Source: JM Bullion 2/1/2021). As Job stated, "He ransoms us from death." Not just physical death but eternal death. Our salvation through the Lamb of God is priceless as our inheritance is eternal life with Him which is more than the human mind can imagine.

Peace
Connected in Him, I stand
GHR

PSALM 119.10

Yodh: Comfort to the Righteous

The psalmist opens with God's ownership of his life as God created and formed him. He prays for understanding to learn God's commands. As one living in faith, he prays that those in faith that see him will rejoice in the life of the afflicted that he continues to walk in faith despite his failings.

For what he knows is that God's love is unfailing. That is comfort with a capital C! The psalmist in the Psalm 1:6 says this about the righteous, "For the LORD watches over the way of the righteous, but the way of the wicked will perish."

If the LORD watches over the way of the righteous, He will surely have compassion (verse 77) because of God is eternally faithful. The psalmist knows that the wicked will get their just do in God's time just as Psalm 1:6 reminds us. The prophet Isaiah reminds His people, "Let them (wicked) see Your zeal for Your people and be put to shame; let the fire reserved for Your enemies consume them." (Isaiah 26:11) He is hopeful that those who walk in faith will see that he is walking in God's path according to His commands. His heart is blameless, says the psalmist and confident that he will not be put to shame.

Dr. H. C. Leupold in his *Exposition on the Psalms* says, "(God's) steadfast love is comfort in affliction." He also said, "The heart is the center of all thinking activity." As Dr. H. C. Leupold remarks, God's steadfast love for us is comfort to the righteous.

Peace
Connected in Him, I stand
GHR

PSALM 119:11

Kaph: Hope's Building Block

The continuing theme of affliction is once again noted in this stanza. The psalmist remains steadfast in his faith despite the world and its temptations to ignore God. He opens this psalm stating that his soul faints as he longs for God's saving grace. He also states positively that he continues to put his hope in the Word. Yes, salvation comes through faith; and faith by hearing; and hearing by the Word of God, says scripture. So, hope's building block is faith in Jesus Christ, the Savior of the world.

The psalmist is pleading for God to have mercy on his affliction and asks, "When will you comfort me?" (verse 82) The subsequent verse may seem a little bizarre as he states, "I am like a wineskin in the smoke." What? Doing some research, I found that placing a wineskin full of wine in the smoke of fire provides a mellowing of the wine bringing it to earlier perfection. The psalmist compares his affliction to the wineskin in smoke that the affliction will refine, mellow, or ripen his character. (Source: biblehub.com). But the psalmist is unsure of how long he must wait. And will his enemies, who continue to persecute him, ever be punished? Will God take note of their continued indiscretions?

The psalmist is firm in his belief of God's perfect precepts as they have preserved his life! God's love fills the earth as the psalmist states. His precepts are sure. His compassion is unfailing. Praise the Lord. In closing, listen to the words of the hymnist as he describes hope's building blocks.

My hope is built on nothing less Than Jesus' blood and righteousness;
No merit of my own I claim but wholly lean on Jesus' name.
On Christ, the solid rock, I stand; All other ground is sinking sand.
(LSB 575 v. 1)

Peace
Connected in Him, I stand
GHR

PSALM 119.12

Lamedh: Boundless Nature of God

If creation is not enough to convince you that God's nature is boundless, then listen to these characteristics.

Boundless Nature	Result
He (Word) is eternal, verse 89	No beginning and no end
He is faithful, verse 90	Continues to all generations
His laws, verse 91	Endure forever
He is Creator, verse 91	And all nature serves Him
His commands, verse 96	Are boundless!

The word boundless is almost an infinite term. Listen to St. Paul as he tells the Ephesians about his mission as an apostle of Jesus Christ. "To preach to the Gentiles the unsearchable riches of Christ, and to make plain to everyone the administration of this mystery." (Ephesians 3:8) Here Paul uses the word unsearchable vs. boundless but the meaning seems similar. St. Paul talks about God's riches which were demonstrated in His Son, Jesus. And His boundless nature has extended beyond the Jewish nation, God's people, to the Gentile nation.

Now let's look at the psalmist words. He opens with a statement that God's Word is eternal and stands firm in the heavens. As the table above states, His faithfulness endures forever to all generations. The psalmist is confident that he will never forget God's precepts. His plea for salvation is based on God's grace and he continues to seek God's laws.

The psalmist notes the limit of human acts as perfection has a limit. The limit is sin that began with Adam and Eve, and which continues to all generations. But God's love continues (and boundless) regardless of our infirmities. The boundless nature of God exceeds all human reason. And in original sin, we cannot expect to do anything for our salvation and wholly lean on Jesus' name to His boundless love which was demonstrated in the death and resurrection of His Son, Jesus.

Peace
Connected in Him, I stand
GHR

PSALM 119.13

Mem: The Sweetness of God's Word

The psalmist opens with a statement of his love for God's law and that he meditates on it day and night. His laws (statutes) have made him wiser – especially more than his enemies. What is wisdom? "The fear of the LORD is the beginning of wisdom," says the Proverbs author. As the psalmist learns, he finds understanding and insight as a result of his meditation on God's Word.

God's Word provides much insight, and the psalmist is confident that his study and apprehension is more insightful than his teachers or elders. Is his confidence one of bragging or a statement of understanding of God's precepts? His argument is that he has kept his feet from sinning and has not departed from God's Word.

His next statement in verse 103 is one of a comparison of God's promises to sweetness. What is sweetness? Is there a sweetness barometer? I have found a "Sweetness Index" table that compares forms of sugar (sweetness) to table sugar. The psalmist says, "His promises are sweeter than honey." Well, the table shows that honey is approximately the same sweetness as table sugar.

Sweetener	Sweetness Compared To Table Sugar
Agave Nectar	1½ times sweeter
Coconut Sugar	Same
Date Sugar	Same
Dextrose (Glucose)	¾ the sweetness
Erythritol	60-70% the sweetness
Fructose	More than 1½ times sweeter
Honey	Approximately the same
Lactose	Less than ¼ the sweetness
Maple Syrup	⅓ the sweetness
Stevia	Up to 300 times sweeter
Sucanat*	Same
Turbinado Sugar	Same
Xylitol	Same

* Low Glycemic Index is considered to be <55, Medium is 56-69, and High is >70.

How sweet is the Word of God to you? Listen to the hymnist as he expounds on the sweet name of Jesus to a believer's ear. (*How Sweet the Name of Jesus Sounds*, by John Newton 1725-1807)

How sweet the name of Jesus sounds in a believer's ear!
It soothes our sorrows, heals our wounds,
And drives away our fear.
(LSB 524. v. 1)

May the sweet sound of God's Word give you comfort as you meditate on His Word and consume it as the sweet sound of God's Good News.

Peace
Connected in Him, I stand
GHR

PSALM 119.14

Num: A Lighted Path

The psalmist opens this stanza with an all-familiar passage; and one that I remember from catechism class in my elementary grades. Just ponder the words, "Your Word is a lamp to my feet and a light to my path." (Psalm 119:106) God's Word is a light for sure. In Genesis 1:3 His Word created light overshadowing the formless, empty, and darkness over the deep. St. John in his opening verses of his Gospel reminds us that the Word (Logos) is the life and light of men. (John 1:3-4) In Jesus' earthly ministry we see Him referring to himself as the "light of the world." (John 8:12)

Here the psalmist refers to God's Word as an illumination that lightens his darkened situation. The Word has lighted his path so that he can follow God's righteous laws. He admits he has suffered much but is confident that God's Word will continue to renew his life. He offers praise to God as a thanksgiving for His continuing grace provided him through the statutes of the Almighty.

He has avoided the snares that the wicked had set before him and has not wavered from God's lighted path. In the final verses the psalmist says, "Your statutes. . .are the joy of my heart." (verse 111) Yes, the psalmist can be joyful in all circumstances. I am reminded of St. Paul's instructions to the church at Thessalonica (1 Thessalonians 5:16-17). Listen to the litany of instructions, "Be joyful always; pray continually; give thanks in all circumstances for this is God's will for you in Christ

Jesus." In conclusion, the psalmist has his heart set on keeping God's decrees until life's end.

Peace
Connected in Him, I stand
GHR

PSALM 119.15

Samekh: Faithfulness in Opposition

The psalmist opens this stanza with polar opposite positions. First, he hates those who are double-minded, that is, those who blow with the wind versus the one who loves God's laws. In the latter case, we see a single-minded, never wavering person who follows God's statutes. The psalmist reminds all of us that God is his refuge and shield for he puts his trust in God's Word. Remember St. Paul's "Armor of God?" (Ephesians 6:11; 14-17) St. Paul reminds us to "put on the shield of faith," to avoid the arrows of the Evil One.

The psalmist is adamant when he says, "Away from me you evildoers." (verse 115) This phrase is reminiscent of Jesus' temptations by the devil himself shortly after His baptism. St. Luke tells us that following the third and final attempt, Satan left him for a more opportune time. Later, during His Galilean ministry, Jesus was advising His disciples of his ultimate death (Mark 8:31). The impetuous Peter could not accept it and rebuked the LORD. At which time, Jesus said, "Get behind Me, Satan!" (Mark 8:33)

The psalmist pleads for God to sustain him based on His promise and he will live (salvation). He is confident that God's statutes will uphold him. He will look negatively to those who are deceitful and reject God's laws. They will be discarded like the dross from the silver purification process.

Coupled with the last stanza (119.14), we have God's light to his path and the shield of faith to withstand the flaming arrows of deceit, and ultimately to receive his crown of life. The final verse is the exclamation mark of this stanza as he says, "I stand in awe of your laws." (verse 120)

Peace
Connected in Him, I stand
GHR

PSALM 119.16

Ayin: Cling to the Word

The psalmist desires God's continuing protection. He opens with a statement that he has done what is right; and pleads that God will not leave him and let his oppressors devour him. The psalmist has done what is "righteous and just." (verse 121)

The idea of being forsaken is not a new thing. During the O. T. deliverance from Egypt to the Promised Land, Joshua took over leadership from his mentor, Moses. When Moses passed the torch, he advised Joshua and said, "The LORD will deliver them to you, and you must do to them all that I have commanded you. Be strong and courageous. Do not be afraid or terrified because of them, for the LORD your God goes with you; He will never leave you nor forsake you." (Deuteronomy 31:5-6)

While my eyes have failed me, says the psalmist, he is confident that God will deal with him according to his agape love. We too can be assured that God will never forsake us as children of God. The author claims to be God's servant; and requests God's discernment (keen insight) so that he can understand God's plans for him. He is very bold to say, "It's time for You to act!" (verse 126) Your laws are being ignored or broken, but the psalmist continues to value God's laws more than physical gold.

If we, as God's chosen, get to a fork in the road and feel alone, look to His Word and His promises to make the decision to follow His statutes and cling to His Word. Just as the Israelites felt overwhelmed, we too can get comfort that God is in control. Keep the faith!

Peace
Connected in Him, I stand
GHR

PSALM 119.17

Pe: The Gate is the Only Answer

The psalmist exudes with confidence as he states God's statutes are wonderful and he will obey them. The following verse uses the phrase, "the unfolding," as he proclaims the Word of God that gives light and understanding to the simple. (verse 130) The psalmist asks God to "direct his footsteps," so that he remains on God's path – the path that leads to the gate of the sheep pen, indicated in the N. T.

The N. T. refers to Jesus as the gate in one of His seven (7) examples of His presence. He says, "I AM the gate for the sheep." (John 10:7, emphasis added) The Shepherd of the sheep has only one entry into His sheep pen. And that is the gate. All other entry points are foreign and thus attempt to steal the sheep from the pen. Jesus is the only answer! The psalmist pleads for God's mercy for those who love Him.

"Direct my footsteps," says the psalmist and "let no sin rule over me." (verse 133) The path of righteousness is only a one-way path that is narrow and only lighted by the Word. The psalmist also asks for God to redeem him from his oppressors and to let His face shine on him. And when we are disobedient, the psalmist defines his sadness as "tears flowing from his eyes."

I am reminded of Jesus' teaching on the Sermon on the Mount. Matthew records the example about salt and light when He says, "Let your light so shine before men that they may see your good deeds and praise your Father in heaven." (Matthew 5:16) As we live out our life in Christ, we know that His light is the only answer and that the Great

Shepherd of the Sheep is the ONLY gate by which we can enter His pen. (eternal life)

Peace
Connected in Him, I stand
GHR

PSALM 119.18

Tsadhe: Righteousness is Everlasting

The psalmist dwells on the righteousness of the Holy One; and the laws, statutes, and precepts that are right, just, and true. In this eight-verse stanza, the psalmist comments on the laws of God multiple times. First, he states, "God's laws are right." Then he says, "Statutes are righteous and fully trustworthy." Thirdly, he states, "Your law is true," and finally, "Your statutes are forever right."

"Righteous are You, O LORD," is a powerful opening statement. This is a faith statement! St. Paul, in his opening chapter in the book of Romans, says, "The righteous live by faith." (Romans 1:16) And because of our faith in the Righteous One, we have a "crown of righteousness" laid up for us, says Paul in his letter to his beloved Timothy. (2 Timothy 4:8)

The psalmist expresses that his zeal for God's Word and precepts is tiring. While he loves them, his enemies are ignorant of God's thoroughly tested statutes. He promises not to forget God's "thoroughly tested" precepts. He acknowledges that God's righteousness is everlasting with no beginning or ending. The psalmist is pleading to God to give him understanding so that he might live. But we know that in faith, we receive the righteousness of Christ and share in his sacrificial death, burial, resurrection, and ascension. As sinner-saints, we know that we cannot keep the precepts of God perfectly, thus God sent His Son to be sin for us so that we might be made righteous in His sight. Praise the Lord.

Peace
Connected in Him, I stand
GHR

PSALM 119.19

Qoph: Pray Without Ceasing

This stanza begins with the psalmist "calling out" for God to hear him. "I call with all my heart; answer me!" (verse 145) The next verse in this stanza is similar to the first vis-à-vis calling out to be saved.

The psalmist describes praying day and night (through the watches). The day and night periods were each 12-hours. The night 12-hour period was divided into multiple watch periods. The Hebrew night watches were three each of four hours called the first, middle and morning watch. The Roman night watches were four three-hour watches called "Vigilia" followed by prima, secunda, tertia and quarta. The Vigilia prima began at 6P and lasted until 9P and so on. (Source: Wikipedia.org)

His prayers (meditations) are on God's Word and His promises. Included in his meditation is to preserve his life according to God's love and His promise. (verse 149) He continues to state the proximity of his enemies, yet they are so far from God. He knows that God is always near and that His commands are true. So why do his enemies scheme against him?

Today we know that the Evil One is prowling about seeking whom he may devour. But in faith, we can be assured that God has given us that "shield" that rebukes the arrows of the Evil One. Remember St. Paul in his letter to the church at Thessalonica, "Pray without ceasing." (1Thessalonians. 5:17)

Listen to the hymnist as states his trust in the LORD, knowing full well that God will save him! (*Precious LORD, Take My Hand*, by Thomas A. Dorsey, 1899-1993)

Precious LORD take my hand.
Lead me on, let me stand;
I am tired, I am weak, I am worn.
Through the storm, through the night, Lead me on to the light.
Take my hand, precious LORD; lead me home.
(LSB 739 v. 1)

Peace
Connected in Him, I stand
GHR

PSALM 119.20
Resh: Life's Renewal

The human life is only renewed by the Spirit of God; otherwise, we are helpless in our sin and totally separated from God. The psalmist is calling out for God to see his suffering. The pathway: **suffering→deliverance→defense→redemption.** The psalmist calls out in his suffering for God to deliver him. God defends His faithful, and leads them to a righteous ending (salvation, redemption).

The Bible tells us of God's hand delivers us on many an occasion. In the time of king Jehoshaphat (873-848 BC), multiple tribes/nations were making war against this God-fearing king of Judah. (2 Chronicles 20) People from all over Judah congregated in Jerusalem and in a corporate plea, the King said, "Power and might are in your hand." (2 Chronicles 20:6) God answered their prayer saying, "Do not be afraid or discouraged because of this vast army. For the battle is not yours, but Gods." (2 Chronicles 20:15b) And deliver He did!

The psalmist, like king Jehoshaphat, was confident that God can deliver them from the enemy. "Preserve my life," says the psalmist, "I love your precepts." (verse 159) Your Words are true and eternal. God has truly been a defender of those who trust in Him since the fall of Adam and Eve. While He hates sin, he loves the sinner, and as such, gave the first Gospel to them (Genesis 3:15) to deliver them from eternal damnation. Our lives today have many roadblocks with traps to ensnare us and draw us from the Holy One. For our delivering God does not forsake His followers, ever! We are indeed renewed by the Word, and His Holy Spirit as we walk by faith, and not by sight.

Peace
Connected in Him, I stand
GHR

PSALM 119.21

Shin: Trembling Yes; Stumbling No!

This is the second to last stanza in the ever-lengthy Psalm 119 that speaks almost entirely about the laws and precepts of God. The word "faith" is not used here but is certainly intimated in its many verses. The psalmist opens with a statement that considering his enemy's approach, and that his heart trembles at Your Word. The psalmist rejoices in God's promise like a king who returns in victory over his enemies with assets of victory (spoils).

The psalmist is always giving praise always (seven times/day=the perfect/complete number in the Bible) for God's righteous laws and precepts. He finds great peace in God's Word and His laws while nothing can cause him to stumble (Hebrew: mikshol). The Hebrew word used here is translated as an obstacle, stumbling block, or a cause to fall. While God's Word causes him (his heart) to tremble, nothing can cause him to stumble!

For we know that the love of God's Word is only possible with faith! One cannot love the attributes of God and His laws without faith. Remember St. Paul's words in his epistle to the Romans, "So then faith cometh by hearing, and hearing by the Word of God." (Romans 10:17 KJV) The psalmist has already admitted that his heart trembles as His Word. Thus, by hearing faith ensues!

The psalmist feels great peace in the nearness of his LORD. He waits patiently and continues to follow in God's commands. While we may tremble at the greatness of our God, we need not fear Him for He protects His own from stumbling and leaving the sheep pen.

Peace
Connected in Him, I stand
GHR

PSALM 119.22

Taw: Insightful!

This is the final stanza of the beautiful 119th Psalm in God's Word. Remember, this is an alphabetic acrostic psalm with each stanza beginning with each successive letter of the Hebrew alphabet. The theme throughout this psalm is God and His laws, precepts, and statutes. These final eight verses contain some very insightful pleas from the psalmist. I have prepared a table that attempts to summarize these pleas and the result.

Insight/Request/Plea	Result/Request
Give me understanding (169)	According to your Word
Deliver me (170)	According to promise
Teach me (171)	Your decrees
Help me (173)	With your hand
Save me (salvation) (74)	Your law is my delight
Let me live (175)	That I may praise you
Your laws (175)	Sustain me
Seek your servant (176)	Like a lost sheep has strayed

The psalmist opens his stanza with a hope that his cry for help has reached God's attention. Don't we all feel that way as we offer prayers to the throne of grace? This stanza has reminded me of my mnemonic that I use in my prayer life. ACTS! A is adoration; C is confession; T is thanksgiving and S is supplication (ask). We first acknowledge our

God as Almighty followed by a confession of our misgivings then thanksgiving for His continued blessings and then our requests.

If you look closely you can see all four ACTS in this plea. In particular, he is very distraught about his prior misgivings (straying) and that God would seek him and deliver him from sin.

The psalmist is clearly thirsting for God's Word and the blessings that flow from them. He says, "I long for your salvation, O LORD, your law is my delight." (verse 174)

So, there you have it. 176 verses packed with praises for the Almighty, acknowledgement of His Law, and precepts, and finally, a true faith that the psalmist continues to lean on God's promises to save him from his enemies and deliver him to everlasting glory. Amen and Amen.

Peace
Connected in Him, I stand
GHR

PSALMS: 120-134: INTRODUCTION - ASCENTS

The next 15 psalms in Book V of the psalms are entitled "Ascents." My Prologue to Book V contains a brief summary of the Ascent Psalms. As stated, it is postulated that as the worshippers approached Jerusalem, they would sing these psalms as the roads to the Holy City were ascending.

As with many aspects of scripture, numbers have some relevance. Since there are 15 Psalms of Ascents, is there any relevance? The naming this section is also called, Gradual Psalms, Songs of Degrees, Songs of Steps and Pilgrim Songs.

Authors of these 15 psalms vary with four attributed to David, one to his son Solomon. The length of the psalms varies in length from as short as three verses in (3) and several up to 18 verses in Psalm 132.

The history of this section varies while some may consider these 15 psalms to the 15 steps as the Levite singers ascended as many steps to minister at the temple. Others suggest as they sang songs at the dedication of Solomon's temple during the 15th of Tishri (959).

In modern Christianity, there is some symbolism as the Christians are ascending to the Heavenly Jerusalem. The Western Christian churches have been strongly influenced by these Ascent Psalms, especially by the Rule of St. Benedict. They have been assigned to various gradual psalms.

As we travel through this section of psalmody, let us all consider our walk with Jesus as we ascend to the throne of eternal bliss by way of the blood of the Lamb who has saved us. "Arise, shine for your Light has come," says the prophet Isaiah. Let us all remember the perfect Lamb of God who came, suffered, died, resurrected, and ascended to the right hand of God in Glory.

Peace
Connected in Him, I stand
GHR

PSALM 120

To Hate Peace is to Hate God

This psalm has several attributes of a person of God who lives away from Zion and among deceitful and treacherous people. (Source: *Halley's Bible Handbook*) The first verse gives us a clue to support this hypothesis, "I call on the LORD in my distress." The psalmist is quick to add a response that God answers his prayer. Several verses in this psalm give us a clue of the distant land in which this psalm is set. The term "Meshech" (verse 5) is named for the son of Japheth (Genesis 10:2) and the tribe. It is postulated to be in modern-day Turkey. The second reference to living among deceitful people is in reference to the "tents of Kedar." This is in reference to a nomadic tribe (NW of Arabia) and cut off from the worship of the True God.

The psalmist continues his plea for God to rescue him from the lying lips and deceitful tongues. King Solomon in his book of Proverbs says, "The LORD detests lying lips, but delights in the men who are truthful." (Prov. 12:22) The psalmist is confident that He (God) will punish them with sharp arrows and burning coals. Not just any coal but those of the broom tree which are thought to be the hottest!

Broom Tree: This tree (*Retama raetam*) is a desert shrub of the pea family. It is one of the most abundant plants in the Judean wilderness, the Sinai Peninsula, and the remainder of Arabia. It grows to about 1 to 4 meters in height. The foliage and its roots are used as fuel. Trees are uprooted for the manufacture of charcoal. (Source: *Holman Bible Dictionary; wol.jw.org/en/wol/d/r1/lp-e*)

This psalmist feels woeful as he lives among these deceitful and lying people. He continues by saying, "Too long have I lived among them. . .they hate peace!" (verse 6) If one hates peace, then can they love God? The obvious answer is no! The author is troubled as evidenced by his last thoughts in this chapter. He is a man of peace but when he speaks, he is more of a warmonger. (verse 7)

As Christians, we can express the same feelings as the psalmist as we live among war-like people and unrest in the world. Christians are becoming a shrinking minority, and often ridiculed, and persecuted as the psalmist notes. Let us be ever vigilant that our faith is firmly rooted in the Gospel of Jesus Christ and His promises for us in eternity. As an antithesis to the title, "To love peace is to Love God."

Peace
Connected in Him, I stand
GHR

PSALM 121
Constant Surveillance

I am particularly attracted to this psalm as many of the verses are ingrained in my memory bank from catechism class of my youth. The time of this psalm may be one of post-exile but could also be attributed to the time when the hills of Jerusalem came into view as the sojourners approached the Holy City. From my memory, "I will look to the hills from whence cometh my help." (verse 1, paraphrased) And in his next breath, he says in a rhetorical way, "Where does my help come from?" The City of Jerusalem was situated on the hill and provided physical protection to its inhabitants. In a more spiritual form, we look UP (emphasis added) to God for His divine assistance from our enemies.

The psalmist answers his question quickly as he gives credit to the Creator God who "made heaven and earth." (verse 2) The psalmist notes that God's surveillance is constant. "He who watches over you will not slumber nor sleep." (verse 3b) He references God's creating elements of the sun and moon, but He serves as our shade to protect from the sun's heat.

God's promises are sure indeed! The psalmist exudes with confidence as he writes, "The LORD will keep you from all harm-He will watch over your life." (verse 7) - whether coming or going makes no difference. Our every step is in constant surveillance by the Almighty God – and yes, now and forevermore.

I am reminded of St. Paul and his letter to the church at Philippi. This letter is one of Paul's "Prison Letters." Even in chains, he knows that God is with him, and he continues to rejoice. Paul is comfortable in his situation regardless of whether he lives or dies. He knows that "Christ will be exalted in his body, whether by life or by death." (Philippians 1:20b) God's care for His chosen is ever-close and does not slumber nor sleep. "Let the word of Christ dwell in you richly. (Colossians 3:16 KJV)

Peace
Connected in Him, I stand
GHR

PSALM 122

Zion, The City of God and of Truth

This is the first of several (4) Ascent Psalms by King David, that is, according to the Hebrew text. According to research, the Septuagint (LXX) and the Vulgate do not attribute this psalm to David. H. C. Leupold however, in his *Exposition of the Psalms,* based on the general reliability of the Hebrew text, continues to support David's authorship. The LXX is the Greek translation of the Old Testament that was completed in the 2nd century BC. The Vulgate (meaning "common") is the Latin translation of the Hebrew text completed by St. Jerome.

The timing of the writing of Psalm 122 has been postulated by some to be either during David's time or post-Babylonian exile. The latter theory is somewhat weak as verse four talks about the tribes of the LORD going to Jerusalem. This would not likely have occurred post exile as the 10 northern tribes had been taken into captivity by the Assyrians. Regardless of all the theories, the tone of this psalm gives great joy to the faithful of Israel going up to the City of David. The author opens with those who rejoice by saying, "Let us go to the house of the LORD." (verse 1b) In David's time, the first temple was not yet built so it would refer to the Tabernacle.

Jerusalem is one of the oldest cities in antiquity, dating back to 3,000 -2,800 BC by some sources. The city was built on the plateau of the Judean Mountains. The city was destroyed twice; besieged 23 times; captured 44 times; and attacked some 52 times. (Source: *Wikipedia*) Yet, God's city of Zion still stands, and extends beyond the Old City. Zion, a name for Jerusalem, was previously a distinct part of the city but now refers to the city in its entirety. King David made it the capital city for the Kingdom of Israel and then continued after the northern tribe's defection as the capital of the Kingdom of Judah. The name Jerusalem is also known as the "City of Peace."

So why are the faithful rejoicing? Well, first the Tabernacle contained the Glory of God. Second, the O. T. tells us that all men were required to go to the House of the LORD (at a place He will choose) for three festivals: Passover, Tabernacles and Pentecost (Weeks). (Deut. 16:16) Their attendance would allow them to praise the name of the LORD. (verse 4b) The worship of the Almighty included praying for peace and security of those who love God.

David's closing comments prays for his constituents (calls them brothers and friends) saying, "Peace be within you." And finally, David shows his concern for the House of the LORD.

Regardless of the various names associated with Jerusalem, it is the center of God's people that was not yet known in Deuteronomy; but later King David made it the center of God's people. The Glory of the LORD was present in it regardless of the Tabernacle or the subsequent permanent temple constructed by David's son, Solomon. Now, as modern-day Christians, we await the trumpets of God who will claim us to be with Him in eternity in the new heavens and new earth (Revelation 21:1).

In closing, listen to the words of the prophet Zechariah as the LORD promises to bless Jerusalem. "I am very jealous for Zion; I am burning with jealousy for her. I will return to Zion and dwell in Jerusalem. Then Jerusalem will be called the City of Truth, and the mountain of the LORD will be called The Holy Mountain." (Zechariah 8:2-3)

Peace
Connected in Him, I stand
GHR

PSALM 123

Looking Up!

"Things are looking up," as the old saying goes, that is if you accept it to mean things getting better. That's not how the psalmist uses the phrase. "I will lift my eyes to You, to You whose throne is in heaven." (verse 1) The opening in this psalm is similar to the opening in Psalm 121. The difference in this psalm is the psalmist tells us that he is looking to the heavens and not the hills. Looking up to God in the heavens is not new. The prophet Isaiah in his Book of Consolation (Isaiah, chapters 40-55) gives comfort to God's people as they were being besieged by the Assyrians. Listen to his words, "Lift your eyes and look to the heavens: who created all these?" (Isaiah 40:26) and then, "He gives strength to the weary and increases the power of the weak." (Isaiah 40:29)

The psalmist uses a servant analogy – a slave looks to his master and a maid to her mistress – comparing the faithful looking to the LORD for His mercy and deliverance. The third verse emphasizes this mercy by repeating the phrase, "Have mercy on us." Yes, God's people had endured much! Some theologians place the timing of this psalm to the Persian period when the exiles returned from Babylonian captivity with high hopes but were bitterly disappointed. (H. C. Leupold, *Exposition of the Psalms*).

As Isaiah states, "Who created all these?" (Isaiah 40:26) If God can create by speaking the Word, then He can surely give strength to the weary, and increase the power of the weak. In King Solomon's Proverbs, he states, "When the storm has swept by, the wicked are gone, but the righteous stand firm forever. (Proverbs 10:25) The Israelites have indeed endured much ridicule and contempt from the arrogant (wicked) but as the wise man Isaiah said, "The WORD of our God will stand forever." (Isaiah 40:8b, emphasis added) Amen.

I will leave you with these words from the hymnist of centuries past.
My God has all things in His keeping;
He is the ever faithful friend.
He gives me laughter after weeping,
And all His ways in blessings end.
His love endures eternally;
What pleases God, that pleases me.
(LSB 719, v. 4)

Peace
Connected in Him, I stand
GHR

PSALM 124

If-then

This psalm of David contains various conditional sentences (if-then). In this case, sources suggest David is looking back in a national type deliverance. Let's see the various uses of the if-then examples.

If	Then
LORD had not been on our side when	1. They would have swallowed us alive
• when men attacked; and	2. The flood would engulf us
• angers flared. . . then	3. The torrent would sweep over us
	4. The raging waters would sweep us away

These various conditional situations did not happen. Why? Because the LORD was on Israel's side. David's goal was to remind his people that the LORD continues to provide their deliverance just as He had promised long ago to Abraham, Isaac, and Jacob.

How often do we all have to be reminded that God watches over those whom He loves? Well, David does what is appropriate, and that is to give praise to the LORD (verse 6). His description compares the escaping of the tearing by their teeth and an escaping bird from a fowler's snare.

We too are delivered from the devil's snare as we trust in Jesus and Him alone for our salvation. He has indeed saved us from eternal damnation due to our sinful condition. David concludes this psalm with a well-known phrase often used in worship. "Our help is in the name of the LORD; the Maker of heaven and earth." (verse 8)

> Listen to the hymnist *"My Hope is Built on Nothing Less"*
> His oath, His covenant and blood
> Support me in the raging flood;
> When every earthly prop gives way,
> He then is all my hope and stay.
> On Christ, the solid rock, I stand;
> All other ground is sinking sand.
> (LSB 575, v. 3)

Peace
Connected in Him, I stand
GHR

PSALM 125

Supernatural Protection

As the sojourners continue to ascend to the Holy City (Ascents), they sing, "Those who trust in the LORD are like Mt. Zion which cannot be shaken but endures forever." (verse 1) The Holy City of Jerusalem, with constant outside threats, is protected. By whom? Just as the hills or mountains surround the city, so the LORD surrounds those who trust in Him both now and forevermore. "What a comfort this sweet sentence gives," to quote a famous Easter hymn. (*I Know That My Redeemer Lives,* by Samuel Medley 1738-99)

While the author here refers to natural protectors, we see that God is the supernatural protector as He "surrounds" his people. (verse 2) The psalmist acknowledges that the wicked will not just go away, rather, irrespective of their earthly successes, we see where God will vindicate us and banish them (evildoers) forever.

The timing of this psalm may be in the time of Nehemiah following the return from exile as he was attempting to rebuild the wall surrounding the Holy City. Not only did the Israelites have external enemies, but there were also internal struggles as well. (Nehemiah 6:2) The psalmist says, "Do good, O LORD, to those who are good and to those who are upright in heart."(verse 4)

It is impossible to rid our lives of all evildoers, but we can remain in good spirits as the LORD promises to protect us regardless of the approaching enemy. Our protectorate is none other than our faith that comes by the Holy Spirit of our LORD. When troubles come, we must always lean on Him as Scripture says, "Trust in the LORD with all thine heart and lean not unto thine own understanding." (Proverbs 3:5)

This protector in days of old is the same as today. Remember Paul's admonition to the church at Thessalonica, "May God himself, the God of peace, sanctify you through and through. May your whole spirit, soul, and body be kept blameless at the coming of our Lord Jesus Christ." (1 Thessalonians 5:23)

The psalmist concludes his thought to evildoers who do not turn from their ways. The end result is their destruction. "Peace be upon Israel." (verse 5c)

Peace
Connected in Him, I stand
GHR

PSALM 126

The River of Restoration

This psalm of Ascents is around the time of the post exile period when the Israelites returned to Judah from Babylon. The first verse would suggest that this psalm was sometime after their return since the verb is past tense (brought back). Their time in Babylon was from 587/586 to 537 BC. For over two generations, the nation of Judah was in the hands of their captors. Now that they have returned to their beloved country, the psalmist says, "We were like men who dreamed." In modern times, we might say, "pinch me to see I am awake." I am reminded of the time when St. Peter was imprisoned (Acts 12) during the time of Unleavened Bread. While imprisoned during the festival time, he was chained between two guards with additional guards at the entrance. Now, the Angel of the LORD appeared with light shining bright and said, "Put on your clothes. . . and follow me." (Acts 12:8) Peter thought he was seeing a vision (dreaming). Once free from his prison guards, the angel disappeared.

The Israelites (mouths) were filled with laughter and their tongues sang songs of joy. The psalmist comments on how the surrounding nations were amazed (perhaps even grudgingly) at their return and marveled at what their God had done.

Their songs of joy were short lived. Verse four changes tune with the verb now present tense. They're back. . .but! The people are praying to have their fortunes restored. The psalmist uses an analogy of the "streams in the Negev." The Negev is the desert in south Israel. The stream term is really a wadi which is generally a dry riverbed. But in the rainy season, the dry riverbed is transformed into overflowing waters. This vivid picture of the flooding waters is analogous to the LORD flooding them with His blessings in their time of need.

The last two verses remind us that God causes seed to sprout and to yield its fruit. Planting in an arid condition and not knowing if rain will come, causes some consternation. But in the end, God causes the seed to yield a crop. The sower returns thanks with songs of joy.

As Christians, we too can plant a seed (Word) in those who have not heard. God in His grace and mercy will provide the water to cause the seed to sprout forth and yield its fruit of faith. To God be the Glory!

Peace
Connected in Him, I stand
GHR

PSALM 127

Abundant Blessings

This psalm is one of two psalms written by King Solomon. The other is Psalm 72. This psalm is generally classified as one of wisdom. Not surprisingly, the man Solomon made an unselfish request to the LORD for wisdom (discerning heart – 1 Kings 3:9) as an incredibly young man. 1 Kings 3 tells us that LORD was so pleased with Solomon's request for a discerning heart, that He said, "I will give you a wise and discerning heart, so that there will never have been anyone like you, nor will there ever be." (1 Kings 3:12)

Halley's Bible Handbook comments that this psalm is really "two poems in one." The first theme is temple building and the second family building. The opening verses comment on God's assistance in the building of His house, and then the protection of His city. Without God, their human efforts would not be successful. Solomon uses the phrase "in vain" three times in the opening two verses. Here the psalmist regards our human toil (early and late) is in vain if God is not present. (H. C. Leupold, *Exposition of the Psalms*)

The LORD also blesses the marriage with fruit of the womb. "Children are a reward from Him," says Solomon. (verse 3b) The man and his sons are a team. Solomon remarks about a man's family compared to a quiver full of arrows. Some theologians have suggested these sons provided protection to their father at the gate where trades and other activity occurred.

The psalm is rather short but the point to me is made by God's presence in all circumstances. Whether it's building, protecting, or creating a family, God indeed has His hand in our lives. King Solomon built a permanent house of the LORD which was an extreme edifice to the Glory of God. As people of faith, we too are houses (temple) of the Spirit of Christ who has created faith in our hearts.

Peace
Connected in Him, I stand
GHR

PSALM 128

With Fear, Come Blessings!

From a personal note, I would like to share a family note during a time when our children were school age, and dinner was a family event. Unlike today, there were no cell phones, no internet, just the five of us sharing a meal and having a discussion. It was not uncommon for us to talk about how God had blessed our household, not just in monetary terms but in general, including our faith, job, health, family, and the like.

This psalm is a companion to the previous psalm written by Solomon. In this psalm, the author opens with a matter-of-fact statement: "Blessed are all who fear the LORD, who walk in His ways." Theologians are unsure as to the timing of this psalm, but it is postulated that it occurred during the time of Nehemiah, almost 100 years after their return from Babylon. The population was scarce, and the taxes were hard on the people. (H. C. Leupold, *Exposition of the Psalms*) It is also possible that it was written around the time of the Festival (Feast) of Tabernacles. The feast celebrated the in-gathering of their crop including grapes from the vineyard.

This psalm is part and parcel of the group of wisdom psalms. Wisdom? Yes, because the "Fear of the LORD is the beginning of wisdom, and knowledge of Him is understanding," says Proverbs 9:10. Here the LORD promises fruit from their labors and will yield prosperity! The second part of the blessing promises fruit of the womb including future generations. What more can we say about the LORD and his generosity? The psalmist repeats the LORD's promise in verse four, "Thus is the man blessed who fears the LORD . . .May the LORD bless you from Zion all the days of your life." (verses 4-5) The psalmist is also confident that Jerusalem will also see prosperity despite their current situation.

In modern times, people tend to relate blessings as money. But in God's plan, He blesses those who have faith in Him; and the trust we have in the Son of God who saved us from our treacherous condition. Fearing God is the result of faith; and those who walk in the fear of the LORD will have guaranteed blessings. What a promise!

I am reminded of the prophet Elijah and the widow of Zarephath. Just prior to their encounter, Elijah was fed by the ravens by God's blessing during a famine. Elijah witnessed how he had food and drink based on God's blessing. Then, he was told by God to go to Zarephath and seek a woman who will supply you with food. When Elijah arrived at the city gate, he met the woman and asked for something to eat and drink. She said, "As surely as the LORD your God lives, I don't have any bread." (1 Kings 17:12) Her supply was down to a little flour and oil sufficient for one meal for herself and her son. Elijah said, "Don't be afraid." (1 Kings 17:13) Elijah told her that her flour and oil would not run dry until the LORD brings rain.

The faith of this woman was great even in her extreme need. She was going to share everything she had with the LORD's prophet. Her fear of the LORD yielded blessing beyond human understanding. So, we too can heed the words of Elijah as he said, "Don't be afraid." We must rely on our faith and blessings that flow from faith and trust in the One True God.

Peace
Connected in Him I stand
GHR

PSALM 129

Enemies Abound, But God Reigns Supreme!

This psalm of Ascents is generally regarded as a corporate psalm versus an individual type. Israel is speaking here. It has some of the same attributes as Psalm 124. While the psalmist's identity is not known, he recalls the oppression of his youth. Theologians believe this in reference to their time in Egypt as slaves. But their troubles continue throughout history even to the post-exile period from Babylon, when neighboring nations sought to seek the demise of this tiny nation.

The dating of this psalm is a guestimate and may date back as far as the Assyrian period onward to post-exile from Babylon. The psalm is divided into two stanzas. The first four verses elaborate on the oppressive measures of its enemies. The psalmist describes the oppression like a plowman making furrows down their backs. The author is quick to add a "but" to the oppression which states, "The LORD is righteous, and He has cut me free from the cords of the wicked." (verse 4) The cords described here appear to refer to being in bondage from which the LORD has given them freedom.

The final four verses are written in a prayer-like fashion using words like, "May." The first request is that their (enemy's) life is as short as grass growing on the housetop. This analogy of the short life of grass is used throughout Scripture. The prophet Isaiah says, "The grass withers and the flowers fade, but the Word of our God stands forever." (Isaiah 40:8). Again St. Peter says, "All men are like grass and all their glory is like flowers of the field, the grass withers and the flowers fall, but the Word of the LORD stands forever." (1 Peter 1:24-25) No such crop can be gleaned from the housetop!

H. C. Leupold comments, in his *Exposition of the Psalms*, on the final verse in this psalm as one making an observation that such people (enemies) that have turned against God and Israel (His people) cannot thrive.

My title for this psalm consolidates the historical enemies of Israel and God's people. While they may be many, they cannot compare to God's abundant protection of His people, and the blessings bestowed on their nation. Today, the Christian's enemies abound but the love of God endures forever that was echoed by the prophet Isaiah and St. Peter in his first epistle.

May God keep you in His covenant of grace and, yes, even as flowers fade and grass withers, our faith continues to live to the Day of the LORD. Amen!

Peace
Connected in Him, I stand
GHR

PSALM 130
Waiting Patiently

As the old saying goes, "LORD give me patience and give it to me right now!" That's the antithesis of today's notes on Psalm 130. This psalm is a favorite of the great reformer The Reverend Dr. Martin Luther. Its verses are familiar to me, dating back to my time as a young catechumen in elementary school. The psalm is generally classified as a penitential psalm, yet it is in the Ascent collection of psalms. It makes total sense as sojourners ascended on the roads to Mt. Zion. They sang this song of confession for their sin and crying for mercy.

The psalmist opens with a deep sighing lament, "Out of the depths I cry to you, O LORD; O LORD, hear my voice. Let Your ears be attentive to my cry for mercy." God does not need hearing aids. He hears the pleas and cries of all who believe and trust in Him as LORD and Savior.

The psalmist confesses that he sins much and that if God kept a record, no one could stand before the throne of grace. And then comes that qualifier, "but." For we know that with God there is forgiveness! The prophet Isaiah reminded God's people that those who trust in Him will be saved. "Surely this is our God; we trusted in Him, and He saved us. . .Let us rejoice and be glad in His salvation." (Isaiah 25:9)

Verse five as his soul waits with hope in the LORD. He stated that his waiting period is more anticipatory than the watchman of the final watch waiting for morning's light. The psalmist pleads that Israel will put their individual and collective hope in the LORD and His unfailing love. Why? Because with Him is unfailing love and full redemption.

(verse 7) And that's Good News! Jeremiah, in his book of Lamentations, says: "The LORD is good to those whose hope is in Him, to the one who seeks Him; it is good to wait quietly for the salvation of the LORD." (Lamentations 3:25-26)

Dr. Luther wrote many hymns, but this Psalm was the basis of one of his earliest (1524), and one of eight songs in the first Lutheran hymnal. The German title is *Aus tiefer Not schrei ich zu dir*. Today, Christendom continues to sing this old hymn *"From the Depths of Woe I Cry to Thee."* It still has five verses as does the original. Listen to the Gospel words in the third verse:

> Therefore, my hope is in the Lord and not in mine own merit;
> It rests upon His faithful Word to them of contrite spirit
> That He is merciful and just; this is my comfort and my trust.
> His help I wait with patience.
> LSB 607, verse 3

The short epistle of Jude reminds all Christians that we are to wait patiently and to keep ourselves in God's love. Listen, "Keep yourselves in God's love as you wait for the mercy of our LORD Jesus Christ, to bring you to eternal life." (Jude 21) Wait patiently but keep watch!

Peace
Connected in Him, I stand
GHR

PSALM 131

Haughty or Humble?

This psalm is attributed to King David, although some may disagree with his authorship. H. C. Leupold in his *Exposition of the Psalms*, comments that this psalm is very unpretentious and contains the cardinal Christian virtue of humbleness. Remember the words of Jesus' brother (James) when he said: "God opposes the proud but gives grace to the humble." (James 4:6 from Proverbs 3:34b)

David opens with a positive statement remarking that his heart is not proud nor are his eyes haughty (arrogant). Haughtiness is the polar opposite of humbleness. How far does your pendulum swing? David clearly states that he is not too proud to concern himself with matters that may be meaningless in the big picture, rather, he has "stilled and quieted his soul." (verse 2) I am reminded of a wonderful hymn that all of us should be focused on the LORD. Listen to the words: *Be Still, My Soul, Before the LORD*, by Herman Stuempfle, Jr., 1923-2007.

> Be still my soul, before the LORD,
> For God is always near.
> Before your mind is moved to pray,
> God listens and will hear.
> (LSB 771, v. 1)

David's faith is described as a: "stilled and quieted soul," similar to a weaned child from its mother. David's strong faith statement gives hope to all of us today as to what is tremendously important – faith versus earthly matters. Our soul can only be quieted in the full knowledge of God's saving grace for His believers.

He concludes with a plea for his fellow countrymen to place their hope in the LORD both now and forevermore. (verse 3)

St. Peter stated in his first epistle, as in James' epistle, quotes the Proverbs 3:34 of "Giving grace to the humble." (1 Peter 5:5) As Christians today, we need to avoid the pressures that might engender short term success for the haughty nature. Humbleness before God always wins out over haughtiness.

Peace
Connected in Him, I stand
GHR

PSALM 132

A Dynasty: Eternal Resting Place

This psalm is one of the longer Ascent psalms. The authorship is unknown, but is suggested to be Solomon, David's son, by some theologians. This psalm is a prayer to sustain and bless the dynasty of king David, upon the permanent sanctuary, and the priesthood. The timing of this psalm is also unknown; however, my Bible side note has a question mark by the date of 1004 BC. If accurate, this would have been during David's reign. Solomon's reign was 971-931BC during which the temple was completed and dedicated.

The temple of the LORD was to be the permanent resting place for the Ark of the Covenant, which for a time, was lost until David's discovery and return to its place in Jerusalem. The author opens this psalm as a prayer for the sanctuary. The psalmist asks God to remember his servant David and his hardships. The psalmist remarks on David's focus for a permanent home for God's presence. He says, "I will allow no sleep. . .till I find a place for the Mighty One (YHWH)." (verses 4-5)

The next verse reflects on David's attempt to find the Ark and restore its home in Jerusalem. Here the author mentions Ephrathah (Bethlehem) where David heard where the Ark was hidden. The "field of Jaar" may refer to a town where the Ark was found in the home of Abinadab.

The author shows excitement that the Ark can return to its resting place and that the LORD can be worshipped there. Verse seven demonstrates the author's love for God's house – worshipping at the footstool of his throne (New Living Translation) In 1 Chronicles 28:2,

David outlines his plans for the temple, "Listen to me, my brothers and my people, I had it in my heart to build a house as a place of rest for the Ark of the Covenant of the LORD, for the **footstool of our God.**" (emphasis added)

Verse eight is similar to Solomon's prayer prior to the dedication of the temple. Listen: "Now arise, O LORD God, and come to your resting place, You and the Ark of Your might. May Your priests, O LORD God, be clothed with salvation, may Your saints rejoice in Your goodness. O LORD God do not reject Your anointed one. Remember the kindnesses great love promised to David your servant." (2 Chronicles 6:41-42)

Verses 11-12 begin with a restatement of God's promise (oath) that one of his descendants will sit on the throne – including the son of David. 2 Chronicles records a statement by God to Solomon regarding his faithful service. "As for you, if you walk before me as David your father did, and do all I command, and observe my decrees and laws, I will establish your royal throne, as I covenanted with David your father." (2 Chronicles 7:17-18) God's promises are sure as the sun rising each day. The LORD chose Zion for His dwelling place where He will rest forever. Some have suggested that this section of the psalm is Messianic as Jesus was the son of David, and that we all will rest forever with Him as we follow His statutes.

The psalmist repeats a section from 2 Chronicles 6:41b related to clothing her priests with salvation (verse 16), and the saints will sing for joy. God promises to make the house of David powerful (horn = strength). The dynasty will continue to the Anointed One as a lamp with an unending supply of oil. The psalmist concludes with a continued promise to clothe Israel's enemies in garments of shame. Verse 18b states: "but the crown on his head will be resplendent (Hebrew: blossom, shine, sparkle)."

The "eternal resting" title used here is most appropriate as we continue to see how God's promises are sure. Like David and his heirs, we too can rest on his promises as we continue to walk in faith and not by sight. The son of David continues to reign eternally at the right hand of God in power and majesty. While this earthly journey is short, we can fall asleep in Jesus knowing full well that God will call forth His faithful to be with Him eternally.

These words are from a famous Advent hymn about the promised King to set us free and to give us rest. *Come, Thou Long-Expected Jesus*, by Charles Wesley, 1707-88.

> Come Thou long expected Jesus, born to set Thy people free;
> From our fears and sins release us; Let us find our rest in Thee.
> Israel's strength and consolation,
> Hope of all the earth Thou art,
> Dear desire of ev'ry nation,
> Joy of ev'ry longing heart.
> (LSB 338 v. 1)

Peace
Connected in Him, I stand
GHR

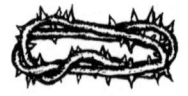

PSALM 133

One in the LORD

Abraham Lincoln once said in a speech in Springfield, Illinois, "A house divided against itself cannot stand." (6/16/1858) The speech was made at the conclusion of the Illinois Republican Convention at which Lincoln was nominated to run for U. S. Senate against Stephen Douglas. The speech, of course, warned of the issue of slavery that was dividing the young country.

In David's Psalm of Ascent, he is clearly speaking about unity. Just exactly the type of unity is not totally clear, but as H. C. Leupold in his *Exposition of the Psalms* quotes Luther saying: "The psalmist attempts to sing the praise of unity in every form." As an ascent psalm, it is a prayer for unity among those who are traveling and worshipping in Jerusalem. It could also be true brotherly (family) unity; and then again, it could be unity of Israel and Judah under king David. Regardless, the unity theme is clearly stated in this short psalm.

In the *Essential Bible Companion of the Psalms*, the author states: "Unity—like precious oil indeed, poured out on the head and running down, dripping onto our hearts—a holy anointing."

In N. T. times, our LORD prayed on many an occasion, but at this particular time His prayer was called His "High Priestly Prayer" as recorded in John 17. In the section where He prays for all believers, Jesus says: "May they be brought to complete unity to let the world know that you sent Me and have loved them even as you have loved Me." (John 17:23)

Following the ascension of our LORD, St. Paul became an apostle as he traveled all over the Mediterranean to preach the Gospel to the Gentiles and the Jews living in the area. In his encyclical letter to the church at Ephesus, he opens with encouraging words of unity to the believers, Jew or Greek. He says: "And He made known to us the mystery of His will according to His good pleasure, which he purposed in Christ, to be put into effect when the times will have reached their fulfillment – to bring all things in heaven and on earth together under one head, even Christ." (Ephesians 1:9-10) Later in his epistle, Paul reminds the church that just as we have been called to one hope – one LORD, one faith and one baptism; one God and Father of all, who is over all and through all and in all." (Ephesians 4:4-6, paraphrased)

May our prayer be like David's that we have unity in the Spirit of God until we are joined together in the heavenly realms.

Peace
Connected in Him, I stand
GHR

PSALM 134

A Call to Service and Praise

This is the concluding Ascent Psalm in Book V. These 15 psalms are also called "Pilgrim Songs." The final psalm is anonymous but is definitely addressing priestly duties. Several settings have been suggested including priests calling the assembly of worshipers to praise. The other scenario is the departing worshipers leaving the priests with an admonition to praise the LORD during the service of their duties.

The first two verses call for the servants of the LORD to give him praise in their duties, especially at night. 1 Chronicles 9, while a genealogy chapter, delineates the priestly duties both day and night. (verses 26-34) "Life up your hands," says the psalmist in their praise to the LORD. The final verse is a priestly blessing to the pilgrims as they depart. "May the LORD, the Maker of heaven and earth; bless you from Zion." (verse 3)

Israel was aware of priestly blessings dating back to Aaron when the LORD gave instructions to Moses for Aaron to bless the Israelites. Today, we hear the Aaronic Blessing frequently at the end of the church service as the pastor blesses the worshipers on their departure into the world. **"The LORD bless you and keep you; the LORD make His face shine upon you and be gracious unto you; the LORD turn His face toward you and give you peace."** (Numbers 6:24-26, emphasis added)

These 15 psalms have been a great lesson for me and hope for you also. As we travel to our various worship sites to give praise to the

LORD, the Maker of heaven and earth, let us sing his praises enroute in preparation for our corporate worship.

Peace
Connected in Him, I stand
GHR

PSALM 135

A Treasured Possession

This psalm is the beginning of a list of five psalms (135-139) that are classed as Psalms of Thanksgiving. H. C. Leupold, in his *Exposition of the Psalms*, calls this psalm a mosaic as its verses mirror others from various O. T. books including Psalms. The timing of this psalm seems to coincide with the post-exilic period as some theologians point to Nehemiah. As a mosaic, the historian Maclaren remarks, "The flowers are arranged in a new bouquet, because the poet had long delighted in their fragrance," as stated by H. C. Leupold in his *Exposition of the Psalms*. Many agree that this psalm was used in the temple worship; and may have been sung antiphonally (responsive).

I have prepared a table that compares various verses in this psalm to other O. T. sources that if not exact are, remarkably similar. (Mosaic nature)

Previous O. T. Reference	Psalm 135
Ps 113:1	v. 1
Ps 134:1	v. 2
Exodus 19:5	v. 4
Deut. 7:6	v. 4
Exodus 19:5	v. 5
Exodus 18:11	v. 5
Jer. 10:13	v. 7
Ps 136:17-22	v. 10-12
Is. 44:12-20	v. 13-18

Jer. 10:6-10	v. 13-18
Ps 115:4-11	v. 15-20

Source: H. C. Leupold, *Exposition of the Psalms*

The psalmist opens with the *Hallelujah* phrase, Praise the Lord. The same phrase is used 10 times throughout the psalm. The first four verses could be a summons for all to praise the LORD from the temple servants to the pilgrims who worship Him. The psalmist reminds all who praise His name that He is good. (verse 4). Jesus himself used that term in his conversation with the rich young man. The man asked Jesus, "What good thing must I do to get eternal life?" To which Jesus said, "Why do you ask me about what is good? There is only One who is good." (Matthew 19:16-17)

The psalmist is truly clear to note that the True God (LORD) is greater than all other gods. The prophet Isaiah says, "And there is no God apart from me." (Isaiah 45:21c) Why? Because He is the creator of all things in heaven and on earth. He rules all nature! The psalmist also reminds us that He delivers us from our enemies, including the slave-driving Egyptians. He also struck down multiple kings including King Og, King Sihon, and all the kings of Canaan. (31 total – see Joshua 12) The result is that all the land was given to Israel as His inheritance.

He made Israel his treasured possession (see Exodus 19:5). They left Egypt as a group of slaves; and arrived in the Promised Land as a treasured possession of the LORD, their Deliverer. The name of the LORD endures forever (verse 13), says the psalmist, and reminds us that he vindicates us (from sin), and has compassion on those who fear him. (verse 14)

He concludes this mosaic by reminding us that all are servants. Beginning in verse 19, he lists the nation of Israel: the priestly line of Aaron, the Levites as priestly servants, and finally ALL who fear Him. (emphasis added).

This gracious and compassionate God has delivered you and me from damnation as slaves to sin just as He delivered Israel from slavery. Together, we are all treasured in God's sight. Listen to St. Peter in his epistle: "But you are a chosen people, a royal priesthood, a holy nation, a people belonging to God, that you may declare the praises of Him who called you out of darkness (slavery to sin) into His marvelous light. (1 Peter 2:9 -emphasis added)

Peace
Connected in Him, I stand
GHR

PSALM 136

His Love Endures Forever

This psalm continues the theme of thankfulness and is marked by a chorus that is repeated throughout the psalm: *"His love endures forever"*. The prophet Jeremiah lived in terrible times for Israel and the Kingdom of Judah. Not only did he experience their captivity by the Babylonians, but he also experienced the end of the monarchy. In Jeremiah, the promise of the restoration is pronounced. Jeremiah then gives us this passage: "Give thanks to the LORD Almighty, for the LORD is good; his love endures forever." (Jeremiah 33:11)

In the Jewish tradition, this psalm is known as "The Great Hallel." This psalm is separate from the section of psalms (113-118) known as the Hallel. This 26-verse psalm has 22 lines of praise that mirrors the number of letters in the Hebrew alphabet. There are four lines for praise to the LORD/God with three at the beginning and one at the end of the chapter.

The psalmist refers to the LORD as "God of gods," and "LORD of lords." These references are taken from Moses' Deuteronomy. Moses reminds the people what God asks of them: "Fear the LORD your God, to walk in all His ways, to love Him, to serve the LORD thy God with all thy heart and with all thy soul" (Deuteronomy 10:12 KJV) Then in later verses Moses says, "For the LORD your God is God of gods and LORD of lords." (Deuteronomy 10:17 KJV). The psalmist recognizes that the world is not monotheistic. So, he enumerates on the wonders of God going into great poetic details of His creation.

The wonders never cease! He then details God's saving deliverance and how He subjected the Egyptians to death and then delivered the Israelites out with His mighty hand! He showed His control over nature by dividing the Red Sea for safe passage then caused the sea to recede and confine the pursuers to their watery grave. God continued to lead His people through the desert of potential death and provided their every need - even with grumbling.

Once they arrived in the Promised Land, God continued His covenant and promise to deliver the enemies to Israel with His right hand of power. Kings were powerless even with their armies.

The final verses are a concluding summary of the praise to God for His marvelous deeds. The Mighty One remembered us in our weakness (lowly estate), freed us from our enemies (physical and spiritual), and provides for our earthly daily needs. Then the final praise statement to summarize the psalmist's beautiful two-part (bicola) lines.

In our time, we too can relate to this "Great Hallel." Like our Jewish brothers and sisters, we too can say, "His love endures forever." I would refer you back to Moses in Deuteronomy 10:12 and his fourfold advice to his people:

- Fear the LORD
- Walk in His ways
- Love Him
- Serve Him.

Peace
Connected in Him, I stand
GHR

PSALM 137
Divine Retribution

This psalm is located in the middle of a group of psalms with a common theme of thankfulness. Indeed, this psalm seems to be out of place! The anonymous psalmist takes a punch at the Babylonians for their blood thirty destruction of Jerusalem. While some indicate this is written during the captive period, the past tense verbs in the first verses might suggest otherwise, possibly a short time after their release but before the defeat of Babylon by the Persians (539 BC). 2 Kings 24-25 record the fall of Jerusalem to the Babylonians. 2 Kings 24:14b suggests that 10,000 Israelites were taken into captivity by Nebuchadnezzar.

As the captives sat by the rivers, they wept tears of remorse as they recounted their beloved city of Zion. The poplar trees brought back memories of similar scenery near the Jordan River. And to top it all, their captors would berate and torment them by requesting they sing a song of joy.

The captives had no reason to sing while in a foreign land. They call down negative things on themselves if they forget their beloved city – losing their skills or in a dehydrated state! They call the City of Peace their highest joy. (verse 6) Why? Because it is where God dwells.

The final verses are calling down retribution on Babylon but also Edom who aided Babylon in overtaking Jerusalem. The O. T. lists sources of God's prophesy against both nations. The Book of Obadiah prophesies again Edom (Esau's descendants); and Isaiah, Jeremiah, and Habakkuk against Babylon.

Can you imagine living without God? The Israelites felt very much alone and abandoned. They recognized their sin and longed to be restored to their LORD God Almighty. As I recount their plight, I think about living today without God. Not a pretty sight. I am a baptized child of God who walks in the light of the Gospel (Good News) of Jesus Christ and Him crucified. I am thankful for my faith imparted by the Holy Spirit that the Evil One and his band cannot overtake me. Thanks be to God for this indescribable gift of faith and protection.

Peace
Connected in Him, I stand
GHR

PSALM 138

A Life Saver

This psalm is generally attributed to David, especially in the Hebrew text. Others, like the Septuagint do not. In fact, some theologians suggest Zechariah had something to do with this psalm, as suggested by H. C. Leupold in his *Exposition of the Psalms*. Many theologians would lean toward accepting the Hebrew text where David is listed as the author versus the alternate translation.

David opens with a mouth of praise for the "true" God as opposed to the multitude of other gods. In the O. T., the Israelites were given strict instructions to worship the one, true God (YHWH), and not to worship any other gods or idols (Isaiah 44:6) The most important commandment in Judaism is the "Shema" which is "Hear, O Israel, the LORD our God, the LORD is one." (Deuteronomy 6:4)

David reaffirms his loyalty by bowing down toward God's holy temple (Tabernacle in David's time), and praises God's name for his loving kindness and faithfulness. God made him bold and stouthearted. (verse 3) 2 Samuel records God's unfailing promise to David, "I have been with you wherever you have gone, and I have cut off your enemies before you." (2 Samuel 7:9)

David is confident that the kings of the earth will praise the LORD. David admits he walks in the midst of trouble but knows that God is his life saver! (verse 7) God's right hand (strength) saves him as He stretches out His hand against David's foes. David is sure that God's promise for him will be fulfilled as the amazing love of the true God endures forever.

Yes, like David, we too can be assured that our loving and faithful God has given us a lifesaving Jesus, His only Son. Only the true God would leave His throne and come down and live among us to do what we cannot. Save us.

Let me close with one of my favorite doxologies from the Hebrews. "May the God of peace, who through the blood of the eternal covenant brought back from the dead our LORD Jesus, that great Shepherd of the sheep, equip you with everything good for doing His will, and may He work in us what is pleasing to Him through Jesus Christ, to whom be glory for ever and ever. Amen." (Hebrews 13:20-21)

Peace
Connected in Him, I stand
GHR

PSALM 139

The All-Encompassing God

This psalm concludes the section of thanksgiving psalms and is authored by David per the Hebrew text; but not in the Greek text of the Septuagint. Like the previous psalm, there is some thought that it is associated with Zechariah. The psalmist is praising the Almighty for his all-knowing and ever-present nature.

From the opening verse, David is in awe of God's knowledge about him. He says, "You know me." That includes when he sits or rises; his thoughts and his speech even before it is spoken. The language is similar to Isaiah 40:28 where the prophet says, "The LORD is the everlasting God, the Creator of the ends of the earth. . .and His understanding no one can fathom."

Verse five is a reminder that we are never out of God's reach as He touches us wherever we go. David says, "You hem me in – behind and before." The subsequent verses are comforting to David knowing that God is always near. He offers up a rhetorical question about going somewhere where God isn't! The poetry that follows describes God's omnipresence from the depths of the earth to the heavens above. Even in the dark, God's love lights up His world.

David is aware that God is involved in all facets of his life beginning with his formation in his mother's womb. "Your works are wonderful," says David and "I am fearfully and wonderfully made." (verse 14) David's son, Solomon, later wrote, "He has made everything beautiful in its time. He has also set eternity in the hearts of men; yet they cannot fathom what God has done from beginning to end." (Ecclesiastes 3:11)

David is awe-struck at God's all-encompassing nature. "How precious to me are your thoughts, O God. . .They outnumber the grains of sand." (verses 17-18)

The final portion of this psalm departs from general theme of all-knowing and ever-present nature of God. Here the psalmist says, "If only you would slay the wicked." Perhaps his dilemma is that if God is truly all-knowing then why doesn't He take care of the wicked that are ever-present in David's time? Not only are they David's enemies but also God's (adversaries – verse 20).

The concluding verses show David's contrition in that, if God searches his heart, what would he find? If there is anything offensive, then forgive my shortcomings and lead me to Your way in eternity. David's confidence is God's all-encompassing nature brings joy to the modern-day Christian. We know that He is ever before us and always guarding our rear. God, the True Shepherd, is a guardian for His sheep in His sheep pen. St. John reminds us that He knows us by name (John 10:3) St. Paul also gives comfort to you and me when he said, "If God is for us, who can be against us?" (Romans 8:31 KJV)

Peace
Connected in Him, I stand
GHR

PSALM 140

But Deliver Me from Evil

This psalm opens a four-psalm section of prayers for protection. David is listed as the author of each of these psalms. In this psalm, David is pleading for deliverance from evil men. (verse 1) The opening words are pointedly direct, "Rescue me!" David had many enemies over his time as King of Israel and Judah. But as *Halley's Bible Handbook* comments, "It drew him closer to God."

Evil men assailed David certainly as the warrior king. God indeed delivered all of David's enemies who sought to overtake him. Now David once again pleads for God to protect him from the men of violence and their evil plans that they constantly stir up. He uses the metaphor of "sharp as a serpent's tongue" and poison on their lips. "Keep me," says David, and "Protect me." (verse 4) David knows that his enemies have set traps to snare him.

This theme of deliverance from evil (one) is certainly recognizable in the Lord's Prayer. Matthew's Gospel records the prayer with plea for deliverance, however, Luke's version does not. David reiterates his faithfulness to his God as God promised to deliver His servant (2 Samuel 7). Yes, the LORD is his strong deliverer and shield in the heat of battle.

David calls down judgment on his enemies. His imprecatory prayer is that their head be covered with trouble caused by the sharpness of their tongues. Furthermore, he calls down coals of fire on them including landing in the fiery pit. David concludes with his confidence in God's justice as He protects those in need.

The final verse is directed to you and me today. "Surely the righteous will praise your name and the upright will live before you." (verse 13) Those who walk in faith know that there is only one God, the Creator, the Redeemer, and the Sanctifier – Holy Trinity. Listen to the hymnist *We Praise You, O God:*

> We worship You, God of our fathers, we bless You;
> Through trial and tempest our guide You have been.
> When perils o'er take us, You will not forsake us,
> And with Your help, O LORD, our struggles we win.
> (LSB 785, v. 2)

Peace
Connected in Him, I stand
GHR

PSALM 141

Check List

David continues his psalm of a prayer for protection. In this case, it's a check list of sorts, that is an effort to keep him on the straight and narrow versus falling into the traps of wicked deeds. Theologians place this writing circa Absalom's rebellion. This psalm has traditionally been considered an evening prayer and used during Vespers. According to H. C. Leupold in his *Exposition of the Psalms*, he states that, "Psalm 63 is the corresponding morning prayer."

The psalmist opens with a request to "come quickly." David is troubled and cries out for his prayer to be heard like incense and his lifting up of his hands (prayer) like an evening sacrifice (sin offering). Why? David is apparently in pain over words and deeds. Jesus reminds us about the words of our mouth in Matthew 12:37. "For by your words you will be acquitted, and by your words you will be condemned." He continues with his check list by praying that God will keep his heart from doing evil as the wicked. The wicked make their sinning seem like a delicacy.

David is open to being rebuked by a righteous man. Solomon in his book Ecclesiastes says, "It is better to heed a wise man's rebuke than to listen to the song of fools." (Ecclesiastes 7:5) So, David's check list includes keeping his mouth bridled; his heart in tune and his eyes fixed on his LORD. (paraphrased from various verses).

David shifts gears slightly and now adds imprecations to the wicked. "The rulers (evil) be thrown down from the cliffs." Verse seven may be difficult to understand but perhaps is better understood elsewhere in scripture. Isaiah is clear regarding the dead and a resurrection, "But your dead will live; their bodies will rise. You who dwell in the dust, wake up and shout for joy. Your dew is like the dew of the morning; the earth will give birth to her dead." (Isaiah 26:19) A note in my Bible margin says, "Gospel assurance."

David concludes his check list by promising to keep his eyes fixed on Jesus, his Sovereign LORD in whom he takes refuge. The author to Hebrews says it this way, "Let us fix our eyes on Jesus, the author and perfecter of our faith, who for the joy set before Him endured the cross, scorning its shame, and sat down at the right hand of the throne of God." (Hebrews 12:2)

David's final statement is his prayer is to pass by the traps of the wicked and maintain his path of safety. Amen.

Peace
Connected in Him, I stand
GHR

PSALM 142

The Cave of Loneliness

As anointed to assume the throne as King of Judah, David was pursued by king Saul to annihilate him. This psalm is likely written during this time frame when Saul was in hot pursuit of David. The subscript of this psalm says, "When he was in the cave." 1 Samuel tells us of David's constant moving about to avoid Saul's pursuit. The 24th chapter continues the story where Saul learns of David's whereabouts in En Gedi (Spring of a kid) on the west shore of the Dead Sea. David and his men were deep in the cave where Saul entered to relief himself. Unnoticed, David was able to clip off a portion of his robe. More to follow on the rest of the story!

David opens this psalm with him crying aloud and lifting up his voice (in prayer) for mercy. David was ready to pour out his complaint to the LORD but prior to that he acknowledged that only God knows his path. David's cry for refuge as no one cares for his life. But then professes that only God is his portion in the land of the living. This idea of "portion" is noted that the tribe of Levi had no land in the 12-tribe division but were given access to a portion of each division for their personal use.

Now, David says, "I am in desperate need." He is in the same cave as his pursuer. He is lonely and continues to move from place to place to avoid Saul. "Rescue me," says David. And rescue He did! David bowed down to Saul and said, "The LORD has delivered you into my hands in the cave." (1 Samuel 24:10) The rest of the story is that Saul was clearly weeping. He said, "May the LORD reward you well for the way you treated me." (1 Samuel 24:19)

David says, "Set me free from my prison." (verse 7) The cave was not only physical but also an emotional plea for God to release him from the pursuers of this world. He is always bent on praising the LORD God Almighty and prays that the righteous will gather about me because of Your goodness to me.

God indeed continued to deliver and bless David throughout his career as the King of Israel and Judah. He handed over multiple enemies to David despite the odds against David's army.

As we read through David's trials, let us all remember that life delivers its punches sometimes to the gut. But we too can rebound just as David did. His faith was so strong that nothing in this world could overcome him and God's plan for his leadership over the people of God. May we remember that when we appear to be in a cave of loneliness, there is light at the end of the tunnel, and God will deliver us from the evil one and his pursuers.

Peace
Connected in Him, I stand
GHR

PSALM 143

The 10 Verbs of Request

This psalm of David is the final psalm in this section (140-143) on the subject of protection. Some suggest this was written by David during Absalom's pursuit of his father. In my initial review of the verses in this psalm, I found 10 definitive verbs requesting God's assistance. The table below lists the verbs and their corresponding verse.

Verse, No.	Verb
V. 1, #1	Hear my prayer
V. 1, #2	Listen to my cry
V. 7, #3	Answer me quickly
V. 8, #4	Show me the way
V. 9, #5	Rescue me from my enemies
V. 10, #6	Teach me Your will
V. 10, #7	Lead me on level ground
V. 11, #8	Preserve my life
V. 11, #9	Bring me out of trouble
V. 12, #10	Silence my enemies

David continues to pen a psalm of protection and deliverance. David opens with a plea for God to hear his prayer and cry for mercy. (#1 and #2) David is confident of God's faithfulness and righteousness for his relief. The enemy of David continues to pursue him and seeks to crush David to the ground, like dwelling in darkness.

As such, he is deep in depression (my spirit grows faint within me) and his heart is dismayed. Even with his constant prayers, he continues to thirst for an answer like a parched land. "Answer me," (#3) says David. And quickly! If God hides his face, then David's doom is clear.

"Show me," (#4) says David, the way he should go. "Rescue me," (#5) for he hides in God's protective governance.

"Teach me," (#6) to do Your will and may Your spirit "lead me," (#7) to level ground. David is confident that God can lead him from the pit of damnation to level ground where all things are possible. "Preserve my life," (#8) because of God's righteousness and "Bring me," (#9) out of trouble.

Finally, David says, "Silence," (#10) my enemies and my foes for I am your servant. David's verbs used here are positive and not just demanding but a personal plea for God's deliverance from his pursuers. From David's initial plea to his final verb of silencing his enemies, we too can be confident in God's great mercy as He promises those in faith to be with them forever.

As we face today's trials, regardless of the source, we too can offer up the verbs of request for deliverance from our trials and tribulations much like David.

Peace
Connected in Him, I stand
GHR

PSALM 144

Battle Song

Psalm 144 is part of a two-psalm collection classed as "Songs of Praise." David is the author of both Psalms 144 and 145. H. C. Leupold, in his *Exposition on the Psalms*, indicates this psalm may in fact be a compilation of previous psalm content. For sure, Psalm 8 and 18 are quoted and possibly others (33, 102-104). *Halley's Bible Handbook* calls this psalm as one of "David's Battle Songs." The timing of this psalm is in question as dates vary from as late as Nehemiah while other suggest that Hezekiah is the king speaking here (Oesterley per Leupold). King Hezekiah reigned from 716-687 BC which would have been prior to the Judean captivity in Babylon.

Regardless of the timing, theologians agree that the contents agree with the life and spirit of David, especially from 1 Samuel 17:47 (Goliath and the Philistines). The battle song begins with *a Hallel* (praise) to the LORD (YHWH) and the Rock who is instrumental in preparing the author's hands for battle. The psalmist calls God his loving-kindness (KJV), his fortress, his stronghold, his deliverer, and his shield. It is He who subdues the enemy. To quote I Samuel 17, "All those gathered here will know that it is not by sword or spear that the LORD saves; for the battle is the LORD's and He will give all of you into our hands." (1 Samuel 17:47) The psalmist realizes that what is man to deserve all that God has done? (verse 3) This verse is a quote from Psalm 8:4, "What is man that you care for him, the son of man that you think of him?" "Man is like a breath," says the psalmist. (verse 4)

The psalmist reminds the reader that God can control all things from His heavenly abode from sending lightening to using His right hand to scatter the enemies. "I will sing a new song to You, O God . . .on a ten-stringed lyre." (verse 9) The lyre (kinnor) is one of the oldest musical instruments in the O. T. Genesis 4:21 first mentions it in the descendants of Cain. Jubal was known as the father of all who played the lyre and the flute. The lyre had a varying number of strings (3-12) but usually 10 which were made from sheep's small intestine. David played the lyre and the nevel (kinnor/lyre but larger and louder). The song of praise was offered to the One who gives victory and who delivers His servant David from the deadly sword. (verse 10) The Mighty One is the only one who can deliver from the deceitful enemy of Israel and Judah.

The final four verses pray for prosperity. Our sons and daughters will be like well-nurtured plants and pillars and their barns will overflow while their flock's flourish. The walls of God's City will not be breached, nor will its people be withdrawn by its captors. The final prayer of the psalmist is the LORD's blessing on all who fear and love Him.

Peace
Connected in Him, I stand
GHR

PSALM 145
The Exalted God and King

What else can we say? Our God is exalted as the King of Kings and LORD of Lords. His name is to be praised by all forever and ever. This psalm, like others before it, is an alphabetic acrostic psalm. The only exception was the letter *nun* (verse 13b) was omitted in the copying process but was corrected and inserted in the Septuagint. Dr. H. C. Leupold in his *Exposition on the Psalms,* quotes his colleague, Dr. A. F. Kirkpatrick from his book, *Cambridge Bible for Schools & Colleges: Psalms IV & V.* "This noble doxology worthily heads the series of Psalms of Praise with which the "Book of Praises" ends. "Thine is the kingdom, the power, and the glory, for ever and ever," is the thought which it expands. It is addressed to Israel's God as the supreme King, whose kingdom is universal and eternal; it celebrates His majesty, greatness, and goodness; His providential care for all His creation; His constant love towards those who love and fear Him. Its most striking feature is its universalism."

As Dr. Kirkpatrick (1849-1940) notes, this is the final psalm of praise (144-145) prior to the *Hallelujah* psalms (146-150). I'm not sure more can be said of this psalm in addition to Dr. Kirkpatrick's quote from his ageless book. But I'll try!

Following the first two verses which gives a resolution to praise the LORD forever, we see the psalmist delve into great detail about God's greatness that the mind's eye cannot fathom. Each generation will tell of His acts and will meditate on His mighty works. Their joy is a celebration of God's goodness to them in their abundance. (verse 7)

The following verse is the summary verse that shows the fundamental greatness of God's character. "The LORD is gracious and compassionate, slow to anger and rich in love." (verse 8) God's compassion extends to all His creation including you and me. Yes, He is faithful in all His promises and loving to everything He made. (verse 13b) More importantly, He holds us up when we fall!

The next two verses (verses 15-16) are called a "Common Prayer." It's a prayer that I learned as a catechumen. I still remember it from the KJV, "The eyes of all wait upon Thee and Thou givest them their meat in due season. Thou openest Thy hand and satisfies the desire of every living thing." The Book of Common Prayer dates to 1549 in the Church of England.

The psalmist gives great comfort in the final verses that show the LORD and His closeness to all those who walk in faith. He fulfills their desires and hears their cry for help. He watches over ALL (emphasis added) who love Him. (verse 20)

The *Essential Bible Companion of the Psalms* offers this comment in its closing Reflection on Psalm 145, "This is a glimpse of the Revelation vision in which John heard, 'To Him who sits on the throne and to the Lamb be praise and honor and glory and power, for ever and ever." (Revelation 5:13b)

Peace
Connected in Him, I stand
GHR

THE FINAL HALLEL: PSALMS 146-150

As the Book of Psalms comes to a close, we see the "Final Hallel." Each of the psalms in this section opens and closes with "*Hallelujah.*" The final chapter's use of the verb praise varies per Alma Brodersen's *End of the Psalter: Psalms 146-10 in Masoretic Text.* She states that there are three different counts based on the reference – up to 13 times.

This section is "final," but this is the third section in Psalms that contain Hallel psalms. The first is 113-118 which is also known as the Egyptian Hallel (or just Hallel). These psalms were used in particular during Passover meals.

Some sources list a host of psalms entitled, "The Great Hallel." They include 120-136. But many only list Psalm 136 as the Great Hallel (Talmud). Psalms 120-134 are called psalms of "Ascent." Only Psalm 134 (the concluding Ascent psalm) opens with Praise the LORD.

The psalms in the Final Hallel were thought to have been composed following the Israelite's return from Babylonian captivity although not really known for sure. The Vulgate and the LXX (Septuagint) attribute Psalms 146 and 147 to Haggai and Zechariah respectively. Each of these prophets served in between 522-509 BC for Zechariah and 520 BC for Haggai. Again, evidence is scant to confirm their authorship.

The first of the Final Hallel is sometimes called, "Hymn of Praise of Zion's Heavenly King." (source: bible.ucg.org). The *Institute of Creation Research* in its publication, *The Hallelujah Psalms*, could be considered a great "Hallelujah Chorus." The word "hallelujah" occurs 22 times in Psalms, which corresponds to the number of letters in the Hebrew alphabet. The author also points out that it is possible (probable?) that these five psalms will constitute the testimonies of praise and thanksgiving that will be sung by this great congregation in the presence of the Lamb.

A Jewish reference includes Psalm 145 called "Ashrei" followed by 146-150. The qualifier of *pesukei dezimra* is added to Hallel to define and differentiate the unqualified Hallel (113-118). The term *pesukei dezimra* is translated "Daily Hallel."

The table below summarizes the three Hallel sections in Psalms.

Hallel Section	Title
113-118	Hallel or Egyptian Hallel
136	The Great Hallel
146-150	The Final Hallel

Total 12 Psalms (Count varies re: what psalms are included in The Great Hallel)

If the assumption that only Psalm 136 is the Great Hallel, then the total number of psalms included in all sections is 12 which corresponds to the number of tribes of Israel.

Please pray that God will open your mind and heart to the coming notes of the Final Hallel. Praise the Lord!

Peace
Connected in Him, I stand
GHR

PSALM 146

God is My Help and My Hope

At first and second reading, I could not help but make a list of the attributes/character of God. Once you read and review the table below, does this remind you of our LORD Jesus who fulfilled all O. T. prophesies? Let's see.

Psalm Verse	God is/does
6	Maker of Heaven and Earth
7	Upholds the oppressed
7	Provider of food to hungry
7	Releases prisoners
8	Restores sight to blind
8	Lifts up the lowly
8	Loves the righteous
9	Watches over alien
9	Sustains fatherless/widows
9	Frustrates the wicked

The first two verses open with four references to "praise." The psalmist promises to give praise to the LORD all his life including his inmost soul which means his entire being. He compares trusting God versus man who is mortal and once dead, their plans are nil! His total hope is in the LORD!

Why is his hope rested in the LORD? Well, his first statement is that He is the Creator of all things: the heavens, the earth, the sky, the seas and everything in it. God is the provider of food to the hungry which is every human being. He provides justice to the imprisoned by releasing their bonds. (NOTE: Our Savior released the bonds of sin for us on Calvary's cross and granted us freedom in His Gospel). He uplifts the lowly and watches over strangers (aliens) and indeed looks after the orphans and widows. He does all these "helpful" things to His creation but in the end, He frustrates the wicked who would seek to devour His people.

Yes, the LORD reigns forever and is the eternal king of Zion. Blessed is the nation that claims this God of Israel. Thus, we have a concluding and resounding Amen in Praise the LORD.

Peace
Connected in Him, I stand
GHR

PSALM 147

The Hallel Continues: An Invitation to Praise

Reverend Dirk J Human, Department of Old Testament Studies at the University of Pretoria, South Africa refers to the five books of the Final Hallel as: "A crescendo that perpetuates the theme of praising YHWH – first by individual (146), then the community (147) and ultimately the whole creation (148; 150). The then-doctoral candidate, Reverend Kilman Cha breaks down this psalm into three sections. The first is an invitation to praise that shows Israel's God as the restorer and caretaker of both humans and stars. The second invitation (verse 7) shows YHWH as the provider of necessities to both animals and humans. The final call to praise (verse 12) shows the God of Zion as He blesses His people with peace and prosperity. (*Ps 146-150: The Final Hallelujah Psalms as a Fivefold Doxology to the Hebrew Psalter; December 2006; Department of Religion, Baylor University*)

The timing of this psalm seems most appropriate for the time of Nehemiah (~445 BC) based on the language, "Building up Jerusalem, gathers exiles of Israel, and binding wounds." (various verses) It is also interesting to examine the transition of the Final Hallel per *Halley's Bible Handbook*. The table below describes the transition.

Psalm	Topic
146	Individual
147	All creation; community
148	Angels and the heavens
149	Saints
150	Let everything that has breath

The psalmist says, "How good it is to sing praises to our God!" (verse 1) Yes, the post-exile Israelites have been freed (second Exodus) from Babylonian captivity. He has gathered them and has healed the broken hearts and bound their wounds as the physician YHWH. He continues noting God's Wisdom when he notes and names the number of stars in the heavens. God is mighty in power and His understanding is infinite, and finally sustains the humble while casting out the wicked.

The second section is God's great provision to all He created and sustains. He dots the skies with clouds and causes rain to water the earth and its inhabitants. He provides food to all both animal and mankind alike. Finally, he delights in those who have placed their faith in Him as they put their hope in His unfailing love.

The final section begins in verse 12. (The LXX separates verses 12-20 into a separate psalm.) Peace and prosperity are important to God's people having been enslaved for decades and separated from the Holy City of God. Not only does He strengthen their gates (wall) but grants peace to its borders. He supplies every need to His people including His control over nature. His Word created and His Word melts the icy blasts. God did not leave His people without instruction (laws and decrees). No, He gave them to its fathers (Jacob) and all generations that follow.

Praise the LORD!

Peace
Connected in Him, I stand
GHR

PSALM 148

Praise Ye the Heavenly Hosts

Everyone and everything praise the LORD! Without exception! I am reminded of a hymn: *Heavenly Hosts in Ceaseless Worship.* Listen to its words:

> Heav'nly hosts in ceaseless worship "Holy, holy, holy" cry;
> "He who is, who was and will be, God
> Almighty, LORD Most High."
> Praise and honor, pow'r and glory, Be to Him who reigns alone!
> We, with all His hands have fashioned, Fall before the Father's throne.
> (LSB 949)

The Final Hallel takes on a new focus. This time it's the angels, the heavenly hosts and all the created light. Genesis 1 records the six days of creation and on Day 4, he created the heaven's lights: the sun, moon and stars. St. John records in his Revelation, that all heaven's angels said, "Worthy is the Lamb, who was slain; to receive power and wealth and wisdom and strength and honor and glory and praise!" (Revelation 5:12)

Verse seven elaborates on everything giving praise to YHWH. Even the sights and sounds of the heavens, the mountains and hills, the fruit trees and cedars, the animals and birds of the air, and all mankind whether kings or princes, Praise the LORD!

My various readings of this psalm created a spirit of awe running down my spine. I cannot fathom the true holiness of my God and Savior. He has done all things well, says scripture. His endless love for

His creation is farther than east is from the west. He is the "horn of my salvation" (2 Samuel 22:3). The psalmist concludes this beautiful Hallel with a notation that he raised up a horn (strength, kingly) for His people. That horn is the horn of salvation that is Jesus the Christ.

The next time you look up to the skies, remember, they too are praising God by their action of light, wind, and clouds for rain. The mountains point to heaven with their snow-capped peaks. The ocean's waves are clapping their hands. The trees, the fields and earth bring forth its fruit in due season giving glory to God.

Peace
Connected in Him, I stand
GHR

PSALM 149
Let All the Saints Rejoice

Sinner and Saint! Yes, I am both. By one man's sin, sin entered the world and so all have sinned and are separated from God. But, God in His mercy, created a path for salvation through His Son. A saint in human terms is different than in Biblical terms. Saints are the whole body of those who are righteous in God's sight based on the blood of the Lamb of God. In O. T. times, they believed in God's promise of a Savior and lived a life of atonement and believed in His presence via the priests selected by God. In N. T. times we live in post-resurrection times but with the same promise as in days of old.

The psalmist is eager to offer a new song for all the assembly to offer praise to the Almighty. The Hebrew word (*chasid*) means saint or pious. This new song was to be a song of praise in the assembly of its saints. Israel and Zion were to rejoice in their Maker with dancing and music. Why? The LORD takes pleasure in its people as they seek His salvation. The psalmist says, "He crowns the humble with salvation." (verse 4) Regardless of their status, their joy is overwhelming – even from their beds.

God's praise can emanate from their throats (mouths) but also with the Word of God which is a two-edged sword. In Bible times, the two-edged sword was a lethal weapon. The N. T. refers to the "Sword of the Spirit which is the Word of God." (Ephesians) The author to the Hebrews says, "For the Word of God is living and active, sharper than any double-edged sword." (Hebrews 4:12) In this psalm the sword is very offensive in conquering nations, kings, nobles, and anyone who is against the LORD of Glory.

The prophet Daniel in his book says, "Then the sovereignty, power and greatness of the kingdoms under the whole heaven will be handed over to the saints, the people of the Most High. His kingdom will be an everlasting kingdom, and all rulers will worship and obey Him." (Daniel 7:27)

Yes, the two-edged sword is used offensively to inflict vengeance and punishment, bind their kings and nobles in chains and shackles, and to carry out the sentence (judgment) written against them. Glory be to the Saints of the Most High! (El Elyon).

As I conclude my almost yearlong study and writing, I am drawn once again to a beautiful hymn that was written in the early 20th century. It's included in the section called "Church Triumphant" in my hymnal of reference. The title is: *Thine the Amen, Thine the Praise.*

> Thine the Amen Thine the praise
> Alleluias angels raise
> Thine the everlasting head
> Thine the breaking of the bread
> Thine the glory Thine the story
> Thine the harvest then the cup
> Thine the vineyard then the cup is lifted up; lifted up.
> (LSB 680)

Let me conclude with my favorite N. T. doxology from Jude. "Now unto Him who is able to keep you from falling and to present you blameless before His glorious throne with great joy – to the only true God our LORD Jesus Christ be glory and honor; power and dominion both now and forevermore. Amen. (Jude 24-25 paraphrased).

Peace,
Connected in Him, I stand
GHR

PSALM 150

The Crescendo of the Psalter

This chapter of the Final Hallel and is the "Grand Finale." Book V of the Psalms is very long and the longest of the five books in Psalms. Theologically, the first three books were hopeless but the final two books brought hope to the Israelites from their captivity in Babylonia. The final book offers a meditative pilgrimage, per Dr. Human in his *"Praise Beyond Words."*

This psalm is the fifth of the "Final Hallel." It is a doxology giving praise to the LORD Most High. This psalm has a 10-fold repetition of praise (1b-5) which has some Biblical significance. First, there are 10 words of creation and then 10 words of the law (decalogue).

This psalm is not worthy of final study. Rather, God in His wisdom has included all who have been made by Him as the embodiment of those who give constant praise and thanksgiving to the One and only True God.

As I mentioned in my initial *"From Beginning to End,"* this psalm is the conclusion or bookend from the earliest of chapters (1-2). The interim chapters have shown God's continued blessing despite His people's sin and their ignorance of His laws and decrees.

We have seen multiple authors and speakers of God's Word during centuries of time, but one thing remains, "His love endures forever." Amen.

May the One True God who has called you out of darkness into His marvelous light, give you insight and wisdom into His Word as you read and study.

To God be the Glory!

Peace
Connected in Him, I stand
GHR

BIBLIOGRAPHY: REFLECTIONS: JOURNEY THROUGH THE PSALMS

By: G. H. Roesener
Saturday's Notes Publishing

Halley's Bible Handbook: by Henry H. Halley; Deluxe Edition, NIV Version; 25th Edition.

Exposition of the Psalms: by H. C. Leupold, D. D.; The Wartburg Press; 1959.

Nave's Topical Bible: by Orville J. Nave; Hendrickson Publishers, 14th Edition, Marcy 2013

Thompson Chain-Reference Bible: New International Version; B. B. Kirkbride Bible Co., Inc., Indianapolis, Indiana, 1990

Life Application Bible: NIV Version; Tyndale House Publishers, Inc. and Zondervan Publishing House; 1988 and following.

Lutheran Service Book: The Commission on Worship of the Lutheran Church – Missouri Synod; Concordia Publishing House, St. Louis, MO.; 2006.

Rose Book of Bible Charts, Maps & Time Lines: Rose Publishing; 10th Edition; 2005 and following.

Matthew Henry's Commentary: biblegateway.com/resources/ Matthew-henry/Psalms

Luther's Small Catechism: Lutheran Service Book, p. 321ff; The Third Article, Apostle's Creed, What Does This Mean?

The Gospel of Mark: The Compassionate Christ: By G. H. Roesener; December 2015.

How Great Thou Art: https://en.wikipedia.org/wiki/How_Great_Thou_Art

Essential Bible Companion to the Psalms: Brian L. Webster and David R. Beach; Bible by Olive Tree.

American Tract Society Bible Dictionary: www.studylight.org/dictionaries/ats.html

Psalms, Volume I: 1-72: C. Hassell Bullock; Baker Book House, August 2015

The Psalms (Old Testament Library): Artur Weiser, 1962.

Strong's Hebrew and Greek Dictionary: www.biblehub.com

Why Does God Always Demand Praise? Essay by C. S. Lewis

Bible Study on the Book of Nehemiah Chapter 3: The Gates of Jerusalem: The Gates of Spiritual Progression; I. Gordon; www.jesusplusnothing.com/studies/online/nehem3.htm

Cambridge Bible for Schools & Colleges: Psalms IV & V: A. F. Kirkpatrick; Cambridge University Press; 1906.

Days of Praise: The Hallelujah Psalms: Henry M. Morris, Ph. D.; Institute for Creation Research; 2017

Praise to God who helps those in Need (Psalm 146): http://bible.ucg.org/bible-commentary/Psalms/Praise-to-God-who-helps-those-in-need/

Ps. 146-150: The Final Hallelujah Psalms as a Fivefold Doxology to the Hebrew Psalter: Kilman Cha; Baylor University, Department of Religion; December 2006

The Washington Post; Psalm 46:1 "God is our refuge and strength," sermon by The Reverend Derrick Harkins; article by Hamil R. Harris; 9/12/2011

Color Meanings, by Jacob Oleson, https://color-meanings.com/biblical-meaning-colors.

The "Sevens" of Genesis 1:1 – 2:3; by William D. Ramey, Literary Analysis of Genesis 1:1-2:3, April 5, 1997, http://Inthebeginning.org.

Psalms, Volume 1; by C Hassell Bullock, Baker Publishing Group, August 2015

Lightning Source UK Ltd.
Milton Keynes UK
UKHW050843080621
384966UK00016B/340